T0293185

Building an Effective Procurement Organization

Best Practices for World-Class Performance

Iryna Povoroznyk

J.ROSS

PUBLISHING

Library of Congress Cataloging-in-Publication Data
Names: Povoroznyk, Iryna, 1981– author.
Title: Building an effective procurement organization : best practices for world-class performance / Iryna Povoroznyk ; translated into English by Charles Rudkin.
Description: 1st edition. | Plantation, FL : J. Ross Publishing, Inc., [2024] | Includes bib-
liographical references and index. | Summary: "Building an Effective Procurement
Organization presents essential steps for advancing procurement practices to a world-
class level, describing the fundamentals of procurement management and how to build
a solid foundation for success. Povoroznyk emphasizes the importance of mastering the
basics before diving into more complex procurement concepts. With clear explanations
and practical examples, this invaluable resource is for anyone looking to develop their
procurement management skills and enhance their organizations' purchasing power.
For entrepreneurs and suppliers, this book will become a source of insider information
about the structure of the procurement service of their corporate clients and the tasks
that owners and managers of companies set for buyers"— Provided by publisher.
Identifiers: LCCN 2024008745 (print) | LCCN 2024008746 (ebook) | ISBN 9781604271966
(hardback) | ISBN 9781604278507 (epub)
Subjects: LCSH: Industrial procurement—Management. | Materials management. |
Business logistics. | BISAC: BUSINESS & ECONOMICS / Production & Operations
Management | BUSINESS & ECONOMICS / Purchasing & Buying Classification:
LCC HD39.5 .P6813 2024 (print) | LCC HD39.5 (ebook) | DDC 658.7/2—dc23/
eng/20240304
LC record available at https://lccn.loc.gov/2024008745
LC ebook record available at https://lccn.loc.gov/2024008746

Direct all inquiries to J. Ross Publishing, Inc., 151 N. Nob Hill Rd., Suite 476, Plantation,
FL 33324.

Phone: (954) 727-9333
Fax: (561) 892-0700
Web: www.jrosspub.com

To all my colleagues and teams whom I was lucky to work with, gain knowledge from, and have experiences worth sharing. And to my parents—Vitaliy and Nadiia—and my friends, who always support and encourage me to follow my passions.

CONTENTS

INTRODUCTION

Effective spend management is one of the key challenges that any company faces. All businesses target higher profits to ensure long-term development and achievement of their strategic objectives—regardless of whether that is to create compelling new products and services or just to make the world a better place. Profits rise not only because of increased revenue but also because of accurate and professional spend management. After removing salaries, taxes, debt payments, and other obligations, a large spend line that remains is procurement.

Many pundits are quick to claim that procurement is a field where it is very hard to achieve transparency. Some companies have multilayer bureaucratic control procedures and are not always sure what tasks the procurement team is supposed to complete apart from processing contracts and invoices for purchases. Beyond this scenario, it is not uncommon that for small and midsize enterprises, a Chief Executive Officer (CEO) is the single person in the company who authorizes each and every purchase.

Leading companies build effective procurement teams that can make strategic decisions and drive business efficiency without the need to involve the genius of the CEO for every deal. They create ecosystems to collaborate with their suppliers and integrate them as their business partners while hitting impressive savings targets and creating new quality products for their clients. This is enabled not by strict procedures or centralized decision making but by the implementation of effective process designs, balanced controls, creative ideas, proper motivation, and trust.

The transformation from a middling to an elite procurement organization is within reach, and this book can help you do it. *Building an Effective Procurement Organization* explains the objectives to set for your procurement function, how to build effective procurement processes, and how to manage your spend in the most efficient way. In addition, if you represent a service or manufacturing entity and want to understand how your bigger corporate customers handle procurement decisions and operate their procurement function, this book will show you. It can provide the knowledge to build your sales strategy and make them your clients. Whether you are knee-deep in the procurement function or just interact with it, this inclusive guide will help you build better relationships and improve your procurement practice.

FOREWORD

Every year, companies spend enormous amounts of money on procurement. Statistics show that, on average, purchases may account for up to 50 percent of sales. For companies operating in the manufacturing sector, it can be even higher—rising to as much as 60 percent. Yet, only a few companies employ a systematic approach to cost management. Top executives and senior management must ask themselves two simple questions:

1. How effectively are we managing procurement spend?
2. Who do we trust to spend the company's money?

Imagine that today, a company spends 43 percent of its revenues on procurement; tomorrow, it buys the same items but from more reliable suppliers for 3 percent less. What if procurement spend was down by 5 percent? And what if by 7 percent? How would this impact company profitability? Obviously, this can make a huge difference to the bottom line.

Where do you start, and what is the first thing you need to think about if you are entrusted with procurement? What is procurement efficiency, how can it be measured, what procurement management systems exist, what are their benefits and drawbacks, and what can be generally expected from this *service* function? How do procurement systems work for large and small companies? How do you find common ground with experts in this field and with those trying to become a supplier to your company?

This book provides answers to these and other questions, as well as practical tools for managing procurement performance. It does not tell you how to negotiate effectively, it does not explain the techniques and tricks that can help you buy goods cheaper, nor does it explain how to perform cost regression analysis or calculate the margin of your supplier. Many books and articles have already been written about such things. Instead, in this book, we will talk about how to build a *procurement system* and thereby maintain a quality business service. The tools that are used to manage procurement costs may differ to some extent for large and medium-size companies. However, there are some common approaches that are relevant to all, regardless of the size of the company or its range of activities.

Procurement management practices vary from industry to industry. Procurement categories in manufacturing, for example, are different from those in the retail industry: while the former primarily purchases raw materials, goods, equipment, spare parts, and services required to support manufacturing cycles, retailers purchase goods to stock their shelves to sell to consumers. Nevertheless, the basic principles are similar in both industries. It doesn't matter to a good procurement professional whether they are buying workwear, a gas turbine, or an avocado. A true professional understands procurement in any field, regardless of category, sector, or company.

Procurement opens up opportunities beyond increasing profits. Despite this, not many companies have a professional procurement team. Why is this? The answer is simple. A procurement specialist is a recognized profession, but a higher education diploma in this field is a rarity. Furthermore, there is a lingering stigma surrounding procurement, a myth that this function in business is little more than document management—basically, an activity that does not create value and, therefore, does not require special expertise. Everyone understands which issues are handled by sales professionals, economists, financiers, lawyers, and logisticians, but not everyone can answer exactly what a procurement professional does.

I have worked in procurement for over 15 years. I became a buyer by accident, like many in the profession. At first, I was translating documents for the procurement department, then I became a buyer myself, and soon I was in charge of procurement as a Chief Procurement Officer in two power distribution companies in Ukraine that, at the time, belonged to an international energy company called AES Corporation. After a while, I took positions in the Czech Republic, Kazakhstan, and Russia. I worked with international teams that were executing large procurement projects across several countries. I started writing this book when I was in charge of procurement at Severstal, a metals and mining conglomerate in Russia with a total annual procurement spend of several billion dollars and a procurement team of around 400 people located in several cities across the country. During my early days in procurement, I was scrambling for information to understand how to manage procurement effectively and build a sustainable system in a fast-changing environment. It was difficult, sometimes very difficult. There were no obvious solutions to many issues, and not everything worked right the first time, but the challenges were all the more interesting. My teams and managers supported me, and I learned a lot from them.

This book is built around the practical aspects of procurement management that come from my own experiences and those of my fellow colleagues in different industries and companies around the world. My knowledge was developed from a variety of industries where companies buy 50,000 unique items a year, from bolts to high-tech production lines, where they maintain their own manufacturing facilities and offices, execute construction projects, manage fleets, buy special equipment, maintain railways and locomotives, etc. The stories and experiences that were shared by my fellow coworkers come from different backgrounds and are unified by a passion for building effective procurement organizations.

You should not expect to find comprehensive answers to all procurement-related questions in the pages of this book. You will not find a detailed breakdown of methodologies created by someone else. My main goal was to create a roadmap to building an efficient procurement management system. This is a good starting point for any professional in procurement or any CEO who does not have a lot of time to go into the details of procurement operations but wants to maximize the function. After reading this, if you are interested in the topic and wish to continue studying it, you will find that there is a lot of interesting and valuable information out there.

I make a special appeal to those who work in state-owned companies. After reading this book, you might question many of the suggestions I put forward. "That's impossible! My company would never support me if I tried to implement such initiatives. The author doesn't understand the specifics of state-owned enterprises." I have heard such comments many times during my presentations at conferences or while teaching at business schools. I have also worked in the regulated procurement systems of Ukraine and Kazakhstan. In my work, I sometimes encountered public procurement law requirements that appeared absurd but were difficult or impossible to circumvent. Nevertheless, everything described in this book, to one extent or another, I applied in public sector companies as well. You may not be able to implement some changes quickly and radically, but the practices described here can be applied in nearly any company. The key is to adapt them and test them in practice.

I sincerely hope that this book will help you find what you are looking for and encourage you to think about the role that procurement plays in your business. Books help in the search for ideas, but the real solutions generally come from people working together on things that matter to them and ultimately achieving results in sometimes very simple but unobvious ways. Real challenges, practices, experiences, and knowledge—mine and those of my colleagues—form the basis of this book. That is why there is a section on teamwork and motivation in procurement—after all, procurement is not just about tenders and contracts but about effective collaboration across the organization.

If you would like to share your thoughts or experiences with me about what I have written here, I would be happy to hear from you. You can reach out to me online via my *Procurement Blog by Irina Povoroznyk* on Facebook or on LinkedIn. I wish you productive reading!

~

> The modern purchasing agent is a more important man by far than he was in older days when purchasing agents were likely to be more of the nature of "rubber stamps," or "buffers," or were bargainers for an extra penny of advantage. A purchasing agent of the modern breed is a creative thinker and planner and a student of many elements of business.
> —Helen Hysell, *The Science of Purchasing*, 1922

ACKNOWLEDGMENTS

The idea to write a book about procurement management came to me several years ago—the first lines were written in 2018. During that time, a lot has changed—new solutions, technologies, books, and research have appeared. However, the literature on procurement management that talks about the *basics*—the things that are most important to build the groundwork for a well-established procurement function—is still scarce, while the effective setup and management of procurement are more relevant than ever.

Pandemics, wars, terrorism, and environmental issues continue to test the strength of supply chains. Building an effective procurement function in which the basic processes are well organized and do not require detailed support is an expertise that is more important than ever. After all, only with robust operational processes can an organization afford a proactive, rather than reactive, model of operation and decision making in complex situations.

When I shared the idea for this book with colleagues and friends, I immediately sensed their support: some suggested topics for coverage; some helped by collecting cases and telling stories from their own practice; some took the time to read the text before the editor saw it and gave me feedback, including additions and corrections; and some invariably inspired me with their presence and the reminder that the results of this work will find an audience.

I am very grateful for the opportunity that led me into private business and procurement. During my work in this field, I met many wonderful people—real professionals—and learned a lot. Some of them later became my close friends. My experience is not just limited to procurement. Procurement covers a wide area of knowledge, but to be successful, you have to understand many things at once and find opportunities for self-improvement. My work has significantly changed me and the way I see myself. I have learned and continue to learn from my surroundings—from my colleagues, mentors, and managers; from teams in which I participated and led; from industry peers, suppliers, partners, customers, and consultants—it is impossible to list them all by name. Nevertheless, I would like to thank by name those who had a direct influence on the creation of this book:

Kira Lapina and Alisa Mityaeva for their friendship, for working together, for encouraging me to work on this text, and for supporting me right up to its completion; Artem Sherekh, Volodymyr Stetsyk, Sergey Stefanenko, Mikhail Berstenev, Rodrigo Ferreira, and Andrey Polygaev for their time, comments, cases, ideas, and help with materials; Maria Arefieva and Dzmitry Bianko for our joint work, real-life cases, and inspiration; Natalija Shapoval and Olha Tereshchenko for an inspiring teaching experience in the Procurement Professionalization Program at the Kyiv School of Economics, when during classroom discussions it became clearer to me what this book should be about, while the lecture materials that I prepared subsequently helped me to structure the text.

I would like to especially thank Kseniya Demidova, Irina Borodina, Vladimir Gibov, Anton Akimov, Ivan Skorobulatov, Andrey Filonov, Anzhelika Novikova, Anastasiya Golovina, Alesya Mikitchina, and many, many others from my former large procurement team at Severstal, with whom we implemented large-scale projects and managed to build a strong procurement function.

I also fondly remember my AES procurement team, where we studied best practices, tried to figure out how to apply them to regulated procurement, and learned, grew, and changed our procurement operations for the better. That experience was transformative for our entire team. I remember many names, but I would especially like to thank Iryna Kit, Maria Solovyova, and Olena Gavrylova—our midnight creative sessions and search for meaning occupy a special place in my memories of that time.

Friends, thank you for your support, trust, ideas, and criticism; for our team results and inspiration; and for the fact that it was with you that we checked what and how procurement actually works. It's hard to list the names of all the people who have influenced me as a buyer and a leader—there are so many great people. Even though a lot has changed over that time, including our roles, company names, locations, and even countries of residence, you will always be my dream team!

At this point, I would like to thank my former managers, without whose influence on me and my career in procurement, this book would not have appeared: Serge Medvedev, Genah Pavlova, George Nizharadze, Brian Thompson, Denis Pavlyuchenkov, and Dmitry Sakhno. I remember with gratitude the time we worked together. Thank you for your trust and support!

Thanks to Ekaterina Syrovatskaya and Dmitriy Kozlov—you helped to find the elements that either move things forward or get in the way, as well as ways to put those findings to good use. Team sessions and finding solutions with your facilitation stand out in my professional experience.

Thank you to the publishing team for believing in this book and dedicating time to make it accessible to the wider public.

Thank you to my peers, the large professional community of procurement specialists and supply chain management professionals, consultants, experts, and readers for your questions, ideas, speeches, useful texts, information, and experiences that I have found so inspiring!

Thank you to my family, relatives, and friends for your patience and warmth even when I am far away. I always feel your unconditional love and support, and this gives me the confidence to move forward.

Thank you to my friends in many different cities and countries. I have made friends through my work and studies in many different locations, and I am glad to have people in my life with whom I can maintain warm relationships despite the distance and these most difficult times we are experiencing.

Thank you to all those who have read these pages and for taking the time to read to the end. I hope you never lose your inspiration; look for it and find it in yourself and in each other. Do not rest on your achievements, but continue searching, researching, and experimenting. It is what keeps life interesting!

ABOUT THE AUTHOR

Iryna Povoroznyk is an expert in strategic sourcing and procurement, operations management, digital platforms, ERP implementation, change management, and strategic organizational transformation. For the past 15 years, Iryna has managed the procurement of one of the largest companies in the metals and mining and energy sectors. She has a proven track record of building highly motivated teams and implementing successful large-scale transformation projects that are considered a best-practice benchmark by industry peers.

A frequent guest speaker at industry events, Iryna has developed procurement education courses for both the public and private sectors in Eastern Europe and lectured on the subjects of procurement transformation, procurement/supply chain efficiency, planning, IT/ERP systems, and digital applications in the supply chain. Iryna has implemented procurement initiatives in 10 countries during her career—exposing her to diverse cultures and business practices in Asia, Europe, the Middle East, and the Americas.

Following discussions with industry peers, colleagues, and students, Iryna wrote this book for anyone who wants to build an effective procurement function within their business and better understand procurement management concepts. She hopes the reader will develop a solid base for the implementation of advanced concepts that will work not only in theory but in practice.

At J. Ross Publishing we are committed to providing today's professional with practical, hands-on tools that enhance the learning experience and give readers an opportunity to apply what they have learned. That is why we offer free ancillary materials available for download on this book and all participating Web Added Value™ publications. These online resources may include interactive versions of the material that appears in the book or supplemental templates, worksheets, models, plans, case studies, proposals, spreadsheets and assessment tools, among other things. Whenever you see the WAV™ symbol in any of our publications, it means bonus materials accompany the book and are available from the Web Added Value Download Resource Center at www .jrosspub.com.

Downloads for *Building an Effective Procurement Organization* include selected tables and a template for procurement function strategy development.

CHAPTER 1

PROCUREMENT SPEND: HOW MUCH IS NOT A LOT?

ASSESSING THE SCALE: WHERE TO START

Corporate shopping is not much different from your everyday shopping in a supermarket. You can be driven by immediate decisions, buy the same things out of habit, have a prearranged shopping list for a family vacation, or grab a product without reading the labels because you just want to try something new.

Imagine that you have $100, and you go to the store to buy milk. There are five kinds of milk on the shelves, all at different prices. Cost is not important; you can afford to spend the whole hundred if necessary. The main thing is that it tastes good and is good for your health. Which one will you buy? Let's say that your choice depends on the milk's characteristics and how much you trust the producer. However, you don't trust cheap products, but you also think it is a waste of time to read labels to discover the exact details about the half gallon of milk you are buying. It may be better to buy the more expensive milk since a higher price probably means that it went through a better quality control system. After all, your health is priceless, so you shouldn't skimp on it. Or another scenario might be: milk is just milk—it's all the same. You check the fat content because that is always prominently displayed and choose the cheapest one with the fat content that you want.

The same exact thing happens with company procurement, but on a much larger scale. If we don't keep track of where and how our money is spent, we inevitably lose it. There is no guarantee that you will make the same amount of money tomorrow as you did today. In the previous case, there is no significant factor other than emotion guiding your choice. This won't work at the company level. Even when sales are good, inadequate procurement management can lead to serious losses that could have been avoided.

Interestingly, many procurement executives, even in very large organizations, are unaware of how much their company spends on procurement per year, exactly what financial results are affected by the cost of procurement, or what procurement health indicators exist and how to analyze them. Often, this information stays, at best, at the level of the head of the department. Therefore, in those companies where procurement is limited to transactional support, execution of contracts, and ensuring delivery of goods or services, even after running a tightly regulated tender, many managers do not invest their time into understanding these numbers. Normally, they are not even part of regular reporting, and their value is not always clear.

Suppose we already know how much the company spends on purchasing each year. How much does this cost compare to the company's revenues?

Try to break down these numbers into the factors that have influenced them and work out why this figure changes or, conversely, stays the same. What does it depend on? What would happen to the overall financial performance of the company if this value changed in one direction or another?

What would be the effect on the bottom line if you spent 5%, 10%, or 15% less on your purchases?

When Etihad[1] embarked on its business transformation with the intention of restructuring and expanding its global footprint by creating a single, transparent chain of command, the first departments to be restructured were finance, HR, and procurement. This was not a random choice. Ensuring effective cost management and interaction with external parties that affect the company's viability, especially during a period of rapid growth, is a critical strategic challenge. The three-year project redefined all the core business support processes for several of the companies that make up the Etihad group. It laid the foundation for further growth by increasing transparency in cost management and focusing on strategic issues, transforming transactional procurement management into strategic partnerships with suppliers, and giving the company access to the best technology in the market.

Sometimes you hear that a company spends *too much* on procurement—but there is no such thing as *too much* or *too little* when assessing total procurement costs. Any value must be compared to something in order to be adequately assessed. Is it a lot or a little—compared to what? What is the effect? Why does it matter? What would happen if this indicator changed? Take a seemingly simple indicator such as the unit purchase price. Even if the price is higher for you than for other buyers, in this particular case, it may be optimal or even low—it all depends on what exactly it includes. Different companies may have different requirements in terms of technical parameters, logistics, and additional services such as training or maintenance. An accurate price comparison can only be made by comparing products or services that are fully identical in composition and features, as well as the range of services that go with them. Identical names do not always indicate that the goods are identical.

A similar question may also be asked about the cost of the procurement process itself: How much does it cost a company to support its procurement activities? Here is a simple but very useful exercise to measure how efficiently a company manages its procurement process: calculate how much it costs to place a single purchase order. To do this, you need to find out how many purchase orders the company places per year and the cost of maintaining a procurement department or staff to handle procurement in the different divisions of the company. If you divide the cost of maintaining the procurement department by the total number of purchase orders, you will get the average cost per purchase order. No matter how complex the processes preceding this stage, it is the purchase order that is the central stage of the procurement process, where the intention to purchase something turns into an obligation for both the supplier and the buyer. It is not uncommon for the average cost of placing an order to reach the $100 to $200 range. Suppose it's an order to deliver a single computer mouse at a cost of $10. Isn't the process of placing the order too expensive compared to the cost of the item being purchased? Now suppose your company places 10,000 purchase orders per year. That's a minimum of $1 million for the purchasing process. What if you buy the same things but spend $100,000 less to support your procurement processes?

Of course, all orders are different and reducing them to an average perhaps does not seem appropriate. But if you factor out the negotiations and the organization of procurement tenders, we see that the paperwork is not much different for both small and large purchases. The effort input for the purchase of paper clips is comparable to the effort input for the purchase of cars. The smaller orders for the purchase of paper clips appear to be a less efficient use of resources: instead of spending time preparing to negotiate the purchase of cars, employees waste time on small tenders and placing tons of micro-orders for paper clips from various suppliers at unfavorable terms, while the cost of one shipment of paper clips is probably much lower than the $100 to $200 spent on the administration of this purchase.

Procurement issues have received increasing attention in recent years. All the prominent consultancy groups have developed dedicated areas to help companies improve the professionalism of procurement organizations and make procurement cost management more efficient. It is now understood that procurement has a significant impact on business success. It has become increasingly critical for companies to bring new products to market quickly and spend less on raw materials, components, and services. This has to be done without compromising quality. Finding alternatives, managing demand, and integrating supply chains with suppliers—and even with clients—requires a well-designed supply chain structure and procurement process within it.

Evaluating the effectiveness of procurement is a complex subject. Conclusions can only be drawn after a comprehensive study of the impact of each aspect of procurement on the results of a particular business. The key assumption is that any procurement system is comprised of two dimensions: (1) the strategic, which affects bottom-line value—including developing category strategies and managing the supplier base, and (2) the tactical, which combines many operational steps that are succinctly described by the term *procure-to-pay*.

PROCUREMENT PERFORMANCE MANAGEMENT

Understanding your current position and identifying areas to focus on is a worthy exercise. Start by assessing a small set of basic strategic and operational indicators. There are dozens of key performance indicators (KPIs) for procurement that can be measured. But which ones are high priority? Which ones will help you quickly understand where to focus your efforts?

The business owner or departmental manager should first look at strategic upper-level indicators, such as performance measurement, unit cost estimates, and key financial indicators relating to working capital and savings that are affected by procurement.

If you're a procurement manager, the first thing you need to focus on is the operational metrics of supply discipline, procurement costs, quality, inventory levels, and transactional efficiency through which you assess the achievement of the strategic goals of the procurement function and the company as a whole. Find out what major projects are currently underway, what their KPIs are, what objectives need to be met to achieve them, and what level of operational excellence in procurement is required for projects to perform as expected.

Many developed procurement functions have advanced reporting dashboards that track dozens of indicators. It usually takes years to develop a monitoring system that will be comprehensive yet manageable. It is not so much that automation takes time and resources, but that the populating of such databases happens gradually as the functionality and the processes develop and the real need for a particular metric is understood.

Before you start creating your own set of metrics, it is important to determine which metrics are the most critical to your organization today. What is most important to your company right now? What is the internal understanding of the value that procurement creates? What are the key results of an effective procurement function? For example, if the company is not doing well in terms of supply discipline while also experiencing frequent interruptions, associated capacity downtime, and failure to meet commitments and plans, then procurement is likely to focus on operational performance and on activities aimed at achieving KPI targets in these areas. If baseline performance is good, then it's time to take the next step and look at other areas for improvement.

In order to set up a procurement performance dashboard, you need a starting set of indicators that you will begin to track. The following list describes several strategic and operational indicators that could be taken as a starting point.

- **Strategic KPIs and procurement quality assessments:**
  - **Procurement's impact on the company's bottom line**—this indicator can be measured by the annual amount of savings the procurement unit generates.
  - **Procurement's impact on working capital**—this indicator is estimated through the annual average inventory level, the average level of accounts payable, and advances on procurement contracts.
  - **Share (%) of total procurement spend covered by long-term category strategies**[2]—calculated as the ratio of the procurement spend share covered by the implemented category strategies to total procurement spend.
  - **Share (%) of procurement spend managed by total cost of ownership (TCO)**[3] **estimates**—this indicator is similar to the previous one and is calculated as a ratio of the share of spend procured based on the TCO value to total procurement spend.
  - **Client evaluation of the procurement service**[4]—clients include both internal and external stakeholders, including suppliers.
  - **Share (%) of reliable suppliers**[5] **to the total number of active suppliers**—this indicator is calculated as the ratio of the

number of suppliers who received high ratings to the total number of suppliers with whom the company worked on at least one order for the supply of goods or services.

□ **Savings (%) on the total volume (value) of purchases**—this measure can also be defined as the ratio of the amount of savings per year to the amount spent to support procurement processes (or to maintain a dedicated business unit). In essence, it tells you how much the procurement department is paying for itself.

- Operational procurement KPIs:
  □ **Percentage of deliveries of adequate quality that were made within the required timeframe**—this indicator assesses the timeliness and comprehensiveness of supplies of the required products and services. Calculated as the ratio of the amount and/or volume of deliveries made on time to the total amount and/or volume of deliveries for the period.

  □ **Percentage of goods that arrived at the warehouse but were not available for production or resale on time as a share of the total volume of deliveries**—this indicator is calculated as the ratio of the total quantity or value of goods that are physically in stock to the quantity or value of the portion of goods that are fully processed in the accounting system and available for use (for instance, goods having been quality checked and ready for release to production or for resale).

  □ **The speed of procurement operations**—this indicator can be calculated either by measuring the end-to-end procurement process or its individual parts. For example, the average time from receipt of a purchase requisition to placement of an order with a supplier or the average processing time for deliveries from a supplier to the warehouse.

  □ **The cost of procurement transactions**—this represents the average cost per purchase order placed and is calculated by dividing the total cost of supporting purchase orders by the total number of purchase orders for the period. Process support costs include staff salaries, costs associated with their activities, infrastructure maintenance costs, and energy and material costs.

  □ **The volume of deliveries that did not pass quality inspection**—this indicator is the ratio of the value of the products and services with quality claims to the total value of all delivered products and services.

- ▫ **Working capital indicators:**
  - ○ The average level of inventories and the amount of obsolete inventories compared to target levels
  - ○ The share of advance payments that are overdue, i.e., products and services paid for, but not received on time
  - ○ The average level of accounts payable in days
- ▫ **Share (%) of framework (long-term) agreements to the total number of agreements**—this indicator is calculated as the ratio of the number of agreements with a duration of more than one year and the possibility of placing multiple purchase orders to the total number of agreements.
- ▫ **Operational indicators that measure the efficiency of resource allocation and the load on the procurement service:**
  - ○ **The cost of running the procurement unit**—considered the ratio of the total cost to run a procurement function to the total value of procurement savings.
  - ○ **The amount of procurement spend managed by one procurement officer**—calculated as the sum of the total annual spend on all categories for which the procurement unit is responsible divided by the number of staff in the unit. It is worth noting that the proportions will be different for different categories. For example, a raw material category may contain only a few items and still account for the largest proportion of costs, while a consumable or spare part may be relatively inexpensive and still have hundreds of items, making the category difficult to manage. Therefore, it does not make sense to calculate this value in relation to specific categories.
  - ○ **The number of active suppliers per procurement officer**—this is the total number of active suppliers divided by the total number of procurement staff. As with the previous metric, you shouldn't make calculations by category—the purpose of this metric is to estimate employee workload and the labor costs involved in managing the counterparty base.

- The number of purchase orders per procurement officer—calculated as an average figure where the total number of purchase orders is divided by the total number of procurement staff supporting them. This indicator reveals the average amount of workload per employee without reference to the complexity of a certain deal.

How to interpret these estimates and understand when the values of individual indicators are acceptable will be discussed in Chapter 2, where we will talk about benchmarking as a way of setting target levels of procurement performance.

The basis for introducing KPIs into management practice is to get a clear understanding of the tasks they address. The main tasks for which KPIs are used are highlighted here:

- **Measuring the achievement of the goals**—what is not measured cannot be evaluated. However, evaluation is not just about numbers. There are also qualitative indicators that can be obtained from peer assessments. It is possible to understand how your objectives are progressing and how close you are to achieving the goal by tracking key KPIs that take these goals into account in measurable terms.
- **Identifying areas for improvement**—only through performance indicators can one understand what the priorities should be in the short and long term and what exactly needs to be improved. KPIs will not always answer the question as to exactly what improvements should be implemented because many factors can directly or indirectly influence the numbers, but only measurable performance indicators will point in the right direction.
- **Increase transparency**—regular tracking of KPIs will enable real-time monitoring of the procurement process and allow us to observe how well the function is delivering on its promises to clients, including internal stakeholders, management, and suppliers. If any of the targets are not achieved, the causes of the problems can be found through the use of intermediate performance indicators.

Successful achievement of the intended KPIs in procurement will lead to the following results:

- **Improved business financial results**—savings and spend optimization
- **Improvement of the company's working capital**—average level of contract advance payments, accounts payable, and inventory balance

- **Timely and full supplies**—delivery rates, On Time In Full (OTIF),[6] and ratio of noncompliant deliveries to total deliveries
- **Compliance with regulatory requirements**—volume of noncompliant transactions, ensuring timely financial period closure and filing for tax refunds
- **Achievement of client expectations**—stakeholder satisfaction index, management assessment of procurement performance, and supplier loyalty index
- **Improved contract performance discipline**—number of claims, quantity, and quality deviations

Each indicator is based on its own set of inputs and has a number of features that need to be considered in practice.

Take, for example, the inventory level metric from the working capital set of indicators. Excessive inventory has a negative effect on working capital, so companies try to minimize inventory. Different industries have different inventory strategies: in retail, it involves managing product assortment and availability to customers; in manufacturing, it involves holding a safety stock of critical spare parts that may never be needed, but its absence could lead to production disruptions. Companies are therefore looking for approaches that would allow them to maintain inventory at an optimal level, where they have enough stock to guard against lost productivity and profits while at the same time ensuring that unnecessarily large funds are not deducted from working capital by being locked up in excessive inventory.

One often hears that the entire responsibility for a company's stock rests on the shoulders of the procurement office because they are the ones who buy in advance to insure against unforeseen additional demand and to make sure they don't buy the same goods twice. But this idea is inconsistent with the reality. The delivery of goods is preceded by a planning process that starts with those departments that need these items—way before the procurement office steps in. The purchasing plan could be influenced, for example, by maintenance plans or construction plans for new units. In fact, it often happens that these plans are not fulfilled for various reasons and the ordered stock ends up sitting in the warehouse. Who has more influence on the stock level then? Is it the procurement department that secured the order and brought the goods to the warehouse, or is it the department that ordered the goods and did not use them in a timely fashion? Going further, the requestor argues that the stock was not used because the delivery was two days late, which shifted the entire work schedule, and therefore high stock levels in the warehouses are the fault of the procurement department. Procurement responds that they could not deliver the goods earlier because the client submitted the requisition two weeks after the required deadline. Also, in general, it is not just the client who influences the delivery time, but also logistics operators, stockkeepers, and even management, who can sign the necessary documents immediately or delay it a month.

Another equally controversial indicator is procurement savings. Let's say the purchasing department has identified that an analog (substitute) version of the equipment or material that the customer has requested is available on the market. The analog is cheaper, and there is no need to change their technology cycle to use it. In this case, it's simple: the savings achieved are a feather in the cap for the procurement department. But what if a technology process change is required to use the analog version? Without the help of engineers and changes in the manufacturing process, making the switch would simply not be possible. What sense would it make to talk about savings in this case?

On one occasion, my colleagues and I argued at length about how to account for procurement saving's contribution made by the procurement department and internal stakeholders when several different departments were contributing to the overall savings. Several suggestions were put forward: a 50/50 split; calculating each initiative effect in proportion to the number of hours invested in the project; involving a third party such as financial controlling to measure the inputs properly, etc. By trial and error, we found that the only correct solution was a very simple one: to share the benefits together without the need to calculate the share of each department's input. It is simply a matter of cross-functional team responsibility for overall performance indicators and working together toward a common outcome where everyone gets rewarded for team results. This approach helps to free up precious resources that can be spent finding new ideas and helping each other rather than on the arguments about the size of contributions to the common cause. After all, if the team wins, everyone wins.

Colleagues have often asked me about the use of service level agreements (SLAs). This management tool may be somewhat controversial. Indeed, while internal clients expect procurement to provide on-time delivery, and this is their requirement for a specific service level, procurement depends on the speed of warehouse operations and the timeliness of each purchase requisition created by the internal client, so it seems unfair to set a one-sided SLA that defines requirements toward procurement only. In order to balance the responsibility between all involved parties in the process, requirements can be defined on the speed of planning, paperwork quality, the speed of shipment of goods to the warehouse, the timeliness of purchase requisitions, and even the quality of technical specifications. In the early stages of procurement process development, SLAs might work well. But if applied excessively and directed to the responsibility of one side only, sooner or later it starts to provoke disputes and the shift of responsibility. One can always say, "I am doing my job, but things are going wrong because my colleague isn't doing theirs," without helping their colleague solve the issue. The expectations toward each other are too formalistic in this case. Such a formal approach might work when processes and functional operations are clearly defined and independent of each other. When it comes to joint initiatives or projects in which it is not very clear at the beginning exactly what the most appropriate long-term performance indicators are and how to achieve results, it is better to learn to communicate and agree on what everyone needs to do for common success rather than spend time defining SLAs. This will bring much more benefit to the common cause.

Another important aspect of working with performance indicators is that, in some cases, setting targets that are too high (difficult to achieve or simply unrealistic) can lead to the manipulation and incorrect reporting of results. Such risks need to be anticipated. Here is an example:

When my team first introduced OTIF to procurement, we set ourselves the ambitious goal of ensuring day-to-day delivery accuracy. At that time, we had already been working in a paradigm of shared, cross-functional responsibility for our performance, including tracking warehouse operations speed. Things did not look good at first: incoming goods were processed with long delays, and the warehouse's stock receiving records could have been better. The speed of this operation was estimated based on the difference in date and time of two events: a shipment notification from the supplier[7] and the goods receipt document. We tightened the target for the time between these two events and started to track in the system when each of the documents was logged. There were no external reasons to indicate that this new target was not achievable. Quite soon, a few warehouses began to show improved results, but at the same time, buyers complained about the speed of goods acceptance in these same warehouses. Upon closer inspection, we discovered that we had not accounted for possible risk: the shipment notification was not created by the suppliers in our systems; it was logged in the accounting system by our storekeepers, just like the goods receipt. It turned out that the incoming goods receipts documents were not created in accordance with the actual timeline but instead were created together with the shipping notification. Employees did it on the same day and time even if the shipment notification from the supplier arrived days earlier. This shortened the timeline of the incoming goods processing, thus improving KPI reports but not the real processing times of deliveries.

Another scenario is also possible. Employees make every effort to achieve the new target, but the goal is unrealistic and unlikely to be achieved unless there is a change in processes, responsibilities, and infrastructure. Even if management is motivated to set ambitious targets and test the team's capabilities, any ambitious goals must be supported by sufficient resources and process improvement. An *ambitious* goal is one that is slightly daunting but still achievable—even if, at first glance, it is not entirely clear how to achieve it. Continuous process improvement, the implementation of adequate controls, and the development of employee competencies will help to achieve these ambitious goals.

My favorite indicator of procurement performance is *return on investment* (ROI).[8] This indicator can be based on various methodologies, and procurement managers can develop their own, too. According to some consulting studies,[9] developed procurement functions deliver savings of 10 times or more their operational costs. The procurement ROI is the ratio of the amount of annual procurement savings to the amount of annual procurement operating costs—including salaries, travel, training, offices, stationery, equipment, utilities, external services, etc.—that are associated with the department's operations. That procurement savings figure will be the subject of a separate chapter, but for now, I will just say that this figure has often helped me justify changes that required heavy investment and quite expensive training for procurement employees. The procurement department manages a large volume of spend, and how well these teams perform depends on how much value they can create for the same money. A procurement department should be able to pay for itself. If this is not happening yet, investment in the development of this function should help.

While KPIs must be used to measure procurement efficiency, I would also like to caution against getting too carried away with them. There is a huge variety of KPIs, but not all of them need to be applied immediately to your organization. In addition to a standard set of KPIs that cover end-to-end processes, each stage of procurement maturity will require a different set of applicable KPIs. Here are a few rules for working with performance indicators:

- **If the indicator cannot be tracked due to lack of data or the organization is not ready for it, do not use it**—there is absolutely no point in trying to achieve something that cannot be measured or understood. Instead, it is better to select metrics that are as close as possible to what you want to measure in order to help guide the achievement of the desired outcome.
- **Use the number of indicators that you are able to remember**—you should not waste your time creating a complex dashboard with 99

indicators that resemble an airplane cockpit. A manager, or any other specialist, will, at best, monitor 10 indicators and is unlikely to look at the rest. Therefore, they will have no influence on the decision-making and operating processes.

- **Always discuss with the team why certain indicators are needed and how they will be measured, as well as define responsibility for their implementation**—test an indicator for a year before introducing it. We regularly calculated them and checked their adequacy through feedback from the procurement team, customers, and suppliers. Only when we were sure that a certain KPI was understood by the team did we introduce it as mandatory, thereby affecting performance evaluations.

- **Some indicators may be tracked over a long-time horizon only**—this applies to those indicators that depend on specific factors such as seasonality and market trends. In the case of a category that has volatile price and supply-demand balances, it is not appropriate to draw conclusions about the effectiveness of cost management over the course of a week or month, but the chosen methods may well be worthwhile over the longer term. It is better to measure effectiveness and savings over the long term when results can be more accurately verified.

PROCUREMENT CUSTOMER EXPERIENCE EVALUATION

One procurement performance indicator that is difficult to find in public sources and benchmarking studies is the evaluation of the procurement function's performance by internal clients (or customers) and suppliers.

While other indicators can be calculated and acceptable values determined, there is always much debate surrounding the objectivity and value of customer evaluations. Service level assessment is a typical indicator for service companies and functions. At the same time, there is a view that such assessment is driven by emotional reactions rather than real facts, thereby harming the teamwork of procurement with related departments. The evaluation of results through customer experience surveys is subjective because people usually forget or take for granted hundreds of successful cases but will always remember that one failure to deliver on time for an important project, thus guaranteeing a bad evaluation. That's just human nature—we more easily recall things that evoke strong emotions. Therefore, stressful situations where someone lets us down are going to be top of mind even if there are 99 brilliantly executed operations for every one single mistake.

The subjectivity of the customer experience indicator is indeed a challenge, as there is no standard methodology for its measurement. Given the specific nature of the work of buyers, especially in cases where the company has a high share of maverick spend or urgent purchases and the timeliness of planning and the quality of terms of reference suffer as a result, the usefulness of such an assessment may indeed be questionable—its sloppy application has a strong demotivating effect on employees.

Some procurement professionals are not very fond of the *service function* term. Indeed, the very concept of a client-provider relationship can prohibit us from understanding that results are achieved through the *joint* efforts of a team of professionals who, in most cases, do not depend on a single function. And in this sense, it is more correct to speak not about the relationship between the client and provider, but about building teamwork when both procurement and those units that order goods and services put their efforts into achieving a common result. All business processes are interconnected, which means that any action or inaction affects the entire end-to-end process. By introducing a customer satisfaction assessment, we reinforce the client-provider boundary.

Nevertheless, procurement is, by definition, a service function. With that said, I am convinced that procurement can do much more than buy and deliver. The tasks it performs directly determine the profitability of the business and, in many ways, also the processes of production and the functioning of the company as a whole through the creation of added value, such as cost savings and faster delivery times for products or services.

The service that procurement provides is the timely and cost-effective provision of goods and services to operations and administrative units so they can help the company meet customer needs. The clients, or stakeholders, of a purchasing service are not just the company's divisions, but also its management and suppliers since the quality of the purchasing service and the reliability of its processes determine whether suppliers can provide a quality service on time without defects. It can also allow a company to buy more of the goods and services it needs without increasing its spend. It's all about the interpretation of *service*. The mere fact that procurement is a service function does not negate the responsibility of its clients for the overall outcome of procurement (e.g., think in terms of the quality and timeliness of planning).

The procurement process begins at the planning stages of the required good or service. And how this first part of the process is carried out determines the quality and speed of all subsequent steps. Within a company, customer-oriented service is always a two-way process since each function *consumes* the results of the other and passes the results of its work in the form of products and data down the chain and returns them to the starting point—the client who ordered the products or services. Let's take a closer look at a customer evaluation performance metric based on the experience of a large telecom company's Chief Procurement Officer.

"It is important to build the right image of the procurement function in the eyes of the client as a business partner, and to do this through the regular collection and detailed analysis of feedback.

In our case, there was no way to make peace with internal customers until we organized the collection of feedback in the form of evaluations from each internal customer on completed procurement transactions. Before that, there was a constant backlash against procurement performance at the CEO and board level—one thing after another was always wrong. It was just the case that negative experiences with procurement were often escalated to the highest level by the internal customer, while achievements and successes were hardly ever brought to the attention of senior management. Collecting systematized feedback from a large sample of respondents showed that this negativity was shown to be baseless, as it turned out that there were far more successes than shortcomings and, in fact, the overall picture was positive. As a result, the negativity was de-escalated, as we were able to operate through facts, not just emotions."

There is an expression (and a book by the same name) that is apt in this situation: "A complaint is a gift."[10] If no one is complaining about the quality of your service, it may not be because the service is perfect, but because it is seen as so hopelessly bad that customers don't even try to tell you about it. And if you don't ask for feedback yourself, you may never know there are problems. I think using and numerically scoring customer and supplier assessments provides clues as to where improvements are needed. Here's why:

- **Scoring makes it possible to navigate the objectives and helps to measure the results**—we cannot say that everything is good if we have collected fewer complaints this quarter than in the previous one. However, a scoring system helps to account for the significance of events and evaluate overall service perception rather than just count complaints and omit the rest of the feedback.
- **Having a measurable value allows you to set a target for improvement**—if the current score is 3, you can set a goal of raising it to 3.25 over a certain period of time. Then, as successes build, raise it again. Do not make a target like this: *no more than five stakeholder complaints in the next six months.* This is meaningless because it may not be commensurate with the actual number of tasks that procurement performs in the same period of time or their complexity.

- **The existence of an evaluation scale makes things easier for questionnaire respondents.** A scale makes it possible to give a score without lengthy explanations. All financial KPIs can be met but yet the procurement function can still score low on *customer focus*. If achieving a financial KPI means creating inconvenience or problems for others and causes misunderstandings among stakeholders, then something is wrong, and the approach needs to be changed.

Even when there is a score-based assessment, how it is done is important: the way in which feedback is collected has a direct impact on the conclusions drawn and how practical they prove to be. Clients are not always capable of being honest when feedback is requested face-to-face. Perhaps they are too embarrassed to criticize their colleagues and are willing to hide certain problems because they do not consider them critical, whereas, in fact, these problems are systemic in nature and could easily be corrected if voiced. Therefore, formalized questionnaires are a good complement to live communication, and their format and content determine how willing respondents are to provide feedback.

Experience shows that asking a lot of questions does not guarantee you will uncover particular insights, but it does make collecting and processing feedback much slower, and if a survey takes more than two or three minutes to answer, it is far more likely to be ignored. The most successful evaluation systems are those where feedback can be given immediately. This is the approach used, for example, by taxi services—the customer can provide feedback and evaluation *on the fly* while the experience details are still fresh in their minds. This method requires the use of automation, and the design of the evaluation system must ensure that colleagues are not overwhelmed with endless feedback requests after each order has been fulfilled. When feedback requests come too often, they are likely to be ignored, too.

Some companies use the Net Promoter Score (NPS) index for internal services evaluation purposes. This indicator asks if the customer is willing to use the same service provider or recommend it to others. In the case of a restaurant or goods manufacturer, using NPS to assess a customer's willingness to return or recommend the company to colleagues and acquaintances is understandable. But internal customers cannot, in principle, refuse to use a company's procurement service: they usually have no authority to buy on their own, and the question of recommending to colleagues or friends when there is simply no other choice makes the index irrelevant.

The following paragraphs contain a brief version of a questionnaire we have used in order to help evaluate the service level of our internal procurement function. It generally provided useful data and gave us reliable benchmarks. A semi-annual questionnaire was sent out to clients with just three statements whose validity the respondents were asked to rate:

1. The goods and services procurement function usually meets your expectations.
2. The quality of delivered goods and services usually meets your technical requirements.
3. The quality of interaction with procurement meets your expectations.

The proposed multiple-choice answers provide varying degrees of confidence, as there are almost no *black-and-white* situations:

- Strongly agree
- Partly agree
- Partly disagree
- Completely disagree

The difference between *partly agree* and *partly disagree* is that the first option is more likely to be chosen by someone who is generally satisfied with the interaction, but with some room for improvement. In contrast, the second option is chosen by someone who is rather dissatisfied with the service.

The evaluation process itself consists of three steps:

1. Conducting a survey using the aforementioned questions
2. Processing the results
3. Requesting detailed feedback on the results of the questionnaire through personal interviews with select respondents.

Why do we need a questionnaire if we have a third step with the same questions being posed in an interview? The logic can be explained as follows:

- Through the results of the questionnaire, we can see which departments have the most issues in interacting with the procurement function
- The questionnaire covers many participants, and interviews are conducted with select groups to discuss the results and propose possible solutions to identified systemic problems

When we add the results of the interviews to the survey score, we get an impressive set of data—comments and suggestions that become part of an operational improvement program or serve as a basis for revising the elements of the function's development strategy.

During the interview, you can use the Customer Journey Map (CJM) toolkit.[11] A CJM is an approach where you put yourself in the client's shoes and try to experience how the process actually works. You can simply observe the process, carry out in-depth interviews, act out parts of the process together with the client, or in the most radical variant, become the client yourself. This approach has proven to be excellent; there is nothing better for identifying areas of improvement than going through the procurement process from the client's perspective.

In addition to interviewing internal clients, it is equally useful to interview suppliers and procurement staff. In order to gather a truly complete picture, it is important that feedback is comprehensive and comes from all process participants.

You can find out from suppliers what difficulties they face in the supply process: what works, what needs improvement, and what possibly triggers unnecessary costs on the buyer's side that they are unaware of—for example, in logistics or labor costs. Don't assume that all suppliers will be silent or try to cover up issues; some will take part in the survey but remain silent about the main pain points, some will ignore it altogether, but there will be those who will want to get involved and give detailed feedback in order to change things for the better. After all, if you ask, there is a chance of getting valuable information, but if you don't ask, the likelihood of this will be zero.

You can find out from the purchasing staff what hinders or helps them in their work, with which clients and suppliers, on what occasions the most difficult interaction issues arise, and what solutions they suggest to overcome these problems. You can get a lot of ideas from your team members, even if they are not always obvious, immediately applicable, or require adaptation— they are nevertheless no less relevant. Ideas arise through conversations, daily interactions, and of course, special surveys that allow for anonymous responses. Surveys do not have to happen often; it is just essential that this channel of communication exists.

KEY CHAPTER IDEAS

- There is no universal method for determining optimal procurement costs. It is only possible to determine whether procurement costs are elevated by comparing average prices with market indicators and the costs of running a procurement unit or performing individual procurement operations through benchmarking.
- Not all procurement performance indicators are necessary or appropriate for a particular company. It is important to focus on the current goals and strategy of the business and then determine which indicators need to be monitored.

- Indicators can tell you that all is well when the reality is not so rosy. You need to correlate metrics with the results of feedback from employees, internal clients, and suppliers. Formalized metrics are only one small part of the big picture.
- Targets should be ambitious but realistic. If they are too high or if there are too many, processes don't change, and employees won't feel empowered to help. There is a good chance that employees will likely just try to game the system than do effective work.
- Do not think of customer satisfaction as a one-way metric. Any indicator depends not only on the performance of the procurement unit but also on other departments. It is a useful practice to introduce shared responsibility between procurement and clients for certain performance indicators, such as savings or inventory levels.
- Interviews with stakeholders and customer-focused procurement assessments are a valuable source of information about areas that may need improvement. However, it is important to review the timing and type of surveys used to get the most comprehensive picture.

ENDNOTES

1. Etihad Airways is the national airline of the United Arab Emirates. Material from the Procurement Directors' Roundtable, 2016.
2. A long-term strategy is usually defined for a period of one to three years or more. The longer a strategy's horizon, the lower the accuracy of the forecasts it makes, as the market is not static. Long-term strategies should be reviewed at least once a year.
3. TCO is the sum of all the costs of acquiring, operating, and disposing of a procurement item throughout its lifetime.
4. The term *client* in procurement means a representative of any department other than procurement that submits a requisition and will directly use or consume the product or service that has been procured.
5. Criteria for supplier reliability can vary and are defined when developing a supplier management strategy. Often these criteria are the promptness of order fulfillment, product quality indicators, quantity of claims, etc.
6. This indicator consists of two parts: on-time delivery and completeness of delivery; it has many variations—different companies calculate it differently depending on their process design.
7. The availability of this document depends on the features of the ERP/accounting system.

8. In this case, it is the return on investment of the procurement function specifically.
9. Kearney's Assessment of Excellence in Procurement survey.
10. Janelle Barlow and Claus Møller. *A Complaint Is a Gift: Recovering Customer Loyalty When Things Go Wrong.* Berrett-Koehler Publishers, 2008.
11. Some useful reference materials can be found in the Addendum with the list of recommended books.

CHAPTER **2**

BENCHMARKING: A PROCUREMENT HEALTH CHECK

WHAT IS BENCHMARKING, AND WHY DO WE NEED IT?

In the first chapter, we discussed why we need to measure the correlation between procurement spend and company revenue and examine how it changes over time within the firm. But it is just as important to know how it compares with other businesses in your industry or globally. This gives you a sense of how your company's performance differs from that of the leaders in your particular industry.

Comparing your performance to best-practice indicators in order to assess progress is called *benchmarking*. Based on this comparison, you can develop an action plan to achieve better results and measure your performance over a specific period of time.

The most widely used sets of indicators for such comparisons and assessments are those published by specialized research organizations, such as APQC (American Productivity & Quality Center) and CAPS Research (Center for Advanced Procurement Strategy). There are some newsletters that you can subscribe to for free that contain benchmarking indicators, and if you submit your data to participate in benchmarking surveys—which often involve not only subscribers but also a selection of volunteer companies—there is an opportunity to receive reports with the most current benchmarking indicators for the surveys with which you participate.

Some of the most common indicators that are available in benchmarking reports include:

- The ratio of procurement spend to revenue
- Lead time from purchase requisition to order

- Percent of savings on total procurement spend
- Return on investment of the procurement function
- The amount of spend managed by the procurement department compared to total company's expenditures
- Percent of staff engaged in strategic procurement management
- The cost of conducting procurement operations for every $1,000 spent
- Volume of procurement spend managed by one category manager
- Inventory turnover rate
- Number of training days per procurement employee, etc.

There are many advantages to benchmarking, but you must be very careful when interpreting the results. For all its obvious benefits, there are some serious drawbacks to the methodology. Let us start by listing the advantages:

- **Benchmarking studies provide a wealth of useful information on which indicators can be measured in general.** This includes the number of delivery claims for every thousand orders and the average purchase order lead time. It also includes methodological data such as the amount of procurement savings by industry or procurement management costs per procurement officer.
- **Benchmarks can be used as a state-of-function check across all activities since they cover a wide range of processes.** If properly conducted and sufficiently monitored, benchmarking allows for a full cycle of improvement: comparison with similar companies, identification of necessary levers, and the tracking of changes.
- **Benchmarking indicators are calculated, not simply set by someone on a whim.** In benchmarking, all indicators are gathered from real cases. You don't have to try to catch up with the leaders right away. Focus on relative performance. If in the process of benchmarking you find that you are significantly behind in one important indicator, then it is usually a good idea to meet the industry average first before attempting to be best-in-class.
- **Best practices become evident and efficiency gains become possible, even if you thought they were not.** Benchmarking provides a good opportunity to assess yourself in an unbiased way. For example, suppose a company's procurement department was only fulfilling 70 percent of its orders on time. Over the course of the next year, procurement professionals took steps to improve the performance to 85 percent. While this 15 percent increase is a good start, and even if some colleagues think this is an industry average, a benchmark can tell you something different. For example, if the norm for this industry

is actually 95 percent, you can reset your thinking and start making incremental adjustments to achieve the final 10 percent.

- **Benchmarks help identify areas for improvement before a detailed analysis is carried out.** You don't need to sort out all the problems at once. Start by identifying the main areas that need to be improved first. Benchmarks can help you quickly and efficiently assess the current situation and prioritize your needs. The results of such comparisons are usually very specific—for example, *the proportion of problem suppliers is 25 percent higher than the average for our competitors.*

A comparative analysis helps to answer three simple and valid questions:

1. **What is good and what is bad?** A snapshot of performance across the board gives a common understanding of the current state and areas of underperformance. There are dozens of indicators that can be used to determine whether procurement is performing well or poorly. But, in order to understand what value would be optimal for a particular company, a single average figure across all sectors or even data about the situation of companies in the same industry is not enough. The first thing to do is to identify the indicators that are important to your business, assess your own performance or lack thereof, and then draw conclusions about yourself and for yourself.

2. **What is to blame?** Analysis of performance drivers, even if based on our own assumptions for lack of better information, triggers a search for solutions or more reliable information to explain why current performance differs from other companies. Here is an example from my practice. For some reason, it always seemed to us that we were slightly behind the best corporations in the industry in terms of automation. The situation showed that, quite simply, they were investing a lot more in IT solutions. We calculated the return on such investments based on our data and concluded that in our case, increasing the number of automated procedures would not increase efficiency (pay off), but would only be a sort of *tribute to trends*, so we just ceased several initiatives as redundant. The decision not to chase best practices is also quite possible—as long as it is clearly justified.

3. **What needs to be done?** Key performance indicator and benchmark analysis show what changes are needed in order to improve competitiveness and provide a great reason for the team to brainstorm where you want to be, where you don't want to be, and what you need to improve in order to accomplish those goals. For example, you might

decide that this year you need to raise indicator X by 15 percent. Or maybe you realize that you need to develop some area simply to maintain your current position—after all, other companies are constantly evolving too.

Now let's talk about the *disadvantages* of benchmarking:

- **Benchmarking participants may not understand the methodology behind indicators and may provide limited or erroneous data to researchers.** This is mostly true of open studies. Most of the data underlying benchmarking is information that companies have agreed to disclose and provide free of charge to their consultants or research organizations in order to build a database. The benchmarking research option where the client company works *with* consultants is preferable in cases where detailed and in-depth analysis is required. The conclusions from such studies will be more accurate because they are based on reliable information: calculations are supported by direct data from accounting systems, and interviews are conducted with a number of employees with different roles inside and outside of the function responsible for different tasks. In many cases, these people can see the situation from different angles. Carefully interpreting the interview results and then comparing them to data the consultant gathers in the course of talking with managers, employees, and stakeholders—rather than using just impersonal and average indicators—will help reduce the risk of subjective data and judgments.

  When analyzing, the consultants will compare the respondents' answers with their knowledge base that was accumulated from projects at different companies. As a result, they are more critical of their clients' value judgments because they possess wider market data from many projects, and their job is to find inconsistencies and areas for improvement. There is also a balance to be struck between the consultant's experience and knowledge base and the client's own ability to think critically.

  Consider a situation where companies respond to a survey on their own, without any external accompaniment or supervision. For example, when asked about the role of a project office in procurement, many respondents had vastly different ideas about what a project office was. Some thought it was a business unit that played a methodological role. Others thought the project office had just an administrative role, monitoring the correctness of tender procedures or keeping project status records. This disconnect can skew survey results as to whether the project office adds value to the company. Ideally, a project office is a team of dedicated staff who draw up the overall methodology of procurement work, develop new procurement management models, work on partnership development, deal with customer experience surveys to improve interaction with internal and external stakeholders, coordinate project work, and more. Reporting and monitoring refer to operational processes that do not determine development strategy.

As you can see, the understanding of similar terminology may be different and can depend on the specifics of the business. It can be a tricky task for external experts to clarify details during the interviews while constructing a benchmarking questionnaire that ensures equal interpretations from all participants. Even such standard notions as "raw materials" or "direct spend" can be interpreted differently by respondents from different companies. The risk of misinterpretation grows when the questionnaires are processed without a detailed review from the CPO (Chief Procurement Officer), who better understands the wider context. In addition, survey questions can be rather sparse in detail, leaving room for interpretation by respondents that, in turn, leads to incorrect answers.

- **Results may be influenced by nonstandardized input data and missing details.** Different companies have different organizational structures and levels of integration and centralization. It is not possible to take into account all the specifics of processes and management systems or all aspects of corporate culture, governance, and decision-making details when analyzing responses from a large selection of companies, even if specific numerical values are provided by them. To give a simple example, different companies may consider inventories with different storage terms as being obsolete. Comparisons of provided data may be misleading because of differences in the operating model or quality standards. The volume of outsourced services related to a specific category or differences in accounting policies may not be taken into account. The number of subsidiaries, the extent to which they are integrated into the overall end-product value chain, the availability and cost of internal procurement, the level of employee authority, differences in terminology, and the structure of cost categorization can all impact data. For example, one company may categorize electric motors as *engines*, while another includes associated services and spare parts in that same category. That will certainly affect the accuracy of data interpretation. Often, only top-level data is provided, which cannot be analyzed in detail, and the final result depends on a large number of factors that are difficult to isolate due to the confidentiality of the data itself.

HOW TO WORK WITH BENCHMARKS

Regardless of the disadvantages, benchmarking is an indispensable tool for determining the strength of the procurement function and setting targets for its development. You just need to learn how to use it. Benchmarking is a good place to start in order to assess the current state of your procurement department and draw up a development plan. Here are some basic rules for doing so:

- **It is not necessary to compare all the indicators available in research studies.** The initial step is to identify a set of benchmarks that are most important to your business, analyze and compare them in the current period to measure how much better/worse you are compared to the past, how you hold up against your competitors, and whether you are in line with industry best practices. How important is this benchmark to the success of the business as a whole? What happens if you don't change or measure this metric? Depending on the conclusions drawn, further steps in developing the function and improving its effectiveness can be planned.

- **Avoid being overly critical or overly positive in your assessments.** No matter how good your company's procurement is, when it comes to comparisons, everyone wants to see themselves as better than they are. But benchmarking comparisons are not a competition, they are a management tool. Double-check yourself; don't be fooled.

- **External and internal benchmark comparisons should be done regularly.** Gradually, with experience, an understanding will emerge of which indicators are truly valuable and which are just noise. You will also become adept at identifying possible influencing factors and correlations. If yesterday it took 30 to 40 days to deliver some products and now it takes 15 days, but stock is not going down, then the problem may not be the delivery speed. The problem may be in consumption planning or some other detail; the race for shorter delivery times may be irrelevant. It is important to accumulate your own base of reference—therein lies the real value.

- **Best practices are a good benchmark until you've actually achieved them.** So, your procurement key performance indicators are the best in the industry—or even in the world. Can you finally relax? Alas, that's impossible. The key to success in this situation is the realization that other companies are not standing still and that if you don't keep evolving, your success will be short-lived. The solution lies in comparing yourself to yourself (from the past) and then setting a higher target or even replacing a target with another one that leads to greater bottom-line results.

- **A full assessment of the function should be carried out with external experts using a proven methodology at least once.** External, independent expertise can help you to check and adjust your views, get your bearings quicker, decide on the main lines of development, and determine the relevant issues for your particular situation. Even the most experienced professionals miss things or suffer from internal corporate blind spots. Working in one place for a long time with the same people can cause you to miss things that may be apparent to an outsider.

Using a single source for benchmarking is unlikely to work. In this chapter, I have mentioned several different sources. You can use all of them to create a benchmarking matrix for your procurement department, drawing from those indicators that are most relevant to your company and current situation. Sources vary in content and level of detail, so it's always worth targeting several sources at once to fill in the gaps. And, of course, we must not forget to compare results with our own numbers. Typically, working capital management indicators, which are directly affected by procurement's performance, are not available in open benchmarking reports because they are also affected by too many other factors: industry conditions, resource load on production, market conditions, category specifics, etc. Progress in such cases can only be assessed by direct comparison with companies of interest or by assessing your own progress year over year.

There are many sources of information to use when comparing and evaluating key procurement performance indicators. But, is it possible to compare purchase prices, key terms of contracts with suppliers, or the level of service for specific categories? The simple answer is yes. Like benchmarking performance indicators, benchmarking prices and terms of transactions can be determined using information from open sources. However, a direct comparison of the prices that two different companies pay for the same item can be a violation of confidentiality agreements, not to mention unethical. In many countries, such actions are prosecuted by law, and antitrust authorities can take tough measures against violators. At the same time, there are open sources of information that might not reveal at what price competitors purchased fuel from a particular supplier but will provide market indicators and stock quote indices, as well as information on the cost of similar purchases, which may be published on public procurement platforms. There are also many online stores and marketplaces where you can find information about up-to-date prices in many categories, especially when it comes to consumer goods and services.

For many categories, specific conditions need to be taken into account, even if the information is available from public sources. For example, for fuel and metals, commodity exchange quotations are available, but they are based on prices for standard specifications. In reality, the price for a specific type and volume of fuel or metal product will be different—it will include processing costs and logistics at a minimum. Therefore, it is important to understand the price structure. Specialized analytical agencies are good sources of information for researching major market players and price structures. There is usually a charge for their services, but it is worth buying a subscription if you want quality, verified information.

It can be difficult to find "standard" guidelines on recommended cost structures for contractual obligations. This is partly due to the fact that every deal is unique and depends on the outcome of the negotiations, which depends on the quality and depth of each party's preparation and how much is known about the purchased category. Market research; involvement of consultancies, lawyers, and financial analysts with the necessary experience in dealing with specific types of deals; and maintaining a dialogue with suppliers can help you understand what the "norm" is. Even if during this research you only get some of your questions answered, it will give you an understanding of what to aim for and how high your goals or requirements should be.

Finally, I would like to mention two important things about benchmarking:

1. **Your own experience will not be enough to foresee everything.** No professional knows all the answers to all questions. But the answers definitely come from communicating with a wide range of procurement professionals at different levels. It is this communication that is the main tool for finding ideas and implementing consistent steps to develop and improve efficiency.

2. **Even a strong team can benefit from external help.** If the possible effects and the timeframe for achieving them cover the costs, it is worth engaging consultants. An external resource can help to accelerate research and have a positive impact—provided the internal and external teams work together effectively.

KEY CHAPTER IDEAS

- Constant improvement requires constant comparisons—ideas don't come in a vacuum.
- A meaningful qualitative comparison should be done with the companies that are similar to yours in terms of operations, revenues, and other parameters. Comparisons with companies that are not similar to yours can also be useful in terms of finding new ideas, but it is still better to compare apples to apples.
- Best practices are a good benchmark until you have achieved them yourself. Set your next-level targets and challenge yourself constantly!
- The risks of benchmarks:
  - **Companies may provide incomplete or unverifiable data.** Due to confidentiality, the data provided for comparison may not reflect the actual situation. It is also possible that the information may be out of date. When making comparisons with other companies, it is important to have an intermediary (independent expert/consultant) who can bring the data to a common denominator if survey participants are not willing to open up their data through direct benchmarking
  - **Benchmarking results are influenced by the organizational model and structure of a company.** Pay attention to what cost accounting/allocation methods are used and how they differ from yours
  - **Lack of detail can be misleading.** If you do the benchmarking yourself, discuss the methodology among your coworkers in as much detail as possible. If you cannot agree on a methodology, comparing indicators and finding performance points can lead to incorrect conclusions

CHAPTER 3

ACTION PLAN: STRATEGY AND TACTICS

DESIGNING A PROCUREMENT FUNCTION DEVELOPMENT STRATEGY

So, a basic comparison of key performance indicators has been made and some conclusions drawn. What's next? What should you do if you see an opportunity to improve your situation, but are not sure where to start?

First, let's get a handle on expectations. Crafting a strategy for the procurement function is, first and foremost, about finding out what the strategic priorities are for your business. These are the foundations for the development of individual function strategies: all activities and actions should be aimed at supporting and improving the company's overall performance, not at satisfying the ambitions of a particular functional group. In addition to internal strategic priorities, external factors also influence the development trajectory of the function. Only by comparing the former and the latter can one understand where to go next.

A company's development strategy usually defines what its long-term goals are in the areas of profitability, business sustainability, operational efficiency, market share and retention, competition policy, social responsibility, and more. Internal customers and management expect procurement to provide the necessary goods and services quickly, efficiently, and cost-effectively, and to have simple and transparent operational processes. Businesses that understand the role and capabilities of the procurement function also expect it to contribute to their overall financial performance through savings on procurement (we'll discuss this separately in Chapter 5). Additionally, the external environment has an impact that cannot be ignored—for example, market conditions, mergers and acquisitions, raw material shortages, supply and demand balance, innovations, and the introduction of new technologies. All of these ultimately affect the strategy of the procurement function, as well as those of other functions and the business as a whole. Figure 3.1 shows the areas of mutual influence on the main strategy planning factors.

Perhaps the most important thing in planning the development of a function is to strike an optimal balance between all influencing factors, as well as grasping real opportunities and available resources. The development strategy for any function should answer the question: How can we meet the expectations of all parties while ensuring the best possible outcome for the business?

Before you start analyzing the gaps between your future (desired) state and the current state, it is important to think about what the main task of your procurement function is. Why does it exist in the first place? What exactly should it be? What should its teams and their activities be associated with? What is the overall vision of the function and, if you will, its mission? After all, it is from this overall vision that the development strategy and tactical plan for its implementation will be derived.

I have come across the view that the mission of any particular department or function is an artificial construct because, traditionally, the mission is defined at a company-wide level and influences the strategic vision and the existence of the business as a whole. Nevertheless, I believe that defining a

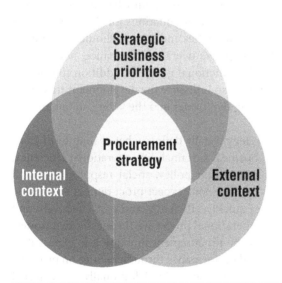

Strategic priorities:
- Profitability
- Sustainability
- Markets
- Operational effectiveness
- Social responsibility

Internal context:
- Speed
- Reliability
- Quality
- Client experience

External context:
- Markets
- New technology
- Attracting talent

Figure 3.1 Influence of internal and external factors, as well as strategic business priorities, on shaping the development strategy of the procurement function (select examples).

function's mission is an important step that plays a noticeable motivating role for the entire procurement team and is a powerful guide for development. The vision for the function is a precise and succinct definition that should be articulated to motivate the staff to achieve their goals. The concept of mission and vision in the context of achieving a meaningful transformative goal is described in the book *Exponential Organizations*.[1] When defining the mission and vision, understanding exactly how you will ensure that you reach them—in other words, which indicator or group of indicators lets you know that you have achieved your goal—is as important as the motivating definition itself.

Here are some examples of the wording of a target vision for the procurement function:

- *Build the most efficient procurement function in the industry*
- *Ensure the fastest rate of industry innovation in procurement*
- *Become the best procurement organization in the region*

The achievement of such goals can be assessed by comparing a set of key indicators across companies or by gaining recognition from industry peers; for example, through a formal competition or open benchmarking.

When we created the procurement mission definition with one of my teams, despite several years of successful transformation and peer recognition, we felt that the results we had achieved might not be sustained and could change under pressure. We wanted unequivocal recognition of the procurement function's contribution to the company's overall results—not only from senior management, which had already been achieved, but also from our internal customers and external suppliers. As a result, we developed a mission statement: "The best partner in securing the present and creating the future."

We realized that we would only be able to measure the achievement of this goal by calculating how client-focused our business unit was. The concept of a *customer-focused assessment* includes many aspects that can be summed up by answering some seemingly simple questions about whether internal clients are satisfied with working with us. We prefer to offer our clients 3–5 statements, which normally address their key interests, rather than using long questionnaires. For example, we would use statements like "The procurement function helps me achieve our business goals," or "I am satisfied with the speed of procured items delivery," or "I always know whom to address for any procurement-related questions." The clients were then asked to what extent they agree or disagree with those statements (strongly agree, agree, disagree, or strongly disagree) and, if desired, they could provide an explanation. The meanings embedded in these questions are much broader than a purely emotional *like* or *dislike* assessment: stakeholders do not select *like* just for being treated politely—although that is also considered—but more for actually helping them achieve their goals.

There is no right or wrong formulation of the unit's purpose or mission, but there is a key rule: the definition should be a team effort and not be imposed from above. To do this, it is important to involve as many employees as possible in the creation of a mission statement. Before our vision for the development of the procurement function was formed, we surveyed the opinions of all procurement employees and discussed ideas at several strategic sessions. It still took us quite a while to come up with a phrase that encompassed the whole set of meanings that we wanted to reflect. I think we managed to solve this on the third or fourth attempt, but the protracted search proved useful in itself when all that pain and effort came up with the correct wording and was adopted by the entire department. We all worked hard to create it, so it was truly *ours*—made and accepted by the whole team and absolutely clear to everyone.

Therefore, let's assume that a meaningful transformational goal for the procurement function (its target state) and the factors affecting the unit's performance have been identified. To put all this into practice, it is important to formalize and communicate the high-level goals and strategy to all employees within the function, as well as to management, customers, and possibly suppliers. This will help to inform stakeholders, share your vision, and confirm that the goal is not simply metaphorical padding, but a real necessity for everyone—employees, stakeholders, and the company itself. In discussions, colleagues are guaranteed to come up with ideas or additional requirements, and you will be able to refine your goals together and agree on how to achieve them.

Setting Strategic Targets

You can now start to develop the strategy itself. Any strategy revolves around a strategic target—what you want to achieve must be measurable in order to evaluate the success of its implementation. One good option is using the *objectives and key results* (OKR)[2] format. This tool has been around for a long time and even though many companies have never used it, it is worth testing. The methodology is convenient, simple, and clear. Here are some of its basic rules:

- OKR is applied when you need to change a business process and make a qualitative leap forward. The *O* in the acronym is not *all objectives*, only those that need to be *in focus*.

- All goals should be supported by measurable *KRs* (key results) with a clear evaluation method. Key results are not practices, but what you accomplish after you have done something.
- OKRs must be sufficiently ambitious (possibly even *breathtaking*).
- OKRs should be flexible—set only for the period or development stage following the current one; they can change from stage to stage depending on the previous results achieved and external conditions (as a rule, targets are set per quarter).
- The principle of inclusion must be respected, where goals and key results are shaped by the team—both top-down and bottom-up. Setting and adopting goals together inspires the whole team to achieve results.
- OKRs do not supersede key performance indicators (KPIs) (e.g., delivery rates or savings), but rather supplement them to quickly prioritize and monitor the achievement of high-level goals.

According to this methodology, top-level key objectives are first defined for each of the development priorities. Then, for each key objective, some key results are defined, which are set both for the long term (e.g., in three years we should achieve 7 percent savings in procurement annually) and for shorter intermediate periods within which you can monitor how well you are progressing toward your key objective.

Here is an example of what this might look like in practice:

- **Priority:** efficiency of the procurement function
- **Objective:** procurement function efficiency should be in the first quartile[3] of global best practice for your industrial segment
- **Key results for Q1 (or the first three months of implementation):**
  - Reduce the average cost of placing a purchase order by 50 percent through process automation
  - Ensure that data on 100 percent of deliveries is available online without delays
  - Develop and approve category strategies for categories X, Y, and Z

There are usually several priorities. They depend on the objectives and goals set for the procurement function. It is important to keep the number of strategic goals to no more than four or five because a larger number would be more difficult to manage. Also, a large number of objectives blurs the focus, and you should be wary of strategies and plans that are overloaded with indicators.

Finding the Gaps

The easiest way to link together all the components of the objectives and identify what is preventing them from being achieved is to perform a *gap analysis*,[4] using a set of KPIs that are critical to you. The method for conducting the gap analysis is as follows:

- For each of the influencing factors, identify what strategic activities the procurement function should undertake and what results it should show to ensure that the company's expectations, strategic objectives, and priorities are met, taking into account the influence of external and internal factors
- Determine the current level of influencing factors by digitizing the appropriate KPIs
- Set short- and long-term targets for your performance indicators
- Compare the current situation with your desired results and identify your weakest areas
- Draw up a list of measures that will get you closer to reaching your targets and focus on what matters most—*achieving them*

An example of a comparison of the current and desired state of the procurement function is shown in Table 3.1. I emphasize that the data in this table are provisional, and the actual analysis will vary from company to company and may contain many more rows.

There are a number of procurement assessment frameworks offered by consultants and procurement research centers that are excellent for guiding the function's development strategy. These studies are oftentimes publicly available on the internet. While such articles often do not provide details of the tools used, they do give a fairly complete picture of their structure, which in itself will serve as a good guide. Of course, these approaches have many common components. However, it is not necessary to adhere strictly to one methodology or the other. Moreover, you should try different methodologies at least once, compare the results, and then select and use the most valuable insights for your organization.

Even a cursory glance at the main methodology building blocks helps in choosing which indicators and tools are important to consider when analyzing the current situation and determining the target state of your procurement function. Don't worry if your interpretation differs from that of the authors of the original methodology. There is nothing wrong with that—only you and your team can determine what is important for your company and what to pay attention to today. Methodology templates only point to a direction and help provide the detail for analysis. No matter which methodology you choose, it is important to develop a strategy and a set of performance indicators for your procurement function that cover all of the organization's core needs as well as reflect the company's characteristics. The fact that a strategy is not built around a single scientific approach (there is simply no one-size-fits-all approach) does not mean that it cannot be successful.

The ensuing lists are example sets of possible basic strategic priorities to help start fleshing out the development strategy of the function, as well as outlining a framework for defining the tactical plan for strategy implementation. The areas of assessment listed complement Table 3.1, which is silent on what specific innovations are required to actually achieve the targets. Some of these indicators can also be used as key results in the OKR methodology.

Check how comprehensive your current situation assessment is and identify key areas for improvement using the control questions in the following lists. Remember, however, that we are only looking at an example, so it cannot be exhaustive. I would also like to remind you that you should not have too many directions and priorities; if the strategy cannot be committed to memory the chances of its survival are drastically reduced. Therefore, the main objectives and indicators that will be the focus of your attention should fit into four or five priority areas. As for operational indicators, such as the speed of individual operations, they only support the strategy but do not have to be part of it:

- **Priority 1: Strategic fit**
  - **Goal:** Ensure that procurement contributes to the overall financial result of the company.
  - **Key results:**
    - Procurement savings: greater than five percent of spend
    - 100 percent of major categories are green-procurement compliant
    - 100 percent of raw material suppliers are routinely certified
  - **Control questions:**
    - How does procurement support the company's development strategy?
    - Does procurement bring innovative ideas from the market to support the company's strategy?
    - How well aligned are procurement's key results with the strategic objectives of the business?
    - Are stakeholders satisfied with procurement's service level?
    - What changes need to be made to the supplier certification process?

Table 3.1 Example of a comparison between the current and desired (target) state of selected performance indicators for the procurement function.

Direction/Influencing Factors	Top-Level Objectives	Current State	Transition State	Target State
		STRATEGIC BUSINESS PRIORITIES		
Profitability	Ensure 18% business profitability	Procurement savings at 2% of spend	Procurement savings at: Year 1: 2.5% Year 2: 3%	Procurement savings at 4% (industry average according to benchmarking)
Sustainability	Ensure the resilience of the business model through a reliable supply chain	On Time In Full (OTIF) supply chain at 90%	OTIF supply chain at: Year 1: 95% Year 2: 97%	OTIF supply chain at 99%
Markets	Ensure a stable gap of at least 15% by market share from competitors	Delivery lead times: 60 days average	Delivery lead times: 15–35 days	Delivery lead times: 5–15 days
Operational effectiveness	Keep operational costs change within inflation rate	Procurement ROI: 200%	Procurement ROI: Year 1: 300% Year 1: 600%	Procurement ROI: ≥ 700%
Social responsibility	Reduce CO_2 emissions by 30% within 3 years	Volume of green purchases: not tracked	Implement green purchasing for 60% of spend	Implement green purchasing for 100% of spend
		INTERNAL CONTEXT		
Speed	Ensure that all requisitions are processed within 3 business days	Average lead time from requisition to purchase order: 30 days	Average lead time from requisition to purchase order: 15 days	Average lead time from requisition to purchase order: 3 days
Reliability	Ensure a delivery discipline rate of 99%	Delivery rate: 90%	Delivery rate: Year 1: 94% Year 1: 99%	Delivery rate ≥ 99%

Continued

Table 3.1 *continued*

Direction/Influencing Factors	Top-Level Objectives	Current State	Transition State	Target State
INTERNAL CONTEXT (continued)				
Quality	Ensure production continuity by reducing the volume of low-quality raw material supplies to 0.1%	Volume of substandard supplies: 10%	Volume of substandard supplies: Year 1: 5% Year 1: 2%	Volume of substandard supplies: ≤ 0.1%
Client experience	Procurement is a reliable business partner	Customer experience evaluation rate: 2.5 points out of 4.0	Customer experience evaluation rate: 3.1 points out of 4.0	Customer experience evaluation rate ≥ 3.5 points out of 4.0
EXTERNAL CONTEXT				
Markets	Strategic supplier partnerships are implemented for all key categories	There are no strategies for managing major categories	Development and implementation of long-term category management strategies for all critical categories	Strategic partnerships defined, negotiated, and implemented for all critical categories
New technology	Ensure procurement function supports implementation of innovative solutions	There is no systematic work and collection of information about suppliers' innovation	Develop knowledge and innovation development program with suppliers	Supplier knowledge and innovation development program implemented and tracked
Attracting talent	Ensure 100% talent pool reserve coverage for all critical positions	There is no system for attracting best talent to procurement organization; skills assessment and development program does not exist	Develop and implement talent attraction program through communication and information events as well as skills assessment and development program for procurement	Developed programs successfully applied to ensure effective talent attraction, retention, and development

- o Is procurement involved in making key decisions that are directly or indirectly related to the implementation of the company's development strategy and cost management?
- o Is the purchasing department involved in the implementation of the company's strategic projects?
- **Priority 2: Organizational compliance**
  - **Goal:** Ensure that the procurement department complies with best practices.
  - **Key results:**
    - o Return on investment in procurement: greater than 700 percent
    - o Relevant service level agreements for different internal clients are agreed upon and fulfilled
  - **Control questions:**
    - o How does the procurement unit's organizational structure fit into the corporate organizational structure?
    - o To what extent can the present organizational structure of the procurement department deliver the intended results?
    - o Is the procurement department's head count in line with target estimates and best practices?
    - o What processes need to be changed to ensure that strategic objectives are met?
    - o Are stakeholders satisfied with the speed and quality of procurement processes?
    - o Is the stakeholder communication system in line with expectations?
    - o Are stakeholders happy with the current organization of change management?
    - o Can processes be made efficient through alternative procurement models (e.g., outsourcing)?
- **Priority 3: Performance management**
  - **Goal:** Ensure that key operational processes are at least as efficient as the first quartile in the industry.[5]
  - **Key results:**
    - o Category strategies are developed and executed for 100 percent of key spend areas
    - o Key operational indicators are in line with best practices (e.g., average time from requisition to order is three days)

- o 100 percent of active counterparties, covering 80 percent of costs, are audited and validated at least every two years
- o The level of automation for procurement operations is at least 60 percent by 2025
- ◻ **Control questions:**
  - o Can we measure all target results (is there enough data to do so)?
  - o How do we assess the quality of the data in our procurement organization? Is it sufficient to achieve our key results?
  - o Are company management and stakeholders informed about the KPIs?
  - o Do employees understand their function, how it affects KPIs, and what actions are expected of them?
  - o What automation tools are available to us? Are we investing enough in automation? How do we measure the effects of automation?
- **Priority 4: Team and competency development**
  - ◻ **Objective:** Ensure knowledge continuity and attract the best procurement talent.
  - ◻ **Key results:**
    - o Have at least two qualified candidates available for each key position
    - o The function's employee engagement index is in the performance zone
    - o Training programs for different levels of competency have been updated and implemented
    - o Attractiveness of the workplace—procurement is among the top three most attractive functions in the company, according to employee surveys
  - ◻ **Control questions:**
    - o Which competencies are lacking in procurement now and which ones will be needed in the future?
    - o What are we doing to attract the best talent?
    - o How are we building the talent pool for key and line positions?
    - o What training programs need to be introduced?
    - o Are we leveraging all the company's capabilities and relationships to promote procurement among employees and possible candidates?

○ How do we manage information and knowledge transfer within the organization?
○ How secure are we against the loss of information and
competencies in key function positions?
○ Is there a dependency on unique personal competencies
in key categories?

This list can be supplemented by other priorities and directions, and one priority can be broken down into several—there are no boundaries or rules. For
example, automation tasks are included under *performance management*, but
this block may be broad enough to occupy a special place in the list of overall
priorities. The previous list serves as the beginning of a process of building
a deep understanding of the function's aims and objectives, as well as setting
directions for the development of the entire procurement system. There are
plenty of articles, books, and methodologies to draw on—the main thing is
to constantly check the strategy for relevance, and update when necessary.
The world is always changing faster than we think, new ideas are constantly
emerging and old ones do not stand the test of time and practice. And that's
okay. Once the strategic objectives are set, it is time to talk about tactics.

REFINING TACTICS FOR STRATEGY IMPLEMENTATION

To ensure that your strategy does not just remain on paper, it is important to
complement it with a detailed plan for implementing the changes needed to
achieve your strategic goals. Let's call it an *operational improvement plan*. This
is the plan that will allow you to monitor whether the function is on the right
track and whether the changes are being implemented fast enough.

Drawing up a tactical plan is as complex and detailed as developing a strategy because in order to decide on a specific set of changes, you need to go
deep into the operational processes, examine them, and look for anything that
might get in the way of your objectives. You need to make a list of practical
steps to implement changes and remove bottlenecks from processes, organizations, and interactions.

First, we must understand the structure of the procurement process.
What is its real state? How long does it take? Who is involved in the process? What obstacles and difficulties does it encounter? Who makes decisions? Are there obstacles or procedures that slow it down or prevent it from
achieving high performance? An overview of a typical procurement process
is shown in Figure 3.2.

If we consider the factors that influence purchasing and its cost and quality, the process chain—even in its most general form—becomes considerably longer (see Figure 3.3).

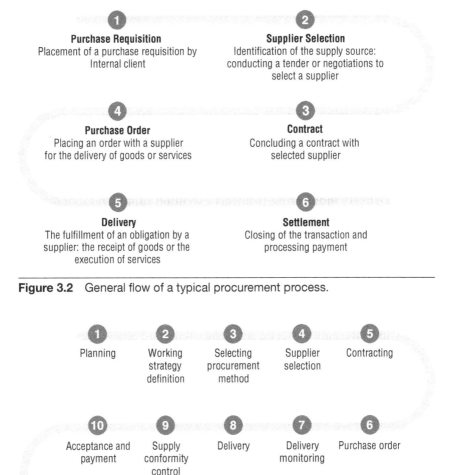

1 Purchase Requisition
Placement of a purchase requisition by Internal client

2 Supplier Selection
Identification of the supply source: conducting a tender or negotiations to select a supplier

4 Purchase Order
Placing an order with a supplier for the delivery of goods or services

3 Contract
Concluding a contract with selected supplier

5 Delivery
The fulfillment of an obligation by a supplier: the receipt of goods or the execution of services

6 Settlement
Closing of the transaction and processing payment

Figure 3.2   General flow of a typical procurement process.

1 Planning

2 Working strategy definition

3 Selecting procurement method

4 Supplier selection

5 Contracting

10 Acceptance and payment

9 Supply conformity control

8 Delivery

7 Delivery monitoring

6 Purchase order

11 Exploitation of the procured item

12 Provision of ancillary services by the supplier

13 Supplier evaluation

14 Relationship management/ partnership development

15 Disposal of the procured item and waste management

Figure 3.3   Procurement process: a more detailed representation.

Let's explain the individual steps in the process:

1. **Planning:** This stage implies the emergence of a procurement request, procurement planning (or budgeting), and preparing a requisition.
2. **Working strategy definition:** Development of a department strategy for the short term (up to one year) and the long term (1–3 years).
3. **Selecting procurement method:** Determining the best method for acquiring the goods or services in the present circumstances, including the provisions of the category strategy, if it was developed.
4. **Supplier selection:** Identifying one or more suppliers from a list of available options.
5. **Contracting:** Drawing up a deal, negotiations, agreeing on terms, and signing a contract.
6. **Purchase order:** Placement of purchase order under which a specific quantity of goods will be delivered, or the scope of services carried out.
7. **Delivery monitoring (contract execution support):** Monitoring of performance according to work schedules and contractual obligations (inspections of manufacturing progress, intermediate quality checks, tests, and trials), intermediate meetings with suppliers, obtaining certificates and permits, logistics arrangements, and customs clearance.
8. **Delivery:** Receipt of goods or service/works deliverables.
9. **Supply conformity control:** Organization and performance of quality and quantity checks, acceptance tests, and processing supporting documents.
10. **Acceptance and payment:** Completion of the purchase order or the entire contract, acceptance of goods and/or services, preparation of accounting and legal documents: invoices, acceptance certificates, processing payment, and confirmations of contractual obligations fulfillment.
11. **Exploitation of the procured item:** Monitoring supply results, following maintenance or repair services, and managing the use of the procurement item and its stock.
12. **Provision of ancillary services by the supplier:** Maintenance, training, and accessories that will be needed during the exploitation process, along with what kind of services and additional supplies may be needed during the object's lifetime should preferably be determined at the very beginning—at the first step in the procurement process when the procurement technical requirements are defined. This will affect the total procurement price at a later stage.

13. **Supplier evaluation:** At the end of the contract or the cooperation period and after enough information has been gathered, the supplier undergoes an assessment. This differs from the prequalification at the beginning of the cooperation period since it is based on real data and the assessments of those who have worked with the supplier during the execution of the contract.

14. **Relationship management/partnership development:** After the fulfillment of contractual obligations and cooperation post-assessment, the category strategy, if it has been developed, is updated and the opportunities for developing relationships with the supplier are assessed. In some cases, decisions are made on developing strategic partnerships if the category is of significant importance and if the parties have enough common interests to develop a mutually beneficial partnership.

15. **Disposal of the procured item and waste management:** During and at the end of the procured item's (equipment and components) lifetime, arrange for the disposal of scrap waste, waste oil products, and hazardous substances; define the methods of handling or using operational by-products; and choose the waste disposal method.

In addition to these operational steps, there are parallel activities to support and organize the procurement process. These may include the following:

- Setting objectives
- Organizational planning
- Development of procurement category management strategy development[6]
- Client relationship management
- Supplier qualification, selection, and evaluation
- Supplier relationship management
- Supplier development programs
- Inventory management
- Reporting and forecasting
- Claims handling
- Optimization of operational processes
- Automation and technology development
- Team development and competency enhancement
- Development of policies and regulations
- Information and communication activities for stakeholders (the list could go on)

As we can see, the reality is somewhat broader than what we are used to imagining about the procurement process. Some stages of the process may run in parallel or change sequence depending on the situation and characteristics of the category. For example, procurement strategy development and planning with a long-time horizon can be done independently from ongoing procurement activities; quality control can be done either before or after delivery or even several times at different stages; and sourcing can be done by a predetermined quota distributed between a narrow range of existing suppliers with whom frame agreements have already been concluded or through supplier selection in an open tender.

Let's take a closer look at what the individual stages of the procurement process entail, along with who is involved in these subprocesses. In the most common procurement model, where companies already have a dedicated department (they often do not have one, especially at the initial stage of development), the following key people are involved in the procurement process:

- Client
- Buyer
- Supplier and/or contractor

In addition, there are other auxiliary functions involved in the process:

- Lawyer
- Logistician
- Financial controller
- Treasurer
- Accountant
- Transporter
- Warehouse worker (storekeeper, forklift operator, etc.)
- Quality control specialist
- Security officer
- Authorized officers (head of the procurement service, tender committee, signatories of legally significant documents, etc.)

Each of these roles contains natural limitations in functionality and expertise, so multiple roles can be carried out by a single employee. Let's look at the pros and cons of combining roles in this way.

In small companies with limited staff, where each employee has to know at least a little bit about everything, many operations are often carried out by the same person. In a company that employs 10 people and spends no more than $1,000,000 a year on procurement, this is a manageable situation—you can pull up the documents for each purchase at any time and literally check them manually for errors or inconsistencies.

But as the number of transactions and procurement costs increase, risks begin to accumulate in the system, and it becomes cumbersome to manage and monitor every transaction reliably. Does the order match the contract? Have all payments gone out on time? Is there any risk of a claim? Have all discounts been received? Does the quantity of goods received correspond to the delivery note?

The larger the procurement load, the more difficult it is to control the process and ensure quality without duties being properly segregated so that each successive participant is essentially in charge of quality control for the operations in the previous step. It is like a continuous chain—each step begats the next one, which must comply with the parameters and conditions laid down in the previous step, thus reducing risks for the whole process. We will discuss the types of risks and how to minimize them in more detail later, but for now, let's look at the most typical roles, their responsibilities, and their constraints in the procurement process (see Table 3.2).

As you can see in Table 3.2, each participant has their own set of responsibilities and their own limitations in their areas of expertise. The introduction of a separation of powers and control functions is well-intentioned—it does reduce the risks of making unwise decisions or authorizing uncoordinated transactions. But, it also creates bureaucracy, which is oftentimes unnecessary and does not contribute to the efficiency of the procurement process; anyone involved can block or delay the process if they are slow or do not fully carry out their duties.

Based on the aforementioned goals of functional separation, all approaches to organizing the interaction of process participants can be divided into two conditional paradigms:

1. We complement each other with our expertise
2. We control each other

Often, one approach or the other will predominate in any given organization, but the optimum situation is a balance between the two.

The option of complementing each other's expertise relies more on trust in the organization, but does not guard against possible incompetence. In the paradigm of total control, everyone in the process chain is responsible only for their part of the work, but not for the whole result. This approach does not allow for open discussion of bottlenecks and suffers from a lack of accountability.

However, in the mixed variant, the participants in the process, while retaining controlling functions, can trust each other and count on assistance and expertise, which implies a joint development of solutions and risk reduction.

The ability to put the principle of *trust, but verify* into practice while professing respect for the work of others, openly discussing risks, and giving

Table 3.2   Typical procurement process role assignments and their constraints.

Role	Role Responsibilities	Typical Limitations
Customer	• Determines the demand • Defines technical requirements • Accepts the procurement results	• May not be aware of the specifics of the market and the links between its players • Primarily focused on closing demand for goods or services to fulfill operational processes
Buyer	• Develops category strategies • Determines the source and terms of supply • Negotiates • Concludes the contract • Places purchase orders • Monitors contract execution	• May not know the specifics of the market in case of urgent unforeseen procurement • May not know all the technical details of the procured item • May not have sufficient training in quality control, law, finance, or risk management
Supplier and/or contractor	• Provides goods or services and performs works • Provides ancillary services and maintains the procured item	• May not understand the real value of the procured item for the client • Their sales strategy may not be aligned with the buyer's procurement strategy
Lawyer	• Ensures that the risks of the transaction are mitigated and that legal requirements are met	• May not know the extent to which procurement has an impact on production outcomes
Logistician	• Determines the optimum route and means of transport • Ensures delivery of the procured item	• May not be aware of the extent to which logistics costs affect the total cost of ownership for the procured item or understand the criticality of timing when selecting the best value logistics option
Financial controller	• Guarantees payment authorization • Evaluates the effectiveness of procurement decisions	• May not be aware of the limitations of the processes; may not have enough information about the details and objectives of the transaction
Treasurer	• Ensures fund availability for transaction payments • Supervises cash flow management	• May not have enough information on the details and importance of the transaction
Accountant	• Performs financial calculations • Keeps records of business transactions	• May not have enough information on the details and importance of the transaction

Continued

Table 3.2 (*continued*)

Role	Role Responsibilities	Typical Limitations
Transporter	• Provides transportation services • Is responsible for the safety of cargo in transit	• Not interested in the final goal of the transaction, responsible only for its part of the operation
Warehouse worker	• Receives goods in the warehouse and delivers them to customers • Keeps records of business transactions	• May not have enough information on the details and importance of the transaction
Quality control specialist	• Ensures quality control or goods and services • Keeps a record of procurement breaches	• May not have enough information on the details and importance of the transaction
Security officer	• Performs supplier compliance audit • Monitors compliance of operations with established rules and regulations • May block the procurement process if risks are detected	• May not have enough information on the details and importance of the transaction
Authorized officer	• Signs off on supplier selections and procurement decisions • Approves category strategies • Signs contracts and specifications • Can block the procurement process if risks are identified or if there is insufficient justification	• May not be aware of operational process specifics

feedback on shortcomings and errors must be a significant cultural component of the organization. This does not replace the manual and automated control of the previous operational stage by the next stage, but it opens up qualitatively new opportunities for the particular team and company as a whole since it involves continuous improvement through regular feedback.

Another important aspect is marginal involvement in the process. Let's look at the contract negotiation stage, a typical subprocess in the procurement chain. Over my years in procurement, I have had to read and sign hundreds of contracts, and there were often a large number of people involved in the negotiation of those agreements. In some cases, I have seen up to 20 signatures on the back of the last page of a contract. An approximate list of standard approvals is given in Table 3.3.

Table 3.3 Sample list of approvals in the procurement process.

Conciliating Party	Approval Role
Procurement officer	Authorizes the transaction by confirming that all procurement procedures have been conducted in accordance with the applicable policies and regulations and that the contractual conditions comply with the tender conditions or agreements reached during negotiations
Warehouse	Confirms packaging, labeling, and dimensions
Logistics officer	Agrees to and confirms the feasibility of the stipulated delivery terms and conditions
Internal client	Approves technical specifications
Specialist X	Confirms internal client approval
Specialist X's supervisor	Approves specialist X's confirmation
Manager of Specialist X's supervisor	Clears the approval of Specialist X's supervisor
Legal department	Checks compliance with legal requirements and structures the transaction and its wording
Security officer	Checks risks and confirms the compliance of the counterparty
Internal audit	Verifies that the procurement procedure has been carried out without breaching regulations
Chief accountant	Checks payment terms and tax requirements
Financial controller	Confirms budget
Financial director	Authorizes the deal
Chief Procurement Officer	Approves supplier selection and signs the contract

The set of approvals in Table 3.3 may seem a bit inflated, but unfortunately it is not far from reality. Let's say a procurement specialist prepares a contract. That person would need to understand what requirements and wording to include in the contract at the drafting stage. This means the specialist would need to discuss the terms with lawyers, finance, internal clients, and other stakeholders that have an interest in the outcome of the deal or will be involved in its execution. In doing so, they may be offered templates with predetermined wording. Thus, when the contract reaches the approval stage at the management level, all services are likely to have already participated in the drafting and negotiation of the text. The approval checklists often do not show the specialists who drafted the contract, but instead, include the names of their supervisors who have not even been closely involved in its drafting. Is it really possible for a busy manager who receives several contracts a day to take enough time to carefully read the contract? Unfortunately, in most cases they cannot because their other work commitments and meetings get in the way. We need to be honest about this reality.

It turns out that the use of a long approval chain for all contracts *without exception* creates the illusion of control where, in fact, it does not exist. But does this mean that approvals are meaningless and can simply be done away with? No. A lot depends on the readiness of the organization, the professionalism of employees, the ability to automate processes and controls, and in the end, whether those involved trust one another.

It is important not to replace control with actions that are meaningless. If a participant in the process has no real influence on the outcome, it is reasonable to conclude that there is no point in them being involved. What does the approval involve: professional expertise and contribution to the overall result or the formal signature of a person who simply has the authority to do so? If we ask ourselves this question and answer it honestly, we can find great potential in optimizing the approval process by developing new rules of engagement, which should be based on complementary expertise and real participation in drawing up the document.

If we go back to the list of typical steps in the procurement process and try to identify who is involved in each of the subprocesses mentioned, we find that it is not only the buyer who is involved everywhere. Lawyers and financial staff are necessarily included in developing transaction terms; internal control or security office representatives, along with technical and engineering specialists, may take part in the supplier qualification process; and it is impossible to develop a category strategy without consultations on the technical, legal, financial, and other aspects of the company's business and markets. The options for involving different specialists at each stage are endless. The same item can be bought in a hundred different ways, and each time, for every transaction, the same processes that seem standard and simple will have variations. In addition to the parties directly involved in the procurement process, there are a host of factors that have a direct or indirect influence, such as how quickly and in what way the specialists are recruited into the procurement office or how knowledge and information are managed in the organization.

Preparing a list of tactical changes requires a detailed analysis of deviations from desired scenarios, a critical assessment of each participant's contribution and tasks, the level of competence required, the use of automation, and so on. The use of lean management tools[7] (the simplest of which are detailed process flowcharts); data analysis to verify assumptions about the actual state of affairs; and collecting feedback from employees, customers, and suppliers helps greatly in the analysis.

A COFFEE TRANSFORMATION AT A GLOBAL AIRLINE[8]

The management at a Middle Eastern airline made a decision to implement an extensive digitalization program, and procurement was a significant part of this effort. The first thing that was implemented was data analysis. For six months, procurement was only concerned with analytics. Then, based on the real data, they started to implement category management. Second, they brought in support by inviting three external companies to the project: one to design the target processes, the second to implement them, and the third to test and compile the instructions. The second company monitored the results of the first, and the third monitored the results of the second. Next, they centralized the procurement of the 12 companies that made up the holding company at the head office and, at the same time, reduced the number of procurement staff by 30 percent.

One offshoot of this transformation process was that after six months of working with the numbers, buyers discovered that the company retained an abnormally high number of coffee suppliers. You can imagine how much coffee a global airline must purchase in order to serve all its passenger flights. An open tender was organized; companies that were capable of supplying coffee globally to all offices and locations were invited to participate. Once the tender was concluded and results tracked, coffee spending was reduced by 10 percent.

When drafting an operational (tactical) change management plan, it is also important to identify the links between different activities and their impact on other processes and functions. This will determine how additional changes will be managed and how the involvement of other departments, suppliers, and company management will be structured because changes are often not limited to the purchasing department and have far-reaching effects. It is important not to lose sight of these connections and influences and to synchronize your actions with the plans and projects of your colleagues in other departments, as well as with your suppliers. For example, if a company has planned an upgrade and reconfiguration of equipment for a particular month, but at the last minute, the supplier will not be able to deliver because it plans to overhaul its main production equipment, the coordination of such plans among stakeholders would be one of the tasks of the procurement department.

It is worth noting that while it is important to have a clear plan and sequence of actions, it is equally important to plan quickly; there are times when the detailed planning phase is either omitted altogether or is greatly delayed. Being able to plan on the fly is vital if something goes wrong. Have a change planning process in place that begins with the major points to be achieved. Start with a few activities and gradually add more detail to the plan as you go along. Remember that a complex process is always based on simple actions; start the changes without waiting for the perfect plan to emerge.

CHANGE MANAGEMENT

Change implementation is a multilayered process that includes three main stages:[9]

1. **Planning:** defining the target state and expected results, roadmap, and methods of introducing changes
2. **Implementing:** communication, executing planned activities, training, tracking results, and adapting the action plan
3. **Supporting:** monitoring results, collecting and processing feedback, adapting approaches, and summarizing change results

A detailed operational action plan supports the strategic change plan by laying out overall strategic priorities of the company or function. It requires a well-designed training program for participants in the processes that will be affected by the change. It may be necessary to update their motivation system and make sure that communication is crystal clear at the start of, during, and at the end of the change process. Gathering feedback during a change implementation helps adapt approaches and methods, fine-tunes the nuances of stakeholder interaction, and manages expectations.

The concept of *change management* comes from project management. When introducing small changes to separate processes, we often tend not to perceive them as a project activity and do not purposefully engage in activities that will support and entrench the changes. We seem to wonder why we should go to such trouble to develop a change implementation roadmap or communication plan if there is only one instruction to change. But how do we make sure that everyone affected by this change will be ready to accept it and start working under the new rules? Do employees understand exactly why they need this change in the first place and what is required of them? How can you make sure that the changes do not just remain on paper?

When our procurement team at Severstal started the project to introduce a category management approach to procurement, we had a plan. We understood exactly how we would assess competencies, determine who and what to teach, what the structure of category strategies would be, how to evaluate results, etc.

We created a project procurement office and a methodological unit, whose tasks included the development of target processes, training, communication, and support and control over implementing changes. Together with the methodological unit team and the project office, we dealt with processes, consolidated category developments, and implemented digital solutions. At the beginning of the category strategies development process, we closely supervised category managers, participated in working groups, helped with analytics, conducted training, developed document templates, and organized status meetings where category managers gave updates on how the implementation of the approved initiatives was progressing.

We introduced steering committees where we met to assess our progress and discuss next steps. We monitored ourselves and asked for feedback: freshly minted category managers talked about how far they had progressed in analytics and in creating category strategies; a group of methodologists dealt with initiatives in process automation; and a reporting group looked for the most convenient formats for management reports and selected relevant performance indicators. We held meetings with our stakeholders and company management and received help from consultants. The process gathered momentum, we worked at a fast pace, and everything generally went according to plan.

Finally, we completed the active phase for introducing the change. The new approaches had not yet taken root everywhere in the organization, but the main changes in the organizational structure and to the team had been made, and the program for developing category strategies with timelines, goals, and schedules had been launched. We had also decided on the most important indicators and were already learning new approaches to the process. We told the entire organization, our internal customers, and our suppliers how our processes had changed and how responsibilities had been redistributed among several procurement teams. Some of the teams focused on developing category strategies, some on ensuring current supplies, and others on back-office operations of order placement and processing of payments.

Soon the consultants left, leaving us to work within the new processes on our own. It seemed that we had gotten through the most difficult stage. We began to hold fewer steering committee meetings when suddenly interesting things began to happen. First, complaints from our internal customers, who had never liked the changes very much, became more frequent. The new ways of working were unpopular because we had redirected people toward developing category strategies and dedicated less attention to operational indicators. Nobody cared much about the fact that the implementation of the category strategy measures promised an across-the-board improvement of all interaction processes, thus saving time and money—for the internal clients, supplies "here and now" are always of paramount importance. A client would ask a long-standing buyer when his spare parts would be delivered and, instead of getting the necessary information, would be redirected to another person in the procurement back office[10] since the buyer was not responsible for processing purchase orders anymore.

Then we began to fall behind in developing category strategies and failing on inventory management metrics. We had to focus on *urgent* operational tasks: urgent tenders, urgent contracts, urgent requests from management, confusion in communications, etc. People clearly did not want to completely give up their habitual ways of working. Disputes arose over issues connected with the responsibility matrix and personal ambitions: some were assigned to work in category development and some to work in the back office—and for some, the new assignments seemed insignificant or did not match the level of their personal goals. We were confident that we had provided for everything, acted according to plan, talked through all the details, and were careful enough to have the team prepared, but as it turned out, we underestimated the importance of supporting the changes after the formal end of the active phase. It became absolutely clear that we had to change something again.

We decided it made no sense to wait for everyone to somehow get used to the new processes, so we reactivated the steering committees and began collecting more feedback from internal stakeholders and suppliers to find out how our changes were affecting them. We helped keep the change plan up-to-date through proactive actions by bringing the changes to the attention of company management and function heads, monitoring progress, offering active assistance and involvement in complex operational issues, collecting information regularly, analyzing mistakes and failures, holding strategic sessions between different teams, actively involving them in developing proposals for process and communication improvements, giving detailed descriptions of these improvements, and coordinating change implementation at all levels.

We started having informational meetings for procurement employees and clients, where the atmosphere was sometimes heated with a lot of criticism and comments. But it was worth it. I think we were able to achieve a high level of transparency about the changes because we communicated and explained why we were making them. We were honest about what to expect from the changes and what not to expect from them, at least in the foreseeable future, as well as where temporary deterioration was occurring and why. We talked about how much money the company was allocating to support the changes and what was and what was not going well.

The result was the creation of several new reference guidelines, instructions, and an electronic *Procurement Guide* on the company portal—these resources explained in simple terms the workings of the procurement process. We assigned dedicated supervisors to deal with certain stakeholder issues, introduced changes to KPIs, and focused on those indicators that were important for our customers. We reallocated responsibilities and redesigned a number of processes that were better on paper than in reality.

I was very grateful to those colleagues who, after observing the challenges we faced—and there were many of them in the most unforeseen places—did not just criticize but gave suggestions on how to improve the situation, including what would help them adapt more quickly to the changes. I often recall a comment that came up regularly in our client surveys at the time: "Colleagues, we need to talk to each other more." It was as simple as that! During times of change, the pressure on the team can be enormous and the workday can stretch on endlessly, so it may seem that extra conversations are a waste of time—after all, there are clear and urgent issues that need to be addressed here and now. But that is not the case. Many urgent issues can, in reality, wait. Time spent openly discussing issues and brainstorming solutions can provide unexpected fixes. Face-to-face discussions beat e-mail newsletters every time.

So, what did our team learn from this experience? Here are the takeaways:

1. **Change does not stop with the end of its active phase; it requires ongoing support.** Even when formal change is complete, continued support is very much needed, otherwise, you can quickly return to where you started. A loss of focus on the part of employees and leaders will inevitably lead to a rapid backslide. Active support must be provided until the collective consciousness of the organization moves on to the new practices.

   It is always easier for people to show the operational results of their work: how many requisitions were processed, how many tenders were held, how many contracts were signed, etc. Looking at the number of processed transactions allows you to tell yourself that the day has not been wasted. But confusion can set in when people are required to be analytical, be creative, and when it is not clear whether initiatives will bear any fruit in the future. It is hard to see any immediate effect from this kind of work as compared to transactional procurement; therefore, people get lost. Procurement leaders must keep them focused on the larger goal.

2. **Both too little communication and too much information can ruin your change efforts.** It is important to talk not only about how changes will be made, but also why they are needed. It is not just the quantity and quality of communication that is important, but also its format. No matter how many newsletters and webinars you conduct, you need

to be prepared for the fact that your message still may not get through to the recipients. Employees lost in their day-to-day work often find it difficult to recognize the need for change. Change can create uncertainty where benefits (personal and professional) may not be completely obvious at first.

Innovation is always accompanied by discomfort because individual habits must change. If something is unclear or causes resistance, the only way to make change work is to gather feedback in every way possible and adapt the action plan to take this information into account. The inconvenience of the transition should be communicated in advance, and you should agree on a timeline, what the interim support tools will be, and how you will work together if things don't go as planned. With this approach, colleagues, executives, and even suppliers will be more understanding and supportive.

It is also worthwhile to caution against providing too much information. When this happens, the interest level of the audience can drop significantly. There is a risk that important information will be missed in the general flow of meetings and messages, or even be mistaken for spam. A careful selection of materials and a communication plan are a must. Asking the intended recipients how often they would like to receive news is the best way to plan the timing of messages.

3. **Training is needed not only for those directly affected by the change but also for other employees in the organization and suppliers.** Each participant in the procurement process has their own perspective, and their expectations are sometimes different: lawyers expect to receive a well-designed document for approval; purchasers expect specialized services, such as finance, to help them; and customers are most often only interested in the end result of the process—the delivery of goods or services on time, in the required quality, and at an acceptable price. At the same time, in spite of their different functions, all participants of the process are in the same boat, and overall success depends on everyone's actions. Therefore, it is important to not only maintain awareness of the changes, but also to hold regular training sessions for all parties involved. You cannot just do training once—it has to become a part of a structured change support process. These sessions usually end with productive discussions of joint actions to improve practices. Trainers should not only deliver information to participants but also gather feedback from them.

4. **What the changes mean to the individual is equally or more important than what they mean to the company as a whole.** Communications, training, improvement plans, ambitious goals, etc., have absolutely

no meaning for a specific employee until he or she knows how exactly the new approaches to their work will help him or her personally. This can only come from practical examples of real changes that people can observe, participate in, and feel the immediate effect of—as opposed to abstract stories from managers or far-flung company goals. The following are two stories on how change might be perceived when it starts and what it leads to if done in collaboration with the clients.

One of our internal customers kept complaining about the poor quality of the bearings they were receiving from suppliers, but ironically kept creating rush requisitions to get them. Our analysis showed that we were paying an average of 150 percent of the normal price for each rush order, and that purchasing through open tenders did not allow us to screen out poor quality suppliers. We involved this internal customer in fleshing out distinct issues as part of the creation of a category strategy. They clarified technical requirements, conducted screenings and evaluations of suppliers, chose a short list of those with whom we would work in the future, and implemented a process of quality control at delivery. The situation quickly became transparent and much more manageable for both procurement and the client.

In another situation, a buyer was processing several hundred requisitions per month and simply could not find time to qualitatively study supplier relationships and contract terms. An endless pipeline of requisitions, orders, and accounting documents did not allow enough time to keep things in order and meet targets. After a reallocation of responsibilities and the transfer of part of the operations to the back office, the timeliness of placing orders and financial clearance increased significantly. The employees of the procurement front office no longer had to worry about a backlog of hundreds of packages of unprocessed documents, and consequently, the indicators began to improve. Such results will not go unnoticed—information from personal experiences quickly comes up in discussions, people share their stories with each other, and an expectation of positive changes begins to take shape.

There are three factors that should always be taken into account when introducing change within the organization:

1. **Security**—people fear for their future, so it is important for them to understand whether they will keep their job after the change, what their income will be, what their workplace will look like, etc. All of these are basic requirements; the second level of Maslow's Pyramid,[11] if you will. And until the employee has received an answer to whether they will

keep their job or the internal client is persuaded that the changes will not break the supply chain and be an unnecessary risk, you should not count on a quick acceptance and adaptation to the change. You need to be as honest and open as possible about how changes will affect daily processes, and if you are not sure, you need to admit it.

2. **Values**—people are guided by their inner values and patterns of behavior. If a person does not like working in a team or lies about what is really going on, you probably will not be able to re-educate them. Our values are ingrained in us from early childhood. They determine our perception of the world around us and our ability to adapt quickly. It is difficult to influence these values and the way a person acts in times of change: whether they will understand the new processes and help their colleagues or start complaining and try to destroy the change process from within. Ideally, teams should include both supporters and critics because criticism oftentimes contains valuable suggestions. However, if the team is dominated by toxic critics, it is time to consider who will stay with the team and who should leave.

3. **Recognition**—nearly everyone likes to be praised and it is necessary to notice and celebrate successes; otherwise, and especially in periods of change, workdays turn into a series of endless challenges, difficult tasks, and high workloads. Even those who really try to "embrace the new" can lose motivation and stop supporting change when their efforts and results go unnoticed. It does not matter if it is a manager or a back-office specialist; even the smallest achievements deserve encouragement and acknowledgment.

KEY CHAPTER IDEAS

- The development strategy of the procurement function must support the overall development strategy of the company and cannot be implemented in isolation from its strategic priorities.
- The procurement function's development strategy is a document that describes the target state through a set of parameters that are the most important for your company, as set by the overall corporate strategy.
- Strategy requires a plan with specific timelines and clearly defined roles, which can be quickly adapted if external or internal circumstances change.
- KPIs should not be too unwieldy. Ideally, they should be memorized and implemented in a focused way, without dispersing into dozens of indicators, most of which are derived from each other.

- Before making an operational improvement plan, it is worthwhile to understand not only the basic performance indicators of the procurement function, but also how the procurement process is built and the main tasks of the team.
- The approach to change management includes three key stages: (1) planning the change, (2) implementing the change, and (3) supporting the change. Change must be supported by a clear implementation plan and continuously supported to ensure long-lasting results.
- Change management must be systematic and continuous, even after the active stage of implementation has ended. To do this, use such tools as steering committees and checklists of initiatives, as well as collecting and processing feedback.
- People must feel secure in their job when implementing change, including how it works within their value system and how their extra effort to implement the change will be recognized.

ENDNOTES

1. S. Ismail, M. Malone, Y. Van Geest, and P. Diamandis. *Exponential Organizations: Why new organizations are ten times better, faster, and cheaper than yours (and what to do about it)*. Diversion Publishing, 2014.
2. OKR (objectives and key results) is a methodology created in the 1970s by Intel President Andrew Grove and described in his 1983 book *High Output Management*.
3. Quartiles are values that divide a table of data (or part of it) into four groups containing approximately equal numbers of observations. The first quartile is the top 25 percent. When applied to business rankings, it means the leaders. The division into quartiles is often used to determine the degree of compliance with best practices in benchmarking: leaders, followers, laggards, and outsiders. Use benchmarking to measure progress.
4. Gap analysis is a method of strategic analysis that compares the current state with the target state and identifies the *gaps* that need to be filled in order to achieve the latter. It can be used to analyze the gaps between current and desired performance indicators and to plan corrective measures to achieve them within a specified time.
5. Can be measured through benchmarking.
6. Read more about category strategies in Chapter 4.

7. Lean production is the concept of managing a company based on a constant effort to eliminate all types of waste. Lean production involves the involvement of every employee in the process of business optimization. The basic idea of lean production is to maximize benefits for the end customer while minimizing the cost of resources.

8. Proceedings of the Open Roundtable on Procurement Management, 2019.

9. PDCA (Plan-Do-Check-Act) methodology or *Deming's Cycle*; PROSCI© https://www.prosci.com.

10. The tasks of the back office will be discussed in more detail in Chapter 6.

11. Maslow's pyramid is a simplified hierarchical model of human needs reflecting Abraham Maslow's theory of motivation.

CHAPTER 4

CATEGORY STRATEGIES: A MAGIC PILL OR A RECIPE?

WHAT ARE PROCUREMENT CATEGORY STRATEGIES?

Many companies are implementing a category approach to purchasing management. In practice, this means that everything that the company buys is classified and/or divided into so-called categories, such as groups of goods, services, and works that are similar in technical characteristics, supply base, markets, etc. Items in one category can overlap with another in some characteristics or even include the same items. For example, they may have a common use, a similar production technology, a common supply market, or a common end user. Fuels, paints, cable and wire products, building maintenance, and bank services are all examples of procurement categories. Similar procurement management approaches can be applied to the items that make up a category or subcategory, and for each of those, a category strategy can be developed—a document describing the procurement approach for that specific group of products or services.

Covering the entire spend base with category strategies is not an easy task. Developing a strategy for a single category can take several months, given that in addition to analytics and planning for a particular category, you need to request information from suppliers, conduct market research, carry out negotiations and interviews with internal clients and suppliers, and allocate time for feedback. The Kraljic Matrix[1] (see Figure 4.1) can help you prioritize what needs to be done first. This classic procurement tool has not lost its relevance despite being many decades old. It is also simple and easy to use. Depending on the level of importance to the business and the level of risk associated with

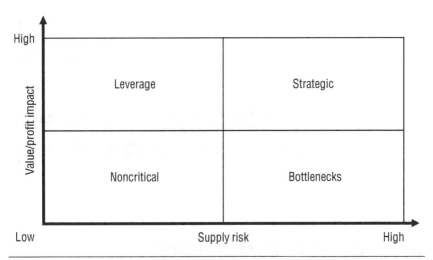

Figure 4.1   The Kraljic Matrix[2]

supply, each category falls into one of the matrix's four segments. Their names speak for themselves: *Bottlenecks, Strategic, Leverage*, and *Noncritical*:

- **Bottlenecks:** low value/supply cost to the company, but high supply continuity risk/complexity; in the event of problems with the supply, the risks of loss for the company will significantly exceed the cost of the item itself
- **Strategic:** categories with high economic value to the company and high supply risks/complexity; these are usually the categories that are a priority for developing category strategies and creating alliances with suppliers to ensure continuity of supply and reduce risks to the business
- **Leverage:** categories with high economic value to the company which maintain a significant share of total purchases, but have many potential low-risk suppliers in the marketplace, thus reducing supply risks/complexity
- **Noncritical:** categories that have little business impact, low cost, and many suppliers

Some believe the matrix is outdated because it does not take into account a number of factors, such as the weight and importance of the category for the supplier or the nuances of interactions between stakeholders. Nevertheless, this tool is still very relevant. It can help evaluate procurement decisions from different angles and users can always use their own criteria instead of the originally suggested—be it the axis of *willingness to cooperate* or any other factor that you need to take into account in a particular situation. The matrix is great not only for classifying categories, but also for segmenting suppliers related to those categories. It is a foundation where one evaluation parameter can be paired with another. For example, evaluating the importance of a category based on its value and the balance of competitive forces may be insufficient. Within even the most ordinary categories there may be cheap little items vital for business, in which the risk of shortages would be unacceptable. Within the category *bearings* for metallurgical companies, there are both relatively low-risk common-use bearings and rolling mill bearings, which can be considered a unique category with their own balance of risks, opportunities, and unique category strategy.

Ideally, procurement strategies should be developed for all categories. Yes, it will take some time, but classification will allow you to reallocate resources and develop a plan for step-by-step processing of the entire cost base, considering wider strategic business priorities.

How a Category Strategy Can Help

Creating a category strategy involves several analytical steps, including a study of market conditions, the nature of consumption and demand, the technical characteristics of the item being purchased, the supplier base, and other conditions affecting the purchase. Based on these findings, a strategic plan for managing the procurement of a particular category is developed.

The strategic plan includes a detailed description of the procurement process organization, the approach to the relevant procurement procedures, the list of preferred suppliers (which considers the current interaction and target conditions of work with these suppliers), and any other issue that may affect the supply in terms of cost, quality, speed, and effectiveness of the process.

But what exactly can a category strategy do to help optimize operational processes? For example, how does it affect the supplier selection process? Let us look at a case study from the oil industry.

For many years, a large Latin American oil company purchased *X-trees* (specialized equipment for controlling pipe flow in oil wells) without considering the cost of their subsequent maintenance. Such myopia is not uncommon in equipment procurement. For suppliers, the main profit from such sales is not the equipment but the after-sales service. An attractive offer

(continued)

for the equipment allows suppliers to get not only a contract for its delivery but also long-term benefits due to high prices for life-cycle services and spare parts. At one point, the oil company decided to conduct a tender to choose a supplier of this equipment, considering the maintenance cost of X-trees for a period of 15 years, which equals the product's life cycle. This completely changed the methodological approach to cost management. It required careful thought given the length of such a contract—it is quite difficult to predict costs and price changes over such a long horizon. Yet, the team introduced specific markers to the contract that could trigger a revision to the cost of services if certain conditions were met. This managed to reduce the total cost of ownership for the entire equipment life cycle by around 30 percent.

Usually, in cases where no procurement strategy is defined for a category, the rules for a particular procurement procedure are set primarily based on the value of the purchase of a particular batch of goods or volume of services. For example, when the purchase amount exceeds a certain threshold, the procedure is more complex and contains additional requirements, such as controlling the number of suppliers competing in the tender and/or the participation of a special tender committee that makes the final decision on the purchase.

Such an approach is oftentimes used in public procurement. The same principle is followed by private companies when determining which procurement procedure to apply; if the procurement cost is relatively low or the item is procured from a single source, a simplified procedure or quick online purchase is allowed that does not require a lot of time. In cases where the procurement cost is high, the procedures become more complex, the requirements are tightened, and the process takes much longer. This approach is largely justified—the more expensive the purchase, the more attention should be paid to all the details of the process. But there is also a major disadvantage.

In the absence of a category strategy, the cost of procurement is often determined based on a specific one-time purchase requisition rather than the aggregate demand for products and services over a certain period of time.

When there is no procurement strategy, the business loses sight of the total volume of all purchases of the same category over a longer period (e.g., a year), misses opportunities to gain economies of scale, and loses an estimate of the total cost of ownership. For example, when selecting specialized equipment, such as a new bulldozer or front-end loader, where there is no developed category strategy, the decision to purchase a particular piece of equipment would be based on the cost of the machine itself. A more advanced approach would also take into account the cost of spare parts needed for major repairs and maintenance, types of engine oils that are needed, etc., so that the future *total* cost for that machine is consistent with the projection on which the purchasing decision was based. Other significant items that we too rarely think about when purchasing heavy equipment are the ability of our employees to operate the machines efficiently, the availability of sufficient repair facilities, additional equipment and competencies required to maintain them, as well as the need to keep a special emergency stock of critical spare parts. This is the key difference of the category approach—purchasing decisions are not made ad hoc, but consider all influencing factors, including indirect ones.

The category approach helps find the best ways to manage total cost through an in-depth analysis of all the direct and indirect factors that affect it, from the supplier base and specifications to quality requirements and assessment of supply risks. For each category or group of categories, if they have dependencies, a standard analysis and set of measures are developed and outlined in a category strategy or *category book*.

The category book contains a description of the methods and tools for working with the procurement category, its main analytical indicators, conclusions regarding the optimal methods and sources of procurement, a description of approaches to working with the market, and a program to support cooperation with suppliers. It also includes measures aimed at improving the efficiency of cost management and improving interaction between the parties involved.

Developing a category book is always a unique iterative process that, when fully implemented, helps you constantly find new ways to reduce procurement costs in a particular category.

In the process of developing a long-term category strategy, demand forecasts are built, and various parameters are assessed, such as the market trends and supplier base, historical costs, technical parameters of the purchased product, customer needs, details of internal and supplier processes, as well as correlations with other categories that can help optimize the spend basket as a whole. The category strategy reviews both external market factors and internal short-term and long-term plans for development, modernization, transition to new solutions, and changes to business processes that affect interaction between the involved parties. All these factors, including costs that are acquired during the entire period of product operation, affect the *final* cost.

In order to cover such a wide range of issues, teamwork within the organization and with suppliers is essential. A category team usually consists of a category manager and one or several analysts and experts, who are often technical specialists. The elaboration of specific conditions may also require the involvement of legal and financial staff. As the work unfolds, they will need the expert support of colleagues and suppliers on a variety of issues—from the specifics of processes to verifying applicable standards and conditions for using the purchased product.

The easiest and fastest way to generate procurement savings is to achieve economies of scale.

Achieving economies of scale is also the aim of an overall procurement strategy—you purposefully consolidate the volume of purchases by category across all company divisions and enlarge the volumes you offer to suppliers, expecting improved prices and delivery terms in return. It is very likely that you will be able to negotiate better purchasing conditions and lower prices simply by making a larger order. Companies that have just started systemizing procurement cost management often start here, and rightly so. Applying such a solution is *low-hanging fruit* or an *easy win* when it comes to procurement savings. It is worth noting, though, that for categories that are in short supply, the consolidation of volume can have the opposite effect—suppliers may not be willing to bundle supplies in larger quantities, preferring to work with more customers.

Benefits Beyond Savings

Imagine that all your costs have already been consolidated, discounts from suppliers have been received, and payment terms have been improved. What are your next steps? How else can you save money on purchases? At this stage, you will have to look for additional levers—and the deeper the category is developed, the more complex they become, and the more effort is required for their implementation. The category management approach helps to find additional savings and increases the efficiency of the purchasing process.

In cost management, there are only a few optimization methods that work for most categories: consolidating volumes, unifying contract terms, and optimizing the supplier base. All of these are easy wins. However, they do not provide the opportunity to unlock all potential benefits. Maximum results require the development of category-specific initiatives. Each category is unique because it depends on the specifics and characteristics of the item being purchased and the relevant market segments. A category book is precisely the tool that unlocks this uniqueness.

Category development is an iterative process that is never complete; initiatives and levers that are relevant today may become obsolete tomorrow because the market players change, new technologies emerge, or your internal requirements or goals evolve. A category strategy usually remains relevant for a few months to three years, but even during this period, you can never say, "That's it. It's done. We can relax now." Even if you have a complete and verified category strategy, its elaboration and updating never stop.

One supplier took a significant share of the market for supplying coffee to offices in a city simply by changing its strategy for calculating the cost of the product supplied. Prior to the change, it invoiced customers for two items: the cost of the coffee itself, which was calculated on the basis of the number of cups made by the machine, and a fixed amount for the cost of operating the coffee machine. But one day, one of their clients gave the supplier a great idea: remove the fixed amount of operating costs and bill only for the coffee. The price per cup was now to include the cost of the coffee, a markup to cover the operating cost of the machine, and the targeted profit. This approach turned out to work to everyone's advantage. The operational and depreciation costs ceased to be fixed and moved into a variable cost category dependent on the number of cups of coffee consumed. At the same time, the price per cup of coffee was clearer for clients and allowed for budget reallocation and optimization of cost management levers both for the supplier and the clients.

In addition to describing a specific category's operational purchasing model and demand management approaches, the category book defines rules for qualifying and evaluating suppliers, which can also change over time due to a variety of factors. A mandatory component of any category strategy is identifying and comparing buyer positioning (strength of demand) and supplier positioning (strength of supply), describing the supplier relationship management approach, identifying key suppliers, performing a detailed analysis of the technical characteristics of the purchased goods and services, and defining a set of requirements for the purchasing process.

A detailed category strategy protects the business from losing time in a crisis scenario because an alternative procurement plan has already been developed and can be implemented quickly—all you need to do is check market factors and put it to work, something that usually takes hours or days at most. Without a category strategy, it can take weeks or even months to readjust and find new sources of supply.

During the trade war between the United States and China in 2018–2019, the U.S. government imposed duties on a number of categories supplied from China. The special tariffs on imports and sanctions affected goods with a total annual import value of about $360 billion.[3] Among them were components for the production of wind turbine towers. Rodrigo Ferreira, at the time the purchasing director of a leading U.S. company in the industry, recalls that during that period, his company sourced 90 percent of the tower turbine components from China. The duties imposed increased procurement costs by 30 percent overnight, and it took about six months to reduce dependence on Chinese supplies and renegotiate contracts—during which time the company had to incur inflated costs because there were simply no other sources of supply. It took some time to find alternative sources of supply, renegotiate contracts, and stabilize supply.

This story is a prime example of how the lack of additional sources of supply can lead to a crisis. Developing alternative category purchasing plans for unforeseen events is an important part of category strategies. Vendor failures, natural and man-made disasters, the financial strength of vendors, and the reliability of your own processes are myriad factors that can adversely affect the supply chain. I had a situation early in my career when due to the poor calculation of warehouse capacity and a sharp increase in the volume of purchases, our goods had to stand idle at the gates of our own warehouse for more than 10 days. We were sure that this was simply impossible, but such factors as warehouse equipment failures, warehouse employees' holidays not timed with work schedules, sick leaves, and sudden changes in major construction projects led to a lack of reserve capacity, causing an emergency situation even in our well-developed procurement organization.

How to Define the Categories

Before moving on to the process of creating category strategies, it is necessary to decide on a list of them. To do this, all purchases must be categorized in some way, and the purchasing costs must be divided into conditional category groups.

There have been attempts in various markets to create industry-specific category classifiers. I think these attempts will continue to be made, but for now, there is no unified classification for procurement categories. Directories maintained centrally by government agencies that regulate the standards in certain industries or by scientific communities that focus primarily on the technical properties of the classified products do not consider the market setup and/or other features of the procured item. In this regard, the best approach is to create your own category classifier using the following criteria:

- Common or similar application of a product or service
- Complementary or closely related components (e.g., equipment and spare parts or services for the same)
- Common or similar production technology or methodology of work execution or services rendering
- Related or shared supply markets (e.g., common manufacturers or suppliers)
- A common point of contact for suppliers on the buyer's side
- A common end user

There have been cases where we initially allocated certain products into different categories, but as time passed, we concluded that it was better to combine them into one. This can happen, for example, when manufacturers of different components merge, or there are changes in the technical parameters of the purchased product. Certain categories even turned from goods categories into services categories when instead of providing spare parts, suppliers started to offer maintenance services, the cost of which included spare parts. In such cases, the two cost categories of *spare parts for pumps* and *pumps maintenance services* were combined into one general category called *pumps maintenance*.

Sometimes the nature and model of a supply organization can change; for instance, suppliers of complementary goods and services could join forces and offer one contract instead of two at more favorable terms. Such changes may also entail reallocating products or services from one category to another. There is nothing wrong with this, as long as the list of categories is clear to you and your partners. The list of procurement categories is internal company information that does not affect the work of suppliers.

It is worth paying special attention to the relevance and quality of the data you have. If they are incomplete or contaminated with duplicates, incorrect descriptions, or accounting errors, then you will have to work on cleaning up and organizing the data so they can be used as the basis for decision making in the future.

It is not enough just to know that *we buy $100,000 worth of electric motors a year*. You need to know exactly which motors are purchased, their capacity, their application, who the manufacturers are, what their average service life is, and how much money, time, and resources are spent on their repair, maintenance, and renovation. The more detailed the data, the better because they determine the comprehensiveness of the analysis and the search for cost optimization opportunities. It does not matter if the data are saved in a centralized digital system or in Excel—what matters is that they are there.

Any database is better than no database at all. Start small and gradually increase the level of automation of data collection, thereby increasing the reliability of your information. Do not wait until you can buy and implement an automated system in a year—you can incur serious losses before that time. It is better to do at least something right now for at least one category: try out the approach, check assumptions, and record any results—even negative ones—because they are lessons that help draw conclusions about what *not* to do.

THE CATEGORY STRATEGY DEVELOPMENT PROCESS

You can find different descriptions of the category strategy development process, but their differences are never distinctive—the set of actions required for creating a category strategy is the same for any methodology. Whatever method you follow, it is critical to ensure the following:

1. **Understand your category spend, demand, and technical characteristics.** During the initial stage, the category manager analyzes all available information on a given category: the list and number of items purchased; their distribution into subgroups by technical parameters; consumption frequency, prices, value, and common characteristics; determination of the use of the purchased item and principles of consumption accounting; inventory structure and supply base; the share of purchase orders for each supplier; details of the procurement process from demand to delivery; and process and operational risks.

   The input sources for this stage are the company's own database of purchasing history, prices, suppliers, and current purchasing policies. Other inputs are internal demand forecasts and understanding how the company's overall development plans can affect the category, such as whether consumption dynamics or technical requirements could change in the near future. Information is collected not only from accounting systems but also by interviewing customers, suppliers, warehouse employees, members of the accounting department, etc.—everyone who, in one way or another, directly *works with the purchase.* When a category strategy is developed for several businesses at once, each of which has its own database, it is important to determine the principles for consolidating this information for consolidated analysis.

Particular attention should be paid to customer requirements regarding technical parameters and quality, demand patterns, how the product is used, and other operational factors affecting a procurement process or cost. Defining a client for a particular category may not always be as obvious as it seems at first glance. For example, the planning department plans purchases and generates requisitions, so in a formal sense, it can be considered as the client. However, in reality, the real client is the person who directly uses the purchased item in their work—the craftsman who performs repairs or the manager who relies on the services carried out by another party. It is these people who have first-hand knowledge of how a purchase requisition plays out in the real world.

2. **Understand your supply base and market conditions.** The task here is to understand the specifics of how the market functions for a particular category. This includes research on market conditions and key market players, trends, possible mergers and acquisitions among supply chain players or factors affecting them, supply chain dependencies, pricing models and forecasts, geographic and geopolitical factors and risks, and an analysis of supply and demand balances. It is at this stage that the buyer and supplier positions are assessed—the determination of the level of competition and commercial leverage that can be exploited when dealing with the category. As a result of an analysis of market conditions, principles of pricing, and interaction principles between suppliers, the degree of competition, the balance of supply and demand, trends in new technologies, the impact of legislation, and standards requirements will become clearer.

After the initial analysis of the category and market, it is necessary to periodically refresh the data and be able to react quickly in case internal or external circumstances change. Gaps in communication, an accident at a supplier's production facility, trade restrictions, changes in legislation, or mergers and acquisitions may happen unexpectedly and require a quick reaction, so up-to-date information will guard against rash decisions.

3. **Define levers to manage category cost and ensure supply continuity.** The input data here are the information and conclusions obtained in the previous two stages. Based on the analysis, hypotheses are built on where and how it is possible to improve prices, change demand structure, adjust technical parameters, reallocate volumes between suppliers, change the supplier selection process, adjust quality requirements or other contract terms, reallocate operations between supply chain participants, and much more. All ideas that emerge should be discussed, verified, and recorded within the working group. Each hypothesis is then ranked in terms of its importance; complexity of implementation; impact on costs, processes, and specifications; potential savings, etc. Use any additional criteria that are important to you. Based on this ranking, the order in which certain activities will be implemented is determined, and the improvement hypothesis is tested. In addition, the optimal purchasing procedure is also defined.

Usually, after just a basic analysis, we can see those easy wins, for example, opportunities to consolidate purchasing volumes. There is a widespread belief that the more suppliers in a category, the better. This is a myth. The presence of a large number of suppliers during a tender can be a plus since it creates competition among participants. However, a large number of active suppliers within the same category with whom the buyer has contracts, or frequently changing suppliers and splitting the total volume of purchases between them, inevitably leads to higher costs. One of the most universal and effective cost-saving measures, oddly enough, is to reduce the number of active suppliers instead of expanding it.

It is by reducing the number of active suppliers that consolidation, also called *economies of scale*, becomes possible, which in turn, leads to reducing the average cost of placing a single purchase order for the company. The greater the number of active suppliers, the higher the administrative costs; the greater the number of small purchase orders, the greater the likelihood that prices are not optimal.

Having too many suppliers is almost as bad as having a monopoly supplier— ensuring consistency in service levels might become mission impossible.

4. **Dedicate time to sourcing and selecting qualified suppliers.** It is necessary to gather information about prospective suppliers—their capabilities, location, characteristics of required goods or services, etc. For this, an inquiry with a set of questions is sent to all relevant suppliers. In the procurement dictionary, this kind of inquiry is called a request for information (RFI). After RFI responses are received, suppliers are rated based on their compliance with minimum requirements. This evaluation eliminates those who do not meet these standards and leaves those who can be further invited to participate in the supplier selection process. The result of the RFI is a short list of suppliers who fit the buyer's requirements and can supply products and services with the required characteristics.

The RFI is followed by the request for proposal (RFP) or request for quotation (RFQ), a tender and/or negotiation process where short-listed suppliers are invited to submit their proposals. In most cases, pricing is determined through a competitive supplier selection process in which the buyer solicits bids with specific terms, conditions, and purchase prices and then determines how much of the purchase volume they are willing to allocate to one supplier or another. There is an important point to make here. Some might believe that it is simply enough to announce a tender, and the best offers will fly to them like bees to nectar. This is yet another myth.

Excessive or unrealistic requirements can drastically reduce competition, scaring away reliable suppliers. Purchasers imposing knowingly excessive requirements and then choosing the cheapest offer may find themselves in a situation where the contract is signed, but the counterparty is unable to fulfill the agreed-upon terms. Problems with complete, on-time deliveries or issues with quality are common. The data and results of the analysis collected during the previous stages of category strategy development will help to draft realistic requirements and choose the optimal format for the supplier selection procedure. It is necessary to define not only the main conditions for the purchase, such as price, delivery, and payment terms, but also associated factors, such as service support, its duration and cost, exact technical parameters, warranty indicators, the structure of discounts

It is not only the buyer who chooses the supplier, but the supplier also decides who to work with and on what terms.

and surcharges, transportation and unloading conditions, and quality control procedure—everything that the market can offer. The analysis of these proposals makes it possible to select the optimal terms of purchase and determine the supplier with whom the contract will be concluded.

It is important to keep in mind that choosing just one supplier to provide a significant portion of your purchasing volume may be beneficial in the moment but is shortsighted as a long-term solution. You must assess the risks and benefits of sharing volumes among different suppliers as you work through your strategy. In many cases, it may not be a good idea to give the bulk of the volume to a large supplier, even if their terms are more attractive than those of their competitors. Instead, it may be better tactically to distribute some volume among several suppliers in order to develop their capabilities. Smaller suppliers will be able to leverage this opportunity and gradually become competitors to larger players in the category, providing advantages and diversifying possible sources of supply in the long term.

5. **Execute the strategy and update it as needed.** After the contract has been signed, a no less important stage begins that requires significant involvement from the buyers and control over strategy implementation. Developed initiatives go beyond the contract, and continuous improvement initiatives such as further process enhancements and the implementation of innovative solutions together with suppliers should be pursued. In the absence of strategy execution control, the risks of failing to fulfill contractual obligations and achieve strategic goals rise.

   After a change of supplier as a result of a tender, it may be necessary to draw up a transition plan with the new contractor. Such a change can be particularly painful in the case of services. For the customer, it is about arranging for the service provider's representatives to have access to the premises, providing storage for tools and equipment, issuing work orders, monitoring the contractor's employee's compliance with safety standards, and so on. When there is a change of contractor teams, it is important to perform a control inspection of the equipment that is being transferred to the vendor and record its condition. In some cases, a change of contractor may lead to the dismissal of internal specialists on the team, and any related conflicts need to be resolved in a professional manner with the help of the client.

   It is important to discuss all open issues with internal clients and counterparties (old and new) in advance in order to build a transition plan that will reflect all areas of interaction from one supplier to another. This includes establishing rules for working together, seeking feedback from all stakeholders, and implementing ways to cooperate and minimize risks. Best practice requires:

- A continuous evaluation of each counterparty's work and the interaction processes between buyer and supplier
- The classification of best practices and their extension to other categories or suppliers
- A regular review of the entire category strategy in order to keep it up-to-date

The continuous analysis of achieved results identifies mistakes and bottlenecks in the existing approaches to category management. This helps to objectively assess the market situation, find additional ideas, and optimize solutions.

Practical Implications of Category Strategies

A category strategy can be short term, with a horizon of up to one year, or long term, lasting three years or more. It all depends on the criticality of the category and the opportunities and benefits that may be derived from it.

For example, the *stationery* category may not be that critical for companies in the mining and metals industry. Yes, such companies use a lot of paper and other office supplies, spending substantial amounts on them annually, but they get lost in the background of more significant costs. Therefore, devoting significant resources to managing this category is an unaffordable luxury. Coupled with the fact that competition in the stationery category is high, it generally receives the minimum necessary attention—for example, there are normally no strategic partnerships with suppliers. The main goal in this case is the creation of a transparent process supported by electronic catalogs or procurement through marketplaces that will help keep prices under control.

At the same time, for other categories such as rollers, bearings, electric motors, and others that are more significant in terms of cost and impact on production processes, strategies should be developed to create value over the long term. Here, special cost management levers are possible, including the creation of joint ventures with suppliers, which itself requires a serious market assessment and significant investment. The longer the planning horizon, the more likely it is that plans will have to be adjusted, so all long-term strategies should be verified and updated at least once a year.

It is not uncommon for category managers to come to unexpected conclusions that contradict conventional wisdom when developing category strategies. For instance, it is widely believed that competitive bidding provides the best results. However, this is not always the case. Everything depends on the specific category and market peculiarities in that category. In some cases, not only will the tender not help determine the best offer, but it can cause negative consequences: risks of poor-quality supplies or the disclosure of confidential information on competitive advantages that may harm the interests of the buyer.

The following examples are from different companies. First, let's look at the case of consultancy services procurement.

When you choose outside experts to help you solve a particular problem, the first thing to focus on is not price but rather on making sure that the consultant's expertise is the right fit and that your teams can effectively collaborate. If the screening process reveals that there are two or more companies that meet these criteria, then price negotiation is appropriate.

It is important to understand in advance on what terms a consultant usually works, what their limitations are, what the pricing range is for their services and where that positions them in the market, how interested they are in your project, and how critical it is for you to work with them. If your company's procurement is not regulated by law, which requires a formal tender procedure, then the best way to choose your provider is to negotiate with each of the participants and then determine with whom you are ready to work. It's incorrect to call this negotiation process a tender because a *tender* is a competitive procedure, usually involving the submission of bids at the final stage and the selection of the winner who offered the lowest price, all other things being equal. But in our example, the capabilities and the terms of the bidders are likely to be unequal, and the decision will be made on the combined advantages and disadvantages of all elements of the proposal, including not only cost but also specific people on the team that define the contractor's ability to complete the task.

In this example, I am not considering consulting services in finance, product, or process certification since there are usually standardized protocols where the consultant acts as an auditor rather than a developer of innovative solutions for the client. In standardized audit or certification cases, the team interaction factor is not very critical to the final result of service delivery because the auditor must remain independent.

Let's look at another case.

A company's traditional light bulb supplier informs them that it can no longer supply the type of product specified in the contract because it has switched to the production of other types of light bulbs. According to corporate procurement policy, in such cases, the buyer has to hold a new tender and select a new supplier. But is this really necessary, and does it add value for the company? A category strategy can foresee such scenarios in advance and determine which similar products can be considered as alternatives, what the pricing review approach will be, which conditions will require a new tender, and which suppliers should be approached first if an urgent tender is needed without undertaking new detailed market research and the screening of dozens of light bulb suppliers from around the world.

The supplier selection method depends on many details: the balance of supply and demand, the availability of market players and competition, the internal situation of the customer, etc. Sometimes the market simply does not allow competitive selection due to limited or no competition. In such cases, it is necessary to look for levers to optimize the cost and conditions of procurement through negotiation.

It is generally believed that issuing frequent requests for quotations for the same product or service is a bad practice since it breaks the spending into smaller parts and reduces the savings potential. However, here is a case from an airline company that shows the opposite.

Every morning, an airline books hotel rooms for more than 200 crew members at their home base airport in a major European capital city. There are 27 hotels nearby. The company has signed a long-term agreement with each of them, which stipulates that the room rate may not exceed $75 per day. Every morning, after receiving information on the number of employees that need to be accommodated, the company opens an electronic request for quotations, and all 27 hotels upload their new prices based on the current room occupancy situation. Sometimes the hotels confirm the prices fixed in the agreement but often offer much cheaper rates, sometimes saving half the standard contracted amount. Thanks to this fact alone, the introduction of an electronic platform for these tenders paid for itself in two and a half months.

As you can see, by understanding the nature of supply and demand, as well as the specifics of an industry, it is possible to achieve significant results by acting in a nonstandard way. Even with a framework agreement, it is possible to regularly request prices and gain additional savings.

A separate aspect of working with categories is determining the strategic benefits to the company from the implementation of category strategies.

Along with the fact that the main expectations from procurement lie in operational efficiency and business process support, it is important not to lose sight of the strategic capabilities of the function.

As part of procurement activities, it is possible to create business alliances with suppliers and introduce new solutions offered by the market in areas new to the business, even generating additional sources of revenue. This is the very point where procurement becomes a strategically significant source of value creation.

HOW TO MAKE CATEGORY STRATEGIES WORK

Developing a category strategy is a prerequisite for effective procurement cost management. However, a category strategy cannot work by itself. It requires cross-functional teamwork not just to develop but also to implement it. Without support and attention, even the brightest ideas are forgotten over time, mired in routine, or their potential is unrealized. Organizations that are undergoing procurement transformation and embarking on the path to developing category strategies should be aware of a significant risk: without the proper support from management and internal stakeholders and constant monitoring of the impact of category strategies, initiatives can end up failing completely, even if at first they deliver noticeable results.

At some point, it may feel like everything has been done, procurement strategies for the most important categories have been developed, required activities have been launched, and all that remains is to wait for the savings. But this feeling is deceptive; the category strategy is just a tool. Implementing the valuable ideas found in the strategy development process and achieving results is a complex, multifaceted process

The category approach can be considered a method, a tool, or a recipe, but the result of its application depends on how skillfully it is used.

in which individual employees are required to be able to implement these ideas, while the organization as a whole must apply the results of their work.

Changing the way you work is never easy. When developing a category strategy, it is sometimes difficult to demonstrate intermediate results; a lot of time is spent on analysis, and mountains of information are poured over, but there is no result in the form of a finished transaction or a signed deal. People are bound to become impatient with the new processes and get frustrated when things don't work out right away. As a result, they start to resist the changes that are making them feel uncomfortable. At such times, it is important not to deviate from the chosen path and support the changes in the organization. In order to do this, it is necessary to adhere to a few simple rules that will make category strategies work:

1. **One category manager, even a very talented one, is not enough to develop an effective category strategy.** The most effective category strategies appear as a result of the joint work of a cross-functional team, which consists of representatives of procurement and customer departments and also involves external and internal expertise—economists, accountants, lawyers, logisticians, etc.—and often also suppliers. The main task of a category manager is to skillfully coordinate the work of experts and to attract missing expertise in time. Category strategies alone will not produce results if they are not actively supported by the team that developed the strategy and the stakeholders.

2. **Having a category strategy without a plan for its implementation is likely to end in failure.** To put theory into practice, you need a plan: who should do what, when should they do it, and how it should be done—so that ideas begin to produce results. In addition to organizational and technical activities, it is important to outline a change management plan, which also includes communication. Tell the stakeholders and everyone affected why the change is needed and why you will not deviate from the implementation plan. It can take anywhere from three months to six months to develop a category strategy. That is a lot of time and a lot of effort. The result of such work is about 100 or more pages of text, illustrations, and graphs. In order to draw reliable conclusions, you need to process large amounts of information and talk to many people; you need to search, argue, and negotiate—and this is not a quick process. It takes even longer to implement the developed initiatives, and updating and adapting the document never stops. However, if you outline exactly what needs to be done and what method to use, the task takes shape.

3. **You need steering committees to track progress.** Successful implementation of certain critical category strategies requires involvement high up in the executive ranks. If the Chief Procurement Officer (CPO) thinks he or she has better things to do than listen to category managers' reports about the progress of developing or implementing critical category strategies, they are making a big mistake. Organizing a system of regular steering committee meetings that are attended by the leaders of all procurement departments and relevant C-suite executives is the first task of the CPO. Once he or she relaxes their focus and stops making time to attend such meetings, they can forget about the effective implementation of category strategies. People will not engage if no one is paying attention. It is necessary to meet often enough and dive deep enough into the details to provide timely support and maintain employee confidence in the importance of their work.

4. **Category strategy development should not be confused with operational purchasing.** This rule does not mean that a category manager does not need to know the details of operational processes. On the contrary, they should be aware of everything that is going on so that they can take it into account when developing and adapting category strategies. They must also, on occasion, perform complex purchases and manage the most complex contracts themselves. But that does not mean diving into the selection of each and every supplier. As soon as you start flinging operational tasks at category management employees, the CPO is guaranteed to hear at the next update meeting, "We did not save this money because I had to urgently sign three additional agreements on current deliveries, and I just did not have time to deal with category strategy this month." Functional segregation is the key to the successful implementation of category strategies and improving the efficiency of operational processes.

Current procurement operations will not stop because you have started to draft category strategies; these processes happen simultaneously. Procurement tactics can be changed at any time, and it is important to be flexible in making related decisions. While a new strategy is still being developed, implementation of identified incremental improvements to the current contracts is already possible, as some simple and effective initiatives may already be identified at the start based on the results of the initial analysis. And the sooner you do this, the better.

When a category strategy has been fully developed, it makes sense to have the provisions of the category book *prevail* over standard procurement

A category strategy can and should be developed in parallel with current operational procurement activities and consider actual operational process execution practice.

procedures. This is because the conclusions drawn while working through the category book may contradict standard procurement policies. For example, category analysis shows that it may be better to negotiate direct contracts rather than run a tender to select the suppliers, or it is more advantageous to limit the range of suppliers instead of expanding it. An even deeper analysis may reveal that open electronic bidding for this category does not yield the results that closed negotiations provide, even though procurement policy requires an open electronic bidding procedure to be held. A well-developed strategy should always favor the best approach to supplier selection in that specific category rather than blindly adhering to a standard procurement policy.

The implementation of category strategies is more complicated if a company's procurement is regulated by law. In this case, the law usually introduces a lot of restrictions, which are mainly aimed at fighting corruption, with increasing procurement efficiency only a secondary consideration.

Therefore, many of these rules and requirements can have the opposite effect and lead to policy violations and inefficient spend management. Nevertheless, even in the situation with regulated procurement, it is necessary and important to work on category strategies and conduct in-depth analyses— these will at least help improve processes and supplier selection procedures. It will also ward off risks of insufficient or excessive requirements, not to mention the possibility of achieving additional savings. Regulation restrictions should not become a reason to refuse to develop category strategies—they are an additional tool that can help increase procurement efficiency.

IS A CATEGORY STRATEGY ALWAYS NECESSARY?

An important topic in category management is the small purchases known as the *tail spend*. As a rule, they account for no more than 20 percent of all purchasing costs but often accumulate the largest number of different small-cost products and services. Typical buys are office supplies and minor services or one-time purchases of spare parts where only a few pieces are purchased in a year.

Usually, there is no time to develop a strategy to manage tail spend, and companies introduce simplified rules for such purchases: oftentimes "out-of-pocket" purchases are allowed and there is no contract because the cost of supporting a full procedure for selecting the source of supply would exceed the cost of the purchase several times over. However, if you add up all these small costs, the sum can be significant, opening up opportunities for savings. Have you ever checked to see how much money your company spends a year on, let's say—flowers? Here's another case story.

A company in the oil and gas industry set up an electronic bidding platform, and after it was operational for a year, the company analyzed which procurement spend areas had not yet been optimized. They discovered an interesting fact: the employees in the head office spent thousands of dollars each year on flowers, which they ordered as gifts for guests and partners. The company decided to optimize the process. They found five flower stores near the office, told them they were willing to buy a certain number of bouquets each year, chose 10 standard types that were attractive, and received a decent discount from each store in return. Then they asked the suppliers to upload images of these bouquets into an electronic catalog and told all employees that they could only order flowers from this catalog. As a result, considerable savings were realized.

This example demonstrates that we should not underestimate the costs of even the most peripheral categories. The time spent developing a category strategy for small purchases, even if not very detailed, is likely to pay off, not only in savings but also through a more convenient process for both customers and suppliers.

The results of implementing purchasing strategies can be most unexpected. They are not only about how to buy better and cheaper but also about how to change the balance of supply and demand or even the technology and approach to the production process. Here is an example from Deutsche Post.[4]

Deutsche Post (DP) could not find small electric trucks with an adequate price/quality ratio on the market that fit its specifications. In addition, manufacturers either delayed their response to DP's tenders or offered over-equipped vehicles whose features had no impact on performance but increased the vehicle's cost. There were simply no good options. As a result, the company did something very out of the box—it decided to create its own van. In partnership with some of the leading car manufacturers and startups, DP developed its own vehicle fleet that was every bit as good as those offered by established manufacturers but much cheaper because it did not have to overpay for a brand or cover manufacturers' increased profit margins from electric vehicles.

Small cost categories may contain a lot of hidden savings potential and indirectly affect the efficiency of the company—not through their "monetary" value per se, but through associated costs in time and resources, as well as by how the process is perceived by employees. The more convenient and understandable a process is, the easier it is for employees to use, allowing them to focus on more important tasks that create the next level of value. Going beyond the obvious possibilities, as in the Deutsche Post fleet example, allows for a departure from the *just-buy-what-you-asked-for* mindset and a refusal to succumb to the constraints imposed by the market. However, this kind of insight does not come immediately and only develops from a systematic analysis of real needs and hidden opportunities.

TOTAL COST OF OWNERSHIP AND COST OF PROCUREMENT

Total cost of ownership (TCO) is a separate topic that is worth considering. As part of developing the requirements for an item/service that is being procured, it is mandatory to assess the factors affecting its value and unavoidable additional costs.

For example, consider a company that buys cars. You consider two cars from different manufacturers with similar characteristics; you compare their cost and the terms of purchase, then make a decision. However, paying for the car itself is only part of the cost that the company will have to incur. The labor cost for a standard service hour for one car may be 10 percent more expensive, its key components fail 20 percent more often on average, and the fuel consumption is 5 percent higher. If you are guided solely by the purchase price of this car, you may find yourself spending considerably more on its operation. In most cases, you can estimate the TCO of the product by obtaining data on the use of similar products in the past, collecting feedback from the market, and comparing the information provided by the supplier or manufacturer with customer reviews. An estimate of such costs should be made for the entire anticipated life cycle of the item being purchased. You probably will not have accurate data for such an estimate, especially when we are talking about a new product for which data simply does not exist. Nevertheless, even in that case, you can make an estimate based on assumptions to calculate the potential cost of ownership. If time and opportunity permit, you can purchase or lease one piece of equipment and collect operating data over a short period of time, thereby testing your assumptions.

As part of the TCO evaluation, it is useful to take into account the possible costs of disposing of the object at the end of its life cycle or perhaps calculating the best time to trade it in for a new one to stop spending money on its maintenance and repair—most likely, that point will be the point at which the cost of operation exceeds the cost of buying a new one.

A relatively new metric, the total value of opportunity (TVO), has been gaining in popularity among professionals since it was first proposed in 2003 by Gartner.[5] Initially, the metric was developed to evaluate investment decisions in digital projects in the field of robotization, but it is increasingly being used in other areas of business, including procurement. Whereas TCO includes all direct or indirect material costs, TVO covers an assessment of the long-term *hidden* benefits or opportunities that the solution can bring; for example, the impact on developing the customer base to increase its willingness to do business with the company, thereby creating opportunities for increased profits. This metric is broader and requires a more meticulous approach to decision making. Nonetheless, assessing procurement decisions from this perspective can be very helpful.

However, it is worth cautioning against being overly enthusiastic about TCO or TVO. Without sufficient data, there is a risk of making assumptions that will greatly increase the expected costs, which means that a decision based on them will carry the risk of excessive spend. The way to avoid this situation is to make a common-sense assessment—use only the figures and data you believe are most reliable. If in doubt, do not try to make guesses by reading the tea leaves; simply postpone the question for the future and try to collect the missing data in order to obtain reliable information over the next year or the next few years.

CATEGORY STRATEGIES AND MARKETS

Choosing a higher TCO can also be strategic when the potential cost benefits can't overcome greater external risks to the firm. I can recall a case where a company consciously chose a higher TCO for the purchase of domestic mining equipment during a crisis. At that time, *domestic* mining equipment had a lower purchase price but a higher TCO compared to the *imported* version, but this savings allowed for other investments to be made more comfortably and did not divert substantial funds for a higher one-time payment to the international suppliers. Even though the TCO looked bad, it was a calculated decision that was made in light of the situation and gave the business a different kind of advantage.

As previously mentioned, a category strategy is a living document. Markets change, crisis scenarios arise, and overall internal corporate strategy can alter, so your category strategies need to be flexible. This means that a set of basic what-if scenarios must always be prepared. In times of change, well-thought-out category strategies can be drastically modified. Even companies with a rich history and established practices of effective procurement are forced to take unpopular measures in times of crisis. That's exactly what Rolls-Royce did in 2020. As one of the leaders in building an effective interaction ecosystem with suppliers, the company was forced to abruptly abandon its long-term strategy of cooperation with suppliers and made demands for one-time discounts of 5 to 15 percent due to new circumstances arising from a crisis in its industrial sector.[6]

Many companies undertake tough measures in times of crisis. Dealing with a severe liquidity crisis, one company instructed its buyers to distribute money among suppliers on the principle of: *give an additional 15 percent discount on equipment already delivered or on upcoming deliveries and you will get paid immediately—otherwise, payments would be severely delayed.* This is neither a best practice nor a fair tactic to use on suppliers, but it happens.

How can category procurement management be quickly adapted in times of crisis? Ideally, a detailed category strategy should include an assessment of the various risks that can affect its execution, as well as scenarios for different situations—from financial and geopolitical to epidemiological and even war (as we have already seen in 2020 and 2022–2024)—especially if the company procures globally. All known factors affecting supply reliability must be considered when selecting sources, but it is equally important to develop scenarios for dealing with crisis situations. In other words, you always need a Plan B, or better still, also a Plan C and D.

In practice, it is very difficult to implement a Plan B that is as effective as the original Plan A. You would need tools such as a risk assessment; criticality and cost ranking; supplier evaluation, qualification, and segmentation; and a crisis response plan with team mobilization. Effective mobilization means not only effective teamwork but also a detailed action plan and the elimination of intra-corporate interference and bureaucracy, which saves a lot of resources and nerves. For example, the number of approvals and documents should be reduced where possible. Decisions have to be negotiated and made quickly, taking into account possible unforeseen future risks. Sometimes this means giving more authority to certain employees under set rules. Aiming for results and analyzing your mistakes are much more valuable than adhering to formal written protocols to ensure the continuous operation of your enterprise or business.

Adapting category strategies in a crisis requires quick and decisive action. If something unexpected happens and there is no alternative plan, follow these few simple rules:

A crisis provides an excellent opportunity to test business resilience, including the resilience of your category strategies.

Rule 1: Do not take rash actions. Stress reduces our ability to respond effectively. Actions should be quick, but they should not be rash because your choices now will affect your operations in the future. Simple operational actions come first:

- Carry out a quick audit of all current supplies
- Ensure payment obligations are fulfilled
- Rank supplies by criticality

It is important for the purchasing department to coordinate quickly with finance in order to understand the situation regarding working capital and available funds, to determine what to pay attention to first, and to decide how to plan the settlement of obligations. A quick plan of action can then be drawn up for:

- Canceling or suspending shipments
- Strengthening control over the fulfillment of obligations under open contracts
- Requesting guarantees of deliveries and payments
- Canceling or suspending certain projects, etc.

The criteria for prioritizing actions in such situations are often universal—priorities will be primarily influenced by the criticality and uniqueness of the category itself, along with the supplier's capabilities.

Rule 2: Inform everyone who may be affected by any significant changes as soon as possible. Quick action must be taken to inform all stakeholders, correct documents, and then redraft plans. Communication is one of the most important parts of an emergency plan. Partners and counterparties need to understand what is going on and how you are going to operate and maintain your supply base. They also need to know what to expect because they are also planning their own actions—therefore, it would be good to coordinate their plans with yours.

Rule 3: Use the *emergency override* only as a last resort. The emergency override is a stage that is best avoided. When the approach to category management changes completely and is put into emergency mode, it means that all other measures have not worked, and it is time to take the most unpopular steps to help stay afloat. For example, at this stage, companies start to selectively pay suppliers, or demand to change contract terms unilaterally, reneging on existing agreements. A significant risk is that this can negatively affect a company's reputation and its perception by the market in the long term. There are a few caveats listed here that will help to avoid these dire consequences:

- **Procurement should not operate in a vacuum.** In moments of crisis, one should not forget about the not-so-obvious risks of supplier relationship management, such as suspending or canceling innovative programs. In the future, you could regret abandoning some projects now. Weigh your decisions in terms of their likely long-term consequences. Evaluate critically what affects your company's competitive advantage. Consult. Create a coordinating anti-crisis working group that will include representatives of all functions and where you can get first-hand information about changes in production volumes or changes in the company's balance sheet.
- **Information quality is critical.** In situations where decisions need to be made quickly, having quality analytics is essential. If procurement data is well structured and automated, and all documents are stored electronically, a quick analysis and prioritized action plan should only take a matter of hours. But if a crisis occurs and you are not prepared for it, you will quickly realize that you should have invested in IT systems and building your procurement database.
- **Safety stocks are a vital insurance policy.** Review carefully what you store as safety stock and whether you have prearranged terms with your suppliers in case of crisis scenarios. In 2020, the category *medical masks and antiseptics* was the top requirement. Even though these items are usually low in value, companies do not keep large inventories of them. However, perhaps it makes sense to do so in some circumstances. A more complicated and expensive issue that should also be on your agenda is the storage of spare parts for machinery. I don't think any company can afford to keep spare parts as safety stock for a

one-time repair of all equipment. Instead, you need balanced—
and therefore, well-thought-out—solutions and strategies for
the emergency supply of necessary components, including possibly the in-house manufacturing of special equipment (like the
3D printing of spare parts).

- **After any crisis comes an upswing.** It is only a matter of time
before the supply chain returns to its previous level of activity
as long as it has not been broken by cataclysms or war. Many
suppliers, especially small companies, run the risk of not sur-
viving without proper support from their significant clients.
The strongest and most flexible survive—those who, for example, quickly switch to alternative products or offer new solutions to their customers. Some are replaced by others; this is
the natural order of things. However, if buyers refuse to support
their suppliers in a crisis, afterward, they may find themselves
alone with a monopolist that has seized the market share of its
fallen competitors. If the buyer is stable enough and can afford
it, the best solution is to support those partners who really need
help to survive by ordering from them—it will pay off in the
long run.

ESSENTIALS FOR SPEND MANAGEMENT SUCCESS

So, let us list what is important to practice if you decide to improve the quality
of procurement spend management and implement a category approach:

1. **Record your experiences while you work without category strategies.** Collect data, information, and knowledge, organize it, and record your conclusions based on successes and failures—they will be
useful in the future, probably much sooner than you think! As you
analyze these experiences, you will see what is missing in your spend
management approach and what questions need to be answered.
2. **Don't wait.** The idea that strategic changes can wait until you have
time for them is a trap. This work is just as important as day-to-day
operational support. Things can change at any moment, and it is the
duty of the procurement organization to ensure that it does its part to
keep the business stable.
3. **Do your research.** The key to developing an effective category strategy
is to have an in-depth understanding of the nuances of procurement
processes, how the market works, and how its participants influence

each other, along with keeping track of new technologies and collecting feedback from stakeholders. Research is an interesting task that never gets boring.

4. **Do not put off risk assessment until later.** When developing category strategies, a number of major tasks are taken into consideration: the suppliers are selected, the specifications and sources of supply are reviewed, and optimal solutions are sought. But, often at this time, a detailed risk assessment has not been carried out because of its low probability of use. Do not make the same mistakes that many people have made before you. Having a risk assessment, at least in critical categories, is a valuable advantage. Do not wait for the next crisis to break out. Be prepared for it at all times.

5. **Research current financial instruments and levers.** If you are not aware of the latest developments in financial instruments that can help improve cash flow, ask your finance manager about them.

6. **Ensure that there are quality control procedures in place.** Haste, a heavy operational task workload, and times of crisis increase the risks of failing to meet obligations or being defrauded by unscrupulous suppliers. Make sure you have sufficient quality control.

7. **Support those who are trying to make a difference.** No matter how formal your procurement process is, there is no limit to perfection. Look for opportunities to simplify processes and accelerate decision making, and remember to take the time to dig into the results and thank those who put in the work to achieve them.

KEY CHAPTER IDEAS

- Methodologies for developing category strategies are only a tool. They do not work on autopilot but require constant maintenance and updating. It is unlikely that they will save you anything unless you put in the work, but they can be a much-needed lifeline, not only in daily cost management but also in critical situations.
- Achieving savings through consolidating procurement volume—also called economies of scale—and reducing both the prices and the average cost of placing a purchase order requires optimizing the active supplier base. Most often, this means reducing the number of suppliers.
- Category strategy development is an iterative process that requires constant support, monitoring, and adaptation to changing market conditions.

- Cross-functional collaboration and ongoing routines to track progress are keys to success.
- A category strategy should include several scenarios in the event of changing market conditions or unforeseen circumstances, such as accidents, disruptions in the supply chain of partners, natural phenomena, etc. If circumstances change and there is no plan of action, act quickly, according to this basic algorithm:
  - Mobilize your team and resources
  - Revise your strategy and action plan
  - Make decisions together
  - Eliminate internal corporate bottlenecks

ENDNOTES

1. The Kraljic matrix is a method for analyzing a purchasing spend portfolio and developing category strategies that was proposed in 1983 by the German economist Peter Kraljic.
2. "Purchasing Must Become Supply Management," Peter Kraljic, Harvard Business Review, 1983. https://hbr.org/1983/09/purchasing-must -become-supply-management.
3. How China Won Trump's Trade War and Got Americans to Foot the Bill. SupplyChainBrain, January 13, 2021. www.supplychainbrain.com.
4. "Tired of waiting on the auto industry, the German postal service built its own e-trucks." QARTZ, December 16, 2017. www.qz.com.
5. TVO Methodology: Valuing IT Investments via the Gartner Business Performance Framework. www.gartner.com.
6. "On the mistakes of others: Two sides of the same Rolls-Royce communication." Mind, October 7, 2020. www.mind.ua/ru.

CHAPTER 5

PROCUREMENT SAVINGS: EVERYTHING YOU DID NOT SPEND

HOW TO ACHIEVE PROCUREMENT SAVINGS

Chief executive officers (CEOs) and chief financial officers (CFOs) are often skeptical about procurement cost savings as an indicator of how well the procurement function is performing. Alternately, procurement is expected to deliver value beyond just on-time supply. So, how do you measure this additional value and motivate the procurement team to achieve high performance? What is the buyer's role in achieving savings? What precisely qualifies as savings in procurement? Savings compared to what, exactly? And how are they calculated? In this chapter, we will try to answer these questions.

Quite often, the procurement function has no clear objectives to optimize costs and create new sources of profit because the organization has not yet formed an understanding of how procurement can affect the cost of doing business and how exactly procurement savings are defined. There are many reasons for this, but I would highlight the following:

- No clear idea of what "procurement savings" means
- Lack of open dialogue and the alignment of expectations between the various participants in the procurement process and the finance department
- Lack of or insufficient data to track savings; if they are not systemized and accumulated, it is generally problematic to calculate savings
- Different baselines for comparison and calculations of savings for different categories, which can make the calculations feel inexact; it can be a comparison to the price of the last purchase, planned prices, the prices of alternative commercial proposals, etc.

- Mixing up the concepts of cost reduction and cost avoidance; savings caused by market situation versus savings that are achieved due to proactive negotiations, etc.

As a result, the evaluation of savings may be inconsistent, leading to a loss of credibility. There is a variety of arguments made for discounting savings achieved through the actions of the procurement department:

1. Procurement wasn't responsible for this; it was just favorable market conditions
2. The supplier increased prices; there are no savings here
3. We have never bought this before, so there is no way to make a comparison with a previous purchase, and if we cannot calculate any savings, it means there are none
4. If we have saved money, why can't we see it in our accounts?
5. It would be more meaningful if we saved 2 percent on raw materials rather than 20 percent on spare parts

Such comments always strike me as odd. They are based on a limited understanding of how the procurement department works and how the effectiveness and efficiency of this function are measured. These views ignore how much effort the buyer will spend on developing the supplier base, negotiating, contracting, and disposing of the procured item at the end of its life. It is true that for manufacturing companies, raw materials is the biggest spend category, where even small savings can yield significant benefits. But if there is an opportunity for additional savings on spare parts, materials, and services, why not take them? After all, if you calculate the potential savings in all other categories, even in medium-sized companies, it can add up to hundreds of thousands or even millions of dollars in savings per year.

The reality is that if there is no evaluation of procurement efforts in the form of a calculation as to the effectiveness of the purchase, be it savings or other improvements, there will be no motivation to thoroughly understand and optimize spend. Employee motivation and engagement are significant factors that affect business performance. However, motivation goals are not only achieved by evaluating key performance indicators. If a buyer's effort to optimize cost savings is met with a yawn or remarks like, "There are no real savings in procurement"—which is completely unacceptable—managers can put a fat red X over any dreams of spend efficiency that they might want to achieve. If we expect results, it is unacceptable to devalue the efforts that have been made to achieve them. And to prevent this from happening, we need to agree on how the effectiveness of these efforts should be measured and recognized.

But how should these savings be calculated? What assessment methods are available, and how realistic and tangible are they? It is worth recalling the well-known saying, "A penny saved is a penny earned." On

The essence of procurement savings: you have earned everything that you did not spend.

a par with the sales function, where you can aim to sell higher than the base price and make an obvious contribution to the profit margin, or the production department, where you find ways to increase output without investing huge amounts of money in new equipment, the procurement department can buy everything needed at better prices without sacrificing quality. This contributes to the efficiency of the entire business. The result of such savings is no different from the results of other departments that traditionally "make money."

Procurement cost efficiency has a direct impact on the financial performance of a business. Linking them to key financial indicators is quite simple. Let's take a look at Figure 5.1.

Reducing the cost of procurement, as well as reducing the cost of support for procurement processes, has a direct impact on the EBITDA (earnings before interest, taxes, depreciation, and amortization) of the company. All other things being equal, without special efforts to save costs, EBITDA would be inevitably lower. The chief procurement officer must understand exactly how procurement costs and savings are reflected in the company's P&L (profit and loss statement) and their closest ally should be the CFO.

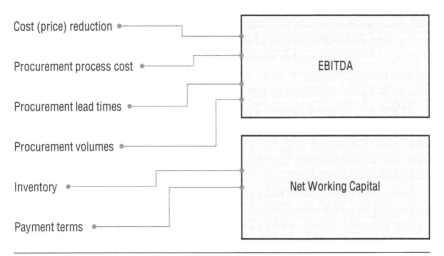

Figure 5.1   Procurement savings and its impact on financial performance.

A former procurement director of a major telecommunications company once told me that management did not believe in the feasibility of procurement savings because this indicator was not strictly tied to the company's financial results. This changed after the evaluation methodology was refined with the help of the finance department. The performance assessment changed dramatically and even convinced management to use some of the savings for bonuses paid out to cross-functional team members who participated in the development of the category strategy that led to the confirmed savings.

The most obvious instance where there is no doubt about the reality of procurement savings is savings from the price of a past purchase. For example, we bought switches at one price, and then later, the supplier agreed to reduce it. The difference in price per unit multiplied by the volume purchased is the savings. This is an easy example, but calculating procurement savings is not always as simple as two plus two.

PROCUREMENT SAVINGS CALCULATION METHODS

There are many ways to calculate procurement savings. Some of them are simple and obvious, like the aforementioned example of reducing costs compared with past purchases; others are more complex, where you need to calculate savings through an assessment of the total cost of ownership (TCO) over the long term, taking into account market indicators (exchange rates, inflation, price quotes for raw materials, and market conditions) and trends in technology development. One of the most controversial points, around which the most frequent disputes about the reality of savings occur, is estimating savings for something you have never bought before and for which there is no fair market price indicator. But, even in these cases, there are solutions.

Before we move on to specific calculation methods, let us look at some general concepts of procurement savings. Before we start, it is worth getting a clear understanding of such terms as *cost reduction* and *cost avoidance*. These concepts, as their names suggest, are not identical, and each has its own characteristics and definition.

Some kinds of savings, such as a cost reduction, can be easily seen in an accounting entry: it was $1,000, it's now $900—everything is clear and transparent. But what about situations where prices have risen due to an increase in macro indices? If the current purchase price is higher than the previous one, does this mean that no savings were achieved? No, this is exactly what cost avoidance is all about. So, let's align on definitions:

- **Cost reduction**—is a type of savings where you can calculate the change in the cost of a category compared with historical data. That is, you can confidently quantify how much money was saved: $15 was previously paid for notepads, now the price is $13. The savings is $2. Usually, such savings can be confirmed when the contract with the new prices is signed.
- **Cost avoidance**—is a type of savings where there are no direct historical price data comparisons, or there is an actual increase in price, but the effectiveness of the purchase is evaluated in comparison to the dynamic of market prices, whereas saving is defined as the difference between the actual negotiated price and the probable (expected) price. For example, last year the purchase price of notepads was $13. However, recently there has been a 20 percent increase in the price of paper. Suppliers send a price increase notice of 17 percent for your current year purchases. After negotiations, an agreement is reached to increase prices by just 12 percent. The 5 percent difference represents savings because with no negotiations, the company would have had to pay 5 percent more for the same goods. Let us consider another scenario: buying raw materials in advance against the background of forecasted price increases. It is only possible to evaluate whether such savings have been made after time has passed when it is clear whether the forecasts were correct or not. If your purchase price rose by 10 percent while the market prices increased by just 5 percent, you have direct losses, not savings. These are forecasting risks in cost avoidance that are worth considering.

Both types of savings deserve equal attention and consideration because they directly affect the amount of money spent on procurement. Although cost avoidance is a less transparent way of estimating savings than direct cost reduction, both bring real savings and require special effort. Macro indices change regardless of our will or how well a company is doing. If there is an upward trend in prices in the market, the challenge will not be to reduce them compared to your last purchase, but not to overpay compared to the market, and ideally to buy cheaper than the market. What indicator, in this case, helps determine the market price? It could be:

- **Market indexes**—such as stock exchange indicators, inflation, producer price index, labor cost index, etc.; if you buy for less than an indexed price, then this can be considered savings
- **Median of offerings from suppliers**—who were short-listed for the category supply base; the difference between the median of the offers and the accepted offer is savings

Table 5.1 contains a summary of the most common savings scenarios, and following the table is a more detailed description of possible use cases. Each savings scenario may be used on its own or in conjunction with others. It may happen that in a single transaction, various savings scenarios are applicable—for example, reduction of price and reduction of stock level, transportation costs optimization due to an improved ordering system, logistics routing, and packaging. All these savings should be summed up to calculate total savings. When working on a specific category, a buyer may find many more ways to optimize costs—provided there is a thorough analysis and understanding of key cost drivers.

Table 5.1 Savings scenarios.

Type of Savings	Savings Scenarios	Calculation Methods
Cost reduction	Reduction of price as compared to previous order	Difference in prices between current and past purchase orders multiplied by current order volume
	Substitution	Difference in price between original/earlier procured specification and the substitute multiplied by current order volume
	Free additional supplies or services	The difference in the cost of purchasing additional volume or additional services if they would not have been part of the scope of the original supply
	Discounts or bonuses	The difference in price without discounts and bonuses and the price with discounts and bonuses (for example, discount for an additional purchase volume)
	Make versus buy	The difference between the cost of purchasing and in-house manufacturing, including raw materials, labor, energy, administration, etc.
	Process cost reduction	The difference between production process costs before and after the purchase
Procurement quantity reduction	Demand reduction or cancellation	Purchase cost change after demand volume reduction (Note: it is important to make sure the volume is reduced permanently and the same scope of needs can be covered with less procured goods or services)
	Procurement order volume optimization	Impact of different delivery scenarios and/or purchase order volumes optimization on logistics and storage expenses

Continued

Table 5.1 *(continued)*

Type of Savings	Savings Scenarios	Calculation Methods
Process cost optimization	Reduction of operation and maintenance costs	Difference in the cost of operating and/or repairing equipment before and after the purchase
	Reduction in administrative costs	Difference in the administrative costs to support the transaction before and after the purchase
	Benefits from reduced delivery times	Gains due to faster purchase order fulfillment as compared to previous supplies
Working capital optimization	Payment terms optimization	Getting additional benefits by optimizing the payment terms, including applying special financial instruments like supply chain finance, factoring, etc., as compared to previous/estimated costs
	Inventory stock reduction	The difference between the average cost of inventory and the cost of storage and handling after procurement terms optimization as compared to previous/estimated costs
Other	Reduction in disposal costs	Difference in the costs of disposal of waste from operating the purchased product, production waste reduction, or end-of-life product disposal as compared to previous/estimated costs
	Operating cost reduction	Difference in costs (resources, labor, etc.) spent for putting the procured product or service into operation and for its use as compared to previous/estimated costs

Let's examine the possible use cases for each of the scenarios:

- **Reduction of price as compared to previous order**—as previously mentioned, this is the most common and simplest way to calculate savings, which is to compare the cost of the current purchase with the cost of the one before it. Note that I use the word *cost*, not *price*. The money we spend on a purchase is not just the price of the item being purchased but also the associated costs, such as shipping, paperwork, quality control, etc. If there is no information about the full cost of the purchase, we can limit ourselves to comparing prices, but it is important that they are comparable. For example, if the contract stipulates price adjustments for each shipment depending on volume, the calculation formula will become more complicated, or alternatively, the basis for comparisons can be calculated by deriving the average purchase price for comparable periods. This could also include reducing the TCO.

- **Substitution**—it is often not enough just to find a usable comparable. To make its use possible, an effort must be made to renegotiate specifications, retrain employees, etc. For example, vehicle manufacturers may specify in their manuals the requirements to use certain brands of parts or certain types of oils. Replacement parts and related materials on the original market (so-called original components) are always more expensive than their counterparts on the aftermarket that are made by manufacturers who are not in the ranks of original parts suppliers. If you do manage to get permission to use these substitutes without losing the manufacturer's warranty, then providing the same or improved durability of a part at a lower cost is a direct cost saving for vehicle operation.

- **Free additional supplies or services**—let's say a tender is held for the purchase of new technological equipment. To put it into operation, employees need to either undergo a certified training program, which costs a lot of money, or maintenance is provided on a paid basis during the warranty period for the purchased equipment. If you manage to negotiate free training or free maintenance with your supplier, you have saved money. The free or discounted inclusion of additional services or quantities of goods that were originally only available for a fee provides obvious savings. In this situation, it is worth your time to critically evaluate the real need for such additional services. It is not uncommon for suppliers to offer services that will not create real value for the buyer or where the buyer is highly unlikely to find the time or resources to take advantage of them instead of a discount.

- **Discounts or bonuses**—after buying the same goods for years, the buyer does not see any changes in the terms of the deal; their loyalty and long-term relationship have not been considered by the supplier in any way. Suppose a procurement specialist requested additional preferences from a supplier based on a long history of cooperation. As a result, at the end of each period, the purchasing company began to receive rebates, discounts, or bonuses from the supplier as rewards for making the agreed number of purchases. These discounts and bonuses also represent savings on purchases; without these arrangements, the company would have spent the same amount on purchases and received no compensation.

- **Make versus buy**—with some experience in acquiring and using an item, as well as suitable resources and production facilities, companies often resort to manufacturing certain products themselves instead of buying them from the market. In the chapter on category strategies, there was a telling example of manufacturing one's own car model instead of buying one from an outside supplier. The difference between making it in-house and the total cost of purchasing is the savings. Oftentimes, this is a good option to consider.
- **Process cost reduction**—let us return to the already mentioned example of the selection of oil types. With this type of substitution, not only can the cost of purchasing the lubricants themselves be reduced, but also the cost of the production process can be optimized if the substitute provides a longer running time or longer maintenance intervals. Sometimes, it can even improve the quality of the end product, which can allow for a revenue increase. Savings measures can have far-reaching consequences and affect, directly or indirectly, different areas of the business. Therefore, do not limit yourself to estimating the cost savings of just the item being procured.
- **Demand reduction or cancellation**—this savings method is not about how to get the best price from a supplier but about how to adjust demand and thereby limit the need to purchase the product. For example, a change in supply or equipment configuration can eliminate the need to purchase individual spare parts or maintenance services. This type of savings is possible by altering the way work is done; for example, when a company changes the way it fastens ceiling upholstery in a car, thereby reducing the consumption of special fasteners. The need to purchase additional equipment can sometimes be eliminated by reducing the downtime of an existing fleet by reducing repair and maintenance schedules. It is not uncommon that when examining demand more closely, it turns out that the purchase of certain components has no effect on the quality of the production process and can be successfully performed without their use. Sometimes a purchase requisition may just be because the requestor has a budget that they are afraid will not be renewed, so they try to stock up on the necessary materials or spare parts as a safeguard for the future. Therefore, it is important to identify such situations and prevent these purchases from being made. Such a demand adjustment can only be considered savings if the demand is actually canceled rather than just delayed.

- **Procurement order volume optimization**—by optimizing supplies, shipping and storage costs can be reduced, and by establishing procedures for controlling reorder point volumes, it is possible to improve procurement conditions, as well as change the frequency and shipment size. Optimization of procurement volumes can mean both the reduction and the enlargement of supply batches. For example, it usually makes sense to buy small metalware items in larger batches since they do not take up much storage space, and the labor cost to place each order and register each delivery may exceed the cost of the inventory lot. On the contrary, for mass consumption categories, it may be more profitable to buy in small batches even if there are volume discounts when the discounts provided do not compensate for the additional costs of storage and handling a large volume of cargo.
- **Reduction of operation and maintenance costs**—any of the savings methods described in this chapter can help reduce operating costs by reducing the cost of parts, materials, and services, eliminating the risk of price increases and optimizing payment terms. However, in addition to these methods, there are less obvious ones such as revising equipment maintenance processes and cycles. In these scenarios, the work is not so much about price or the cost of goods and services but rather about the process of servicing the procured item, which consists of finding ways to optimize it by reducing the duration of process steps, their number, and labor costs through automation or outsourcing.
- **Reduction in administrative costs**—certain types of transactions, such as construction contracts or the complex supply of equipment and services, involve cumbersome processes supporting the fulfillment of obligations by both parties: quality control, acceptance procedures, transportation, storage, keeping track of employee working hours and work orders, etc.—all supported by a lot of paperwork. It is possible to save on these costs if these processes can be optimized without reducing quality, for instance, through automation, the consolidation of volumes and operations, and the optimization of the number of people involved in these processes. Savings should be considered when assessing the effectiveness of the concluded transaction with records of the achieved benefits. An example of optimizing transactional and administrative costs are marketplaces that, if the process is set up properly, allow for the removal of procurement officers from the transaction chain by connecting the supplier directly with the customer and providing automatic compliance control of the transaction. There is no point in carrying out complex supplier selection procedures if the

electronic site provides the opportunity to directly select the most advantageous offer among several presented.

- **Benefits from reduced delivery times**—suppose your company produces a product that is in high demand. Due to the growth in sales, you are expanding your presence in the region and have ordered a new production line. The average period of manufacture and delivery of such equipment, according to the contract, will be eight months. During the execution of the contract, the procurement team is involved in the search for the necessary components for the manufacture of this production line and achieves a reduction in the delivery time of equipment by two months. This means you can have your line up and running and start profiting from additional sales up to two months earlier. This benefit is due to the procurement team's efforts. In this case, it wasn't *savings* that the procurement team achieved but *revenue* and *profit acceleration*, which is just as important, if not more.
- **Payment terms optimization**—this savings method is one of the most common and easiest to evaluate. If it is possible to optimize the terms of payment under the contract, this is direct savings. Work with finance to set an appropriate interest rate or internal rate of return for such calculations of savings from better payment terms. These are different in each country and company and depend on the funds available to the organization, what investment tools it uses, and what conditions are offered by banks.
- **Inventory stock reduction**—in many cases companies do not estimate the cost of storing a batch of supplies if it does not occupy much space in warehouses that they own outright. However, even if a company is not paying rent, the cost of storage is not zero; electricity, utilities, building maintenance, and wages for employees who move and account for the goods in the warehouse all affect the cost of storing inventory. The cost of inventory that is recorded also reduces the amount of working capital, reducing the funds that could have been invested in other projects or earning interest. If, after working out the deal, it is possible to reduce the average amount of inventory in stock compared to the same period in the past, this is also a savings lever worth reviewing. Reducing average delivery batch volume, transitioning to a just-in-time delivery schedule, making timely decisions on the disposal of unused stock or its sale, more carefully calculating demand forecasts, and coordinating work between the supplier and the buyer should be worked out in detail. If such levers are used for many categories at once, the amount of savings will increase significantly.

Optimizing payment terms and reducing inventory levels have a direct impact on improving working capital. Table 5.2 is a memo that I have often used to explain to new employees how their actions affect the company's working capital.

Table 5.2   Influence of payment terms and inventory value on working capital.

Indicator	Influence on the Company's Working Capital
Accounts payable (Goods/services received but not yet paid for)	The longer the payment period after goods/services receipt, the better
Advance payments (Goods/services not yet received but already paid for)	The shorter the delivery term after advance payment, the better
Inventory (Goods accepted into storage but not yet used)	The lower the inventory stock level, the better

The acceptable target levels of each indicator in working capital are determined together with the finance department. It is important to keep in mind that not only the purchasing department but the entire company's production process influences inventory levels, so it is not worth setting inventory and working capital level targets for procurement alone; the related key performance indicators (KPIs) should be shared by the cross-functional team and set for all the departments that affect the procurement process. The main objective of measures aimed at saving money in this area is to determine an optimal level of working capital for the company.

- **Reduction in disposal costs**—let us use the example of lubricants. If a substitute increases the durability of vehicle components and the period of time between oil changes, then a reduction in waste and, consequently, the cost of its disposal will follow. The use of new packaging made from other materials that can be reused or resold can reduce waste. Increased mileage on vehicle tires will increase their lifespan and reduce disposal and repair costs for the equipment itself. Leveraging savings through waste management should also be an essential part of category strategies.
- **Operating cost reduction**—it is important to review what resources are involved in the process of putting an item into operation, including how the process is structured, how long it takes, and what auxiliary resources and equipment are used in the process. The procurement department should have a coordinating role in this.

The list of savings scenarios that were described here is not exhaustive. Many factors influence procurement costs; they can be grouped together in different ways and can be added to in a way that is relevant to the particular situation. Savings items such as price reductions, reduced process support costs, and optimized repair and operating costs, together, form the basis of estimating the change in TCO for the procured item. The main thing is to investigate all possible factors that influence cost value.

The topic of estimating savings in procurement is a sensitive one for procurement professionals. There are usually a lot of questions surrounding this issue, and it is not uncommon for a lack of consensus within companies about what exactly should be considered savings. So here are a few more considerations, some of which are widely supported by industry professionals, while others may be a bit more controversial. However, they will all hopefully lead to a better understanding of how to approach the savings topic. It is totally up to you whether or not to take the following considerations into account:

1. **Saving versus the budget is not savings**—perhaps the only indicator from which savings should not be calculated is the amount of funds planned for the purchase or, in other words, the procurement budget. I know companies and specialists that simply use the difference between the budget and the actual cost of procurement to calculate savings. This type of calculation is based on wishful thinking; first we estimate the budget, for which we gather information from the market, then we proceed from assumptions about the future price or even from our own historical purchasing prices. But what was in the past was *in the past*. Yes, understanding how accurate our forecast was is useful knowledge for applying it in the future, but the budget is not a real cost. The size of the budget can be considered more or less realistic if it is based on historical prices, in which case, assuming there are no other accurate scenarios for calculating savings, having such a benchmark is better than having none. Yet, the calculation has a very low level of transparency. A budget is usually drawn up several months or a year in advance. We all know that there is no such thing as an accurate forecast of market conditions. Even if we ask suppliers for prices when we budget, the numbers we get cannot be considered accurate or fair because suppliers know that this is not yet a real purchase order but a budget estimate, so they may inflate the numbers. Suppliers are in the same position as everyone else, and when it comes to predictions, they may get it wrong.

   When a real tender is held, new inputs appear, the terms of reference and commercial conditions are clarified, new companies emerge as participants in the procurement procedure and competition increases, the markets change, quotes may show figures that are diametrically opposed to our expectations, etc. In fact, the budget is a certain value in which we have faith, but it may differ significantly from reality. The reality is the state of the market at the time of purchase, and that moment is significantly separated in time from when the budget was created. A calculation based on something that is just wishful thinking or, quite frankly, fantasy looks extremely dubious.

Are there exceptions to this rule? Probably, yes, if you can make sure that the estimated (budgeted) value of the purchase is formed transparently and carefully verified, although in practice, the greater the time lag between budgeting and the time of purchase, the less reliable the budget estimate will be.

2. **Procurement savings come from the efforts of people, not procedures**—well-designed processes will undoubtedly help improve procurement's economic efficiency. It may appear that you receive the bid, run the tender on the electronic trading platform, sign the paperwork, and then everything moves as if by magic: goods are delivered, services are rendered, and savings are made. However, formalized procedures are only part of the success story. The requirement to collect several bids (usually a minimum of three), tender rules with predetermined steps, and the use of reductions are all proven tools that give results, but they are not only incomplete; in some cases, they can even be harmful. Where a two percent savings can be achieved by meticulous execution of statutory procedures, a balanced mixed approach where different types of controls and procedures are involved, such as the development of a category strategy and artful negotiations (the outcome of which no standardized procedure can foresee), can produce 5, 15, and in some cases, up to a 60 percent savings. The effectiveness of this purchase depends on the balance of procedures and creative solutions, at what point the purchase is made, how the request to the market is configured, and what the terms of reference are.

Decisions about the best strategy and tactics are made by people based on the current market conditions. Buyers can make the effort to work out all the purchasing tactics in detail, or they can stop at the minimum three-bid requirement laid down in your regulations. Even if you establish differentiated requirements for certain categories, for example, a minimum of 10 proposals for the *fixtures* category, it might turn out that these are just the *first* 10 that turn up in the market rather than a carefully selected shortlist drawn up after a detailed sourcing and evaluation of hundreds of suppliers. By definition, the *first* 10 suppliers chosen in this way cannot be considered reliable partners.

3. **The failure to find information on market indicators does not mean it is not there**—sometimes, when we are looking for ways to save money, we do not find enough information on market price indices for a particular category: the information available is too generalized or not accessible, or perhaps it is simply not collected because of the low demand for these data. However, this does not mean that you cannot calculate the necessary indices or derive them from the data that are available within the company itself or from indirect indicators. You can create your own indices to help predict the situation. For example, you can track how the average price changes from year to year and whether there are any correlations with external or internal events. You should pay attention to whether the price of a service usually grows by two to three percent per year and then suddenly jumps by seven percent for no obvious reason.

   It is important to keep track of macroeconomic indices: inflation, the consumer price index, quotations for major commodity categories that directly or indirectly affect the subject of the procurement, etc. To determine the extent to which a particular index affects a product or service, it is important to understand what proportion of the costs depends on it. Information on this can be found in specialized analytical and information agencies. Yes, such reports may be generalized, may not take into account the specifics of a particular country, and are unlikely to find a price index for a particular electric motor in a specific geographic location, but industry-wide global trends are applicable today in almost any category, and the relative price structure of similar motors from different manufacturers will differ only slightly.

4. **Signing a supply contract at a favorable price does not always mean real savings**—it is generally believed that you have already achieved savings by signing a favorable contract. But in reality, it may turn out that the counterparty has not been able to fulfill its obligations or that while fulfilling the contract, additional costs have been identified, such as fixing defects or adjusting equipment. Or it may turn out that the buyer has changed priorities, and the purchase order volume has decreased, with a corresponding fall in the size of the discount. Unfortunately, it is not uncommon for a buyer to be unable to align the prices and configurations prescribed in the contract with the actual

deliveries. The calculation of savings is best done after the obligations under the contract have been fulfilled. It is then that you can sum up and deduce the amount of savings most accurately.

There are situations where delivery times are too long, such as in the case of complex equipment that can take more than a year to produce and then another few months to install. Often the savings from such transactions cannot be put into just one accounting period. For such cases, it is important to determine in advance how the results will be summed: in stages, in installments after the delivery of each batch of products (if we are talking about a long-term contract with the staged placement of orders for delivery), or after the execution of the contract in its entirety.

Savings will be influenced not only by the procurement but also by technical specialists, the finance department, and other functions. To what extent savings will be received in full depends on whether the buyer adheres to all the terms of the contract, fulfills them in a timely manner, and controls the compliance of prices and conditions with the actual delivery.

It is also necessary to provide for situations when, for example, a company decides to invest in the purchase of equipment with long lead times but in the process of project implementation, new influencing factors are discovered, or the market situation changes, and the decision is made to pause or even cancel the project. The work of selecting a supplier and closing a deal has already been done, perhaps with the efforts of many functions other than procurement. In such cases, a decision needs to be made regarding how procurement's performance will be evaluated.

5. **We are prone to wishful thinking**—there are several *creative* ways of assessing a market offer when the calculation is carried out through specially derived coefficients that were developed for a particular purchase or when setting the weight for one or another indicator in the evaluation of the offer. For example, the price of the product itself is assigned a weight of 50 percent in the overall evaluation of an offer; of this, quality could make up 40 percent and financial conditions the remaining 10. Sometimes a complicated formula is derived for evaluating an offer, and such a calculation may look very convincing because a quantitative valuation is assigned to each indicator, and numbers are always more impactful than an expert's opinion on the importance of a particular selection criterion. As a result, there is an illusion that such mathematics can protect against erroneous decisions

and even policy abuse. But in fact, this way of evaluating proposals is much closer to taking a shot in the dark, which has nothing to do with assessing the real advantages of a particular proposal. After all, the weight given to each criterion still comes down to the expert judgment of the decision maker. Why should *price* have a weight of 50 percent? Why not 40 percent or 36.678?

The weighting approach is used to back up a decision with numerical valuations, but in reality, it is more of an attempt to hide behind the numbers in situations when no better methodology is available, and some kind of evaluation mechanism is required. But by and large, this kind of creative math has nothing to do with assessment accuracy.

Any evaluation must be comprehensive and consider the real price, taking into account the cost of working capital, TCO, and real (not imaginary) losses or gains from the acquisition. In such situations, it is best to use only data and information in which you are confident. If there is no certainty but there is a risk of data manipulation, it is better to exclude such data from the assessment altogether.

The optimal way to calculate savings is achieved through using multiple approaches because it allows you to consider the maximum number of factors affecting the value of the procurement. Ideally, accounting for savings should be automatic. Automation can only be feasible if a reliable database is maintained, be it Excel or a complex ERP system. It is fairly easy to automate savings calculations compared to past purchases; the accounting systems usually have all the necessary data for this. But for other methods, the calculation will be more complex, and most likely, only part of it can be automated. In this case, in order to verify the effects, a certain process needs to be introduced to reconcile the savings calculation.

It is always a good idea to involve the finance department as an arbiter in scenarios that do not lend themselves to automation. Without exception, all measures aimed at saving money need to be checked—not only by the procurement managers but also by the financial controlling department before confirmation of the effect. Even with a good level of automation in data collection, it is not always possible to automate the calculation itself, and verification of inputs is a necessary step in the process that will help increase transparency and trust in the results.

Savings targets are undoubtedly an important measure for evaluating procurement performance, but they should not be the primary metric.

In practice, it is not uncommon for current savings targets to be foregone to ensure supply continuity and/or to achieve long-term strategic benefits. In situations of force majeure, such as the 2020 Covid lockdown, many companies abandoned savings targets, and it was the right thing to do because supply continuity and employee safety were at stake and more important.

KEY CHAPTER IDEAS

- Achieving savings does not happen by itself but requires effort and in-depth consideration of the factors that affect the cost of the procurement.
- If the company does not calculate savings or if management does not trust procurement's calculations, it is worth developing and agreeing on scenarios for calculating savings that will be recognized by finance and key stakeholders.
- Savings cannot always be spotted in the accounts; in addition to cost reductions from historical prices, there is the concept of cost avoidance. These effects are just as real as the price difference between current and past purchase prices.
- Macro indices change independently of our will, and inflation is a normal economic process that must also be considered when calculating savings. The task of procurement is to minimize the negative effects of such changes.
- Money is *buried* everywhere—in prices, in the cost of transaction support, in processes, in people, and even in IT systems. Keep an eye on the quality of your databases and invest resources in the collection and systematization of procurement data. Savings are not possible without reliable data.
- Estimating procurement savings is important, but it is not the number one gauge of performance. The evaluation of its effectiveness should include not only the amount of savings but also the long-term effects of procurement, and in certain situations, it is worth dropping a savings KPI altogether to ensure supply continuity.

CHAPTER 6

PROCUREMENT ORGANIZATION MODELS: CENTRALIZE OR NOT?

MAIN FUNCTIONAL PROCUREMENT BLOCKS

The question of how the procurement department should be organized is controversial and hotly debated. Should procurement report directly to the chief executive officer (CEO) or should it be part of finance, operations, or another function? There is little debate that the procurement function is strategic and creates value for the business in and of itself. Its inclusion within other functional areas reduces its ability to influence important business decisions. The procurement service cannot be truly responsible for the cost efficiency of money spent if it still has to report to its internal client (e.g., operations or finance). Not surprisingly, in such cases, procurement is reduced mainly to support operational processes and has no impact on the company's financial results. There are only two money streams—incoming and outgoing. No one would consider the sales function and its responsibility for the incoming flow of funds as being nonstrategic.

How can the function that determines how efficiently the company spends its money be considered nonstrategic?

Just as the sales function must be as close to its customer as possible, procurement must work closely with supplier teams and be able to represent its company at the highest level—negotiating with CEOs, function heads, and government agencies, along with having enough authority to make decisions here and now. The best practice is for the procurement director to report directly to the CEO. Any other options will require the resolution of various internal conflicts, which will inevitably begin to reduce the effectiveness of the procurement service.

111

The organizational structure of procurement activities includes several areas that differ significantly but complement each other at the same time. They can generally be divided into four major units:

1. **The methodology team**—acting as a center of excellence, it is responsible for planning, maintaining databases and directories, process methodology and automation, organizing and conducting assessments of function efficiency and capabilities, developing and implementing training programs, and determining the overall procurement development strategy and key performance indicators (KPIs).

2. **The category management team** (or the procurement front office)—is responsible for developing and implementing category strategies, as well as developing initiatives to improve the cost and quality of supplies and to facilitate interaction processes within the framework of these strategies.

3. **The operational procurement team** (or the procurement middle office)—implements category strategies together with the category management team, directly executes procurement, conducts negotiations, selects suppliers, and tracks deliveries.

4. **The support team** (or the back office)—is responsible for transactional purchasing, routine operations (processing of orders, invoices, etc.), standardized contracting, monitoring and expediting purchase orders, and most transactional procurement paperwork.

The listed units may have different names and be organized differently within the procurement service, but their functionality and the processes of interaction between them must be clearly defined. Figures 6.1 and 6.2 are examples of organizational structures of the procurement functions in a metals and mining company and an oil refining company. The structures include more than three departments, but each of them has its own area of responsibility and may be clearly associated with either a center of excellence or front-, middle-, or back-office functionality. When developing and implementing these organizational structures, not only were global best practices considered, but also the competencies of each company, capabilities that stand behind each of the teams, their physical locations, and the interaction processes each had with other functions in their respective companies.

The operational procurement team can be divided into smaller teams of specialists who deal with specific categories. It often makes sense to divide into teams based on what category is being supported. For example, large construction projects require procurement across a very wide range of categories.

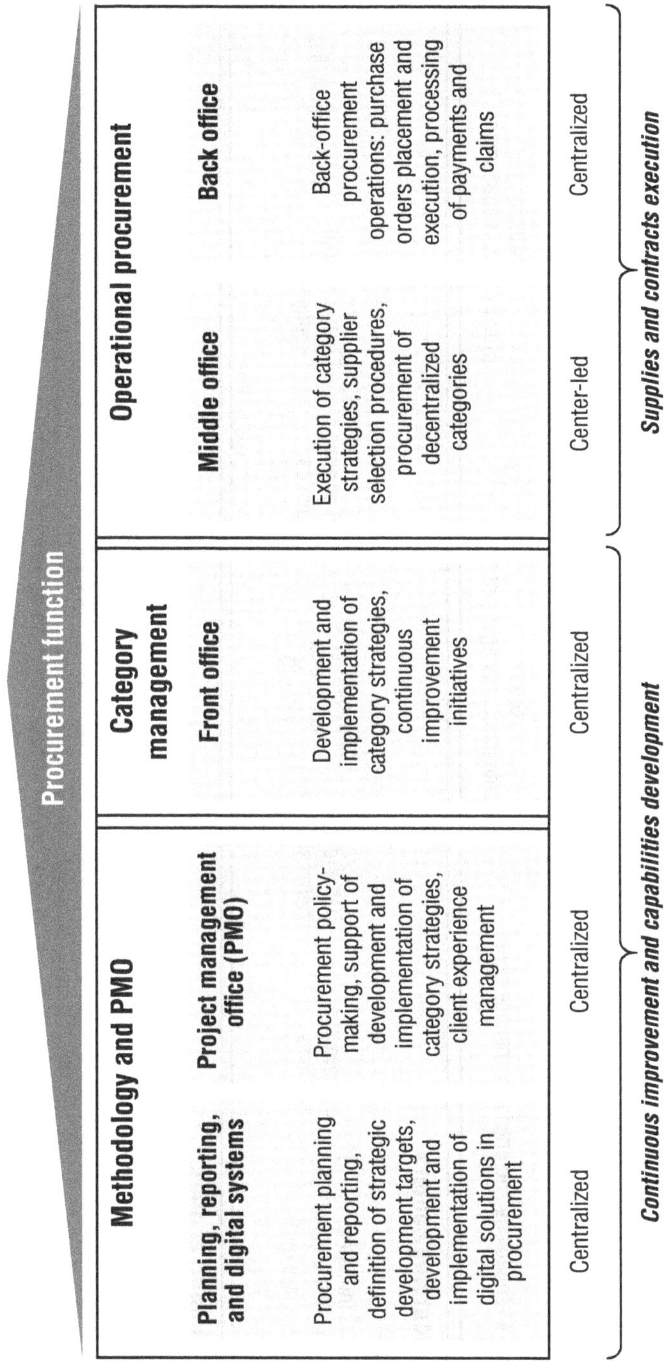

Procurement function				
Methodology and PMO		Category management	Operational procurement	
Planning, reporting, and digital systems	Project management office (PMO)	Front office	Middle office	Back office
Procurement planning and reporting, definition of strategic development targets, development and implementation of digital solutions in procurement	Procurement policy-making, support of development and implementation of category strategies, client experience management	Development and implementation of category strategies, continuous improvement initiatives	Execution of category strategies, supplier selection procedures, procurement of decentralized categories	Back-office procurement operations: purchase orders placement and execution, processing of payments and claims
Centralized	Centralized	Centralized	Center-led	Centralized
Continuous improvement and capabilities development			*Supplies and contracts execution*	

Figure 6.1 Organizational structure of the procurement function in a metals and mining company.

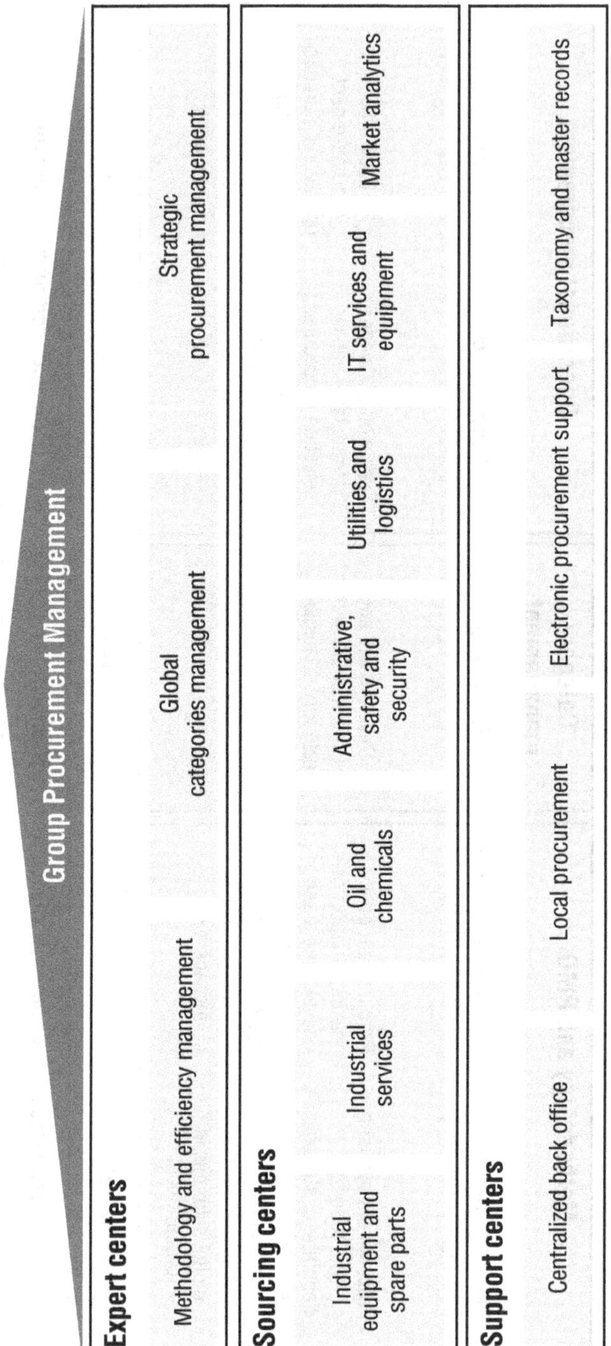

Group Procurement Management

Expert centers

| Methodology and efficiency management | Global categories management | Strategic procurement management |

Sourcing centers

| Industrial equipment and spare parts | Industrial services | Oil and chemicals | Administrative, safety and security | Utilities and logistics | IT services and equipment | Market analytics |

Support centers

| Centralized back office | Local procurement | Electronic procurement support | Taxonomy and master records |

Figure 6.2   Organizational structure of the procurement function in an oil refining company.

However, in practice, it might be more efficient to have one team organized to cover all procurement activities for a particular project rather than having different teams separately procure each category. It all depends on the specifics of the project. When applying segregation of duties in an organization, it is important to ensure that a common knowledge database is available to all participants in the process. This will help ensure that the experience accumulated in each category can be used across the organization and does not create conflicts or misunderstandings caused by a lack of information or uncoordinated communication with suppliers.

Which operational functions are best transferred to the back office should be decided internally. This decision should take into account the readiness of the organization and the employees, the availability of supporting tools (digital, reporting, communication systems), the ability to ensure process transparency, the physical location of departments (though the importance of this factor has decreased after many companies moved to remote work after 2020), the overall team climate, and even such aspects as the level of trust between employees and corporate culture. Some of the basic operational activities that are universal to most companies will be discussed in Chapter 7, *Operational Efficiency: Processes Within Processes.* In this chapter, however, I will provide more detail on procurement centers of excellence.

The functions of a methodological office can, to some extent, be performed by a chief procurement officer and/or leaders of procurement groups when the department has a reasonable number of staff. But in organizations where the team exceeds a hundred employees, and the number of connections and interactions between procurement and stakeholders is counted in the thousands—inside and outside the organization—a dedicated team needs to be set up to consolidate knowledge, maintain databases, ensure knowledge transfer, and onboard new employees. This will ensure that knowledge, expertise, and information are not lost in corporate chaos and can be leveraged and developed further.

The need for ongoing support of key processes does not depend on the organization's maturity level—whether the procurement function has been just created a year ago or already has proven to be an efficient business partner constantly delivering to expectations and setting industry best practices. Setting ambitious goals will inevitably require high-level expertise and significant organizational effort to achieve and multiply success. Things quickly fall apart when communication, change management, and employee training fall by the wayside. Organizational development needs constant support—there is always something to improve. In truth, the list of development tasks never ends because any serious change requires promotion, support, and control;

otherwise, it will quickly amount to nothing. Providing this continuous support is exactly what the center of excellence should do.

Employees who are used to an operational approach to procurement, where everything is just a matter of collecting bids from the market and signing a contract, may find it difficult to switch to a category approach. The category strategy development task assumes that for several weeks, or even months, a manager will be exclusively engaged in the analysis, discussions, and description of the future strategy, and the result of their work will only come to light later. At the time of change, people do not always understand how to explain the meaning of their work to themselves. Just yesterday, one could clearly answer the question, "What did I do today?" by glancing at the pile of approved purchase orders on their desk. Today's results may look like several files that still need to be completed and a vague idea that this *creative* work will build some strategy that the client or supplier may not even support. This atmosphere is complemented by the disapproving glances of colleagues, who continue to do the *real* work of holding tenders and drawing up contracts while you are engaged in something esoteric. This situation is typical of the transformation stage, and things will become difficult for everyone if experts from the center of excellence—who can help visualize the expected end result and train and support others—are not available.

Sustainable development requires continuous change. It may vary in scale, but it must always be supported and advanced. Are there enough tasks to keep the methodology office (center of excellence) busy on a regular basis? The answer to this question is usually "yes." You just have to keep looking for ideas and clearly understand what the goals are for the company and your function.

When people ask me whether procurement needs a center of excellence, I confidently answer, "Yes, it always does." And not only at the stage of active transformation. It should be active all the time.

WHAT PROCUREMENT CENTRALIZATION REALLY MEANS

It is quite common to come across the view that if you centralize procurement, most inefficiency problems will be solved immediately, and savings will become easily achievable. There is also an alternative view that centralization, even if you achieve economies of scale, generates inefficiencies in operational processes and increases indirect procurement costs.

Both of these views contain a grain of truth; however, the reality is somewhat more complicated than the seemingly unambiguous attempts to describe it. Deciding whether to centralize the purchasing function or not is really a secondary issue. Managing the organizational structure is just one of the tools to improve the efficiency of interaction with internal clients and suppliers. Decisions on how to build a procurement organization should be based on the specific objectives of procurement spend and stakeholder relationship management.

Centralization should not be understood as a restriction on local procurement or individual transactions. Centralization can have variations and different depths depending on how centralized categories are managed. According to the degree of consolidation, procurement can be divided into three categories—centralized, center-led, and decentralized:

Centralizing major spend categories allows you to work with the market more effectively and gain economies of scale.

- **Centralized procurement**—usually in holding companies, centralized procurement means centralized control of procurement processes at the level of company management, although this is not true everywhere. Sometimes, centralization means procurement consolidation of one category under a single contract; sometimes, performance targets for procurement teams are set centrally; and sometimes, centralization means consolidation of all procurement spend management within an enterprise. In the full centralization model, all procurement is performed by one team for all other departments or organizational units.

  In developed procurement functions, only the category manager can determine the purchasing strategy and sources of supply for centralized categories. However, not all categories can be centralized. While higher spend categories are managed centrally, the smaller categories might be more difficult to centralize due to smaller order quantities, shorter lead times, or unstable demand.

- **Center-led procurement**—can be described as procurement managed from the center, but procurement operations are not fully centralized. In the example of a center-led organization, purchases are made centrally for several categories but not for all. Center-led may also mean a mixed management model, whereas the strategy is defined centrally, but operational procurement is performed independently by local procurement departments or directly by requisitioners through selected electronic platforms or other ways as defined by procurement. In such cases, common policies may be drawn up, such as unified technical requirements for specific products and services, planning and procurement methodologies, and lists of prequalified suppliers, but purchase orders are processed either by the local procurement organization or by the end users directly.

- **Local (decentralized) procurement**—purchases are made by either the local procurement department or authorized representatives only for the needs of their enterprise or division, where each of them independently defines their procurement policy and procedures.

At Nokia in 2019,[1] procurement units were tied to a specific business unit, and major procurement streams were tied to categories. Regardless of which unit a buyer worked in, they carried out their work within a certain *category stream*. Category managers rotated between categories regularly, and the procurement structure had a separate organizational unit: a project (methodological) office called the Enabling Office. For such a diverse international company as Nokia, a complete centralization of procurement would make it difficult to manage and respond to stakeholder needs. The Nokia approach is an example of a center-led procurement organization.

Whether or not to centralize procurement depends on many factors. There is no one-size-fits-all prescription. I am a supporter of centralization, and centralization is extremely useful when the organizational model is worked out in detail. However, the transition from decentralized to centralized procurement brings much disruption and may cause resistance, which is more or less characteristic of any change. The main thing is that the inconveniences and inefficiencies of the transition period should not outweigh the benefits that centralization provides, which include improved manageability and transparency thanks to process standardization, consolidation of repetitive operations, and the introduction of uniform performance evaluation metrics for the entire organization. Changes at the beginning of the transformation path are likely to be negatively perceived by most employees, who are used to a different distribution of duties and areas of responsibility. If there is a lack of communication of the objectives of the changes, the transition to a centralized management model may, at first, even reduce the efficiency of procurement and complicate processes.

In practice, it is rare to come across examples of full centralization. This type of structure is mainly found in companies where procurement support requires compliance with numerous formalized procedures. Therefore, it is much more common in companies that are owned directly or deal mostly with the government. Each company has its own specifics and its own legacy. But complete centralization, especially in overly bureaucratic structures, does not necessarily mean high procurement efficiency. In most successful large companies, procurement is fully or partially centralized, which increases manageability and transparency. The components by which the effectiveness of procurement, in general, and centralization or decentralization, in particular, are most often evaluated are speed (timing), cost (price), and quality (reliability). Often the most effective approach is a hybrid procurement organization where several approaches to centralization coexist and procurement categories are divided into three groups:

- **The largest, most critical, and most predictable categories are fully centralized**—centralization, in this case, means that all procurement operations for allocated categories are performed centrally, and there is a single point of responsibility for spend management.
- **Smaller but essential categories are partially centralized and managed from the center**—for these, procurement policies and procedures are defined, but the actual selection of the supplier, contracting, and placement of purchase orders are performed in a decentralized manner.
- **The categories for which costs are not critical are decentralized**—often this is the portion of costs that is aptly referred to as *tail spend*. Such categories are often completely decentralized and are procured using simplified procedures due to low cost and poor demand predictability.

A mixed model with management from the center is also possible when procurement is decentralized or carried out by internal clients as long as they follow rules defined by procurement. For example, simplified supplier selection procedures can be established centrally, or a framework contract created, under which it is possible to work with suppliers directly and bypass procurement, as is the case with orders through online marketplaces.

The answer to the question of what and how much to centralize can only be obtained after a detailed analysis of the spend base. Only then will the unique proportions suitable for your company become clear. Proportions will be adjusted over time, taking into account changes in the costs, markets, and the development level of procurement automation.

There is no specific indicator that determines what is considered low spend. It depends on the scale of the company and how important certain categories are to the business. Typically, the *tail* makes up 5–20 percent of procurement spend with the lowest cost per unit and the purchases that are the least critical to the operation of the company.

Similarly, there is no rule on the proportion of spend to centralization. We can apply the Pareto principle and assume that the largest categories, which are about 60–80 percent of all procurement costs, require 10–20 percent of the time and resources to support them, while the remaining 20–40 percent of costs eat up 80 percent of the resources and effort. The categories with small costs often include the largest number of items that require many small processes to support.

There is a tendency for many companies to go through a circular process of centralization. First, the most complex and costly categories are centralized to gain economies of scale and fine-tune the supply process. Then, such categories can move back into the center-led or even decentralized group once demand and market conditions stabilize and processes get automated through digital solutions that improve spend management and require less intervention.

Expectations of the procurement function grow along with client expectations of the business and advances in technology. The corporate procurement process aspires to become as simple and intuitive as shopping in an online store. And, oddly enough, centralization can play a dual role in this; on the one hand, it can help to create such a model, and on the other hand, it can completely destroy it. It is all about the details and the way the chosen model of management is implemented.

Issues of centralized procurement management become especially relevant during mergers and acquisitions. Consolidation does not always increase efficiency.

At an open procurement conference several years ago, a representative of SEG shared the experience of its merger with Siemens. As a result of consolidating procurement processes, the speed of providing key materials for SEG's core products slowed down so much that the company nearly lost significant market share. The conference was held in 2018, several years after the merger, and Siemens had since decided to keep SEG's procurement management autonomous to allow for more flexibility. At the same time, SEG's procurement function was able to leverage Siemens' resources and expertise to streamline its processes and reduce costs.

It's ok to try out a particular approach and initially centralize a few categories or processes, followed by more categories and more processes if the approach proves successful.

FUNCTIONAL MANAGEMENT—SEGREGATE AND CONSOLIDATE

The prerequisite for operational efficiency improvement is optimized processes. It is no secret that one of the most effective ways to improve processes is to standardize and consolidate operations. If the same contract terms are appropriate for different goods or services, we can create document templates, standardize forms for collecting supplier proposals, draft scenarios for supplier audits, etc. This saves significant amounts of time. But there is another component of centralization—consolidating the same type of operations into one. When Henry Ford introduced the assembly line, he was able to significantly accelerate production processes. This approach is now used in many fields. Procurement is also a kind of production line, where in addition to unique creative tasks such as negotiating and writing category books, there are many routine operations that require high speed, attention to detail, and error-free execution. And these tasks can also be accomplished with an *assembly line* methodology.

Dividing the procurement process into components, standardizing and unifying processes, and consolidating similar operations help to significantly increase the speed of a particular step or the number of quality transactions per unit of time. Not that long ago, segregation of routine operations and their transfer to the back office was a fairly rare practice. Today, more and more companies use functional segregation to increase the speed and quality of processes. When we started to optimize procurement processes at Severstal, one of the most significant factors that influenced their acceleration was the further segregation of standard routine operations from front-office teams and the transfer of transactional work to the procurement back office.

We started this process with the most straightforward operations that had well-established rules, allowing us to standardize them painlessly. At the very beginning, these were purchase orders in a number of categories, monitoring order fulfillment, accepting and registering invoices, and controlling the payment process. Over time, this list expanded significantly—in three years, the procurement back office was already servicing requests for standardized contracting, organizing tenders on electronic platforms, resolving certain types of claims, and supporting transactions all the way from contract to payment for 80 percent of the categories. The more we standardized processes, the more activities moved from being unique (which are difficult to optimize) to automated. Our operational performance improved significantly. Here are just some of the results in the first two years:

- The number of processed purchase orders per employee increased by 210 percent
- The number of purchase requisitions processed by one employee increased by 40 percent
- The lead time from requisition to order was reduced by 375 percent
- The 92 percent on-time delivery rate, which long seemed unbeatable for our organization, was raised to a sustainable 98 percent

In addition, the quality of paperwork, payment processing, and transactional data in our electronic systems improved dramatically. What we ended up with was the process segregation shown in Figure 6.3.

The goal of process optimization is not only to speed up or improve the quality of operations but also to ensure their continuity and reliability. Cross-training employees, knowledge transfer, and automation serve this purpose, with processes becoming less and less dependent on the competence of one person or another.

Process optimization is the type of activity that has a start but no clearly defined finish line. It is necessary to *continuously* improve, automate, change, and adapt approaches and methods. Detailed analysis of processes uncovers these improvement opportunities. My colleagues and I drew hundreds of diagrams and tables and used a variety of approaches—from the principles of lean manufacturing to common sense—asking ourselves and others a simple question: *What is next level?*

When we thought the ideas were running out, we generated new analytics, conducted client and supplier surveys, drew Ishikawa diagrams, performed gap analysis, and found new areas for improvement. Each time we were surprised at how much more there was to do.

PROCUREMENT OUTSOURCING

Conducting procurement in-house versus outsourcing the function determines what resources will be allocated to support procurement activities. However, this topic could also be tied to operational efficiency since outsourcing can help to optimize processes and improve the speed and conditions of procurement. It also relates to cost management because outsourcing operations can be a good way to reduce the cost of maintaining the function.

Figure 6.3 High-level distribution of responsibility for individual procurement steps between different units of the procurement function.

The feasibility of procurement outsourcing should be evaluated on the specifics of the business and the maturity of the company. In the following list, I offer a few basic criteria for assessing the viability of such a decision. This list is not exhaustive, but it can be used as a starting point when deciding whether outsourcing will strengthen the procurement organization:

1. **Availability of in-house capabilities**—if the company has its own employees who can effectively support and develop the functionality assigned to them, and their cost corresponds to or is lower than the market rate of outsourcing, then there is no reason to outsource. Outsourcing is justified if it can offer unique solutions and capabilities that create additional value (e.g., savings or other improvements).

2. **The cost of operations**—one of the advantages of outsourcing procurement operations can be economies of scale or more advanced, possibly automated, solutions that the outsourcer applies. The use of such technologies may not be available to the client because of their high cost compared to the total volume of operations, but the outsourcing organization can offer such solutions because it supports a much larger volume of similar transactions. The same goes for categories, with outsourcing organizations sometimes offering more favorable terms of procurement due to economies of scale when they are buying the same items or services for several clients.

   A procurement alliance is a good tool to help better manage spend. When several buyers choose an outsourcer as their market representative and thus combine their purchasing volumes, it makes them more attractive to suppliers. Such procurement alliances are common in select industries, but they need dedicated support and investment from their members to be successful.

   Outsourcing a single category can pave the way for the creation of a wider procurement alliance.

3. **Ensuring competitive advantage**—a category or individual operation may be strategic for the buyer, and, despite the possible benefits of outsourcing, the company may not be ready to outsource the category to a third party in order to protect its market position and confidential information.

4. **Specifics of stakeholder interaction**—a category can be simple to procure, and while working with suppliers may be easy, it is actually a complex interaction with internal clients. Before making the final

decision, assess what the possible risks are of losing focus on client needs, and if it may outweigh the benefits from outsourcing.

5. **Organizational readiness**—a company's level of maturity is the main determining factor when deciding to outsource operations. Recognizing that someone can do your job better than you can be difficult. Engaging with a third party will require more focus and responsibility from those who will remain on the team, including those putting the data and information together that will be shared with the partner. The emergence of a third party could mean downsizing your own team, and that is unlikely to elicit positive feelings and support from employees. This is not a deal breaker, but associated risks need to be accounted for in the change management plan.

6. **Supplier readiness**—a number of large companies work directly with their equally large external clients exclusively, maintaining the confidentiality of their commercial proposals for a particular counterparty. Outsourcing procurement of such categories may be impossible for some due to their partner's refusal to work through a third party or to change their processes.

7. **Risk of client dissatisfaction**—the level of tolerance for errors after outsourcing processes decreases significantly, while at the same time, quality demands increase. Usually, we expect the contractor to do everything many times better and faster than we do. The real reasons for outsourcing, such as management's desire to reduce costs, will be relegated to the background in the perception of clients and employees. Therefore, when comparing *before* and *after*, it is important to determine in advance what counts as a success and how the parties will measure it.

8. **Capabilities of the outsourcer**—the choice of an outsourcing organization is not much different from choosing any other supplier—it is necessary to confirm the qualifications, capabilities, and competencies of the potential partner. It is important to determine how developed the market is for such services and what effects the transfer to outsourcing will have on the company. But there is another factor to consider: how much trust the organizations have in each other. As with selecting consultants, both teams' willingness to work together to improve procurement efficiency is critical. The outsourcing organization becomes an extension of its client, so it is critical to assess the ability of the two parties to work together. This criterion stands out because it is subjective and difficult to quantify.

KEY CHAPTER IDEAS

- The structure of the procurement organization should include four main functional units: methodology, category management, execution, and support. The names of the units may vary, but the important thing is to distribute the functionality so that each area has its place in the structure of the procurement organization.
- Centralization of procurement does not solve all problems and is not necessarily a best practice for your organization. There are three main types of procurement organizational structures: centralized, center-led, and decentralized.
- The most common approach to organizing category management, which is also reflected in the organizational structure of procurement departments, is based on three principles:
  - The largest in spend, most critical, and most predictable categories are fully centralized
  - Most of the smaller but critical categories are partially centralized and center-led
  - Low spend and noncritical categories are decentralized
- Periodic analysis of processes and their deviations is an important prerequisite for supporting operational effectiveness.
- Procurement outsourcing is a real and safe alternative for many companies. The decision on whether to outsource procurement should be made considering the readiness of the organization and other influencing factors, such as the company's processes and the interaction of the parties involved.

ENDNOTE

1. Information on the organizational structure of the Nokia procurement function was presented at the Procurement Roundtable event in 2019.

CHAPTER 7

OPERATIONAL EFFICIENCY: PROCESSES WITHIN PROCESSES

The previous chapters discussed benchmarking and procurement performance metrics, development strategy and operational improvement plans, examples of process optimization, and procurement organizational models. All of these have a direct impact on the operational effectiveness of procurement. Almost everything can be measured, including how well a process is working and whether there is potential for improvement on the following parameters:

- Reliability
- Speed
- Cost
- Convenience

To ensure improvement across all these dimensions, the focus should be not only on end-to-end processes but also on various other aspects of operations—independent processes within processes:

- Emergency purchases
- Planning and control of the procurement process and budget
- Procurement cycle planning
- Demand and inventory management
- Drafting technical specifications
- Selecting suppliers and managing supplier relationships

These processes are part of procurement activities, but are unique in their own complexity, therefore we will discuss them separately in this chapter. Each of these has its own characteristics, performance indicators, and optimization methods.

EMERGENCY PURCHASES

During a meeting with a supplier, the head of the technical function, wanting to encourage and motivate the supplier, says the following: "We need the supply urgently, you are the only one who can deliver fast; we all depend on you. All we need now is to agree on the price." The supplier's reply is as follows: "We are very grateful for your trust, and we acknowledge that you are in a difficult situation now. We can deliver tomorrow, but the price will be 25 percent higher from the previous purchase order." Seasoned buyers can recount many such tales. This example is based on personal experience.

Buying urgently means buying expensively.

Paying a steep price can also happen when technical requirements are not defined, the objectives of the purchase are unclear or blurred, and time is running out. Against this background, a decision is made: let's buy the same thing we bought three years ago. In practice, this means that the analysis of the real market situation has not been carried out due to time constraints or pressure from internal clients. Some price increases are justified if suppliers have to spend extra resources on urgent manufacturing and delivery and/ or buy raw materials urgently at inflated prices. Alternatively, suppliers can exploit the situation, understanding that the client has no other way out and is willing to accept any terms.

Planning punctuality and transaction speed are important levers to improving procurement's economic efficiency.

It is important that the procurement organization be able to track and control the difference between planned and emergency purchases. This, in turn, can only happen when there is a thorough and transparent accounting of all procurement transactional records in a single information repository.

PLANNING AND CONTROL OF THE PROCUREMENT PROCESS AND BUDGET

It is important to note at what point the procurement process begins and what planning in procurement involves. Formally, a purchase requisition is considered the first step in the procurement process. But, in fact, the appearance of a purchase requisition is far from the beginning of the procurement cycle, and the concept of *procurement planning* is much broader than collecting requisitions.

It is at this moment, when the purchase is just planned, that the base for the success and efficiency of future spend and process management is laid. Often at this stage, little thought is given to the fact that the methods of planning for future demand will have serious consequences on decision making and costs. Often when a need arises, we think about how to get certain services and materials quickly. Generally, there is little time to figure out how the organization of the process of obtaining those materials will affect the overall efficiency of the end-to-end process from requisition to delivery and what the long-term consequences will be after the delivery itself. At the procurement planning stage, it is important to bring in the relevant expertise to navigate through the various options. Here is a sample and non-exhaustive list of questions to ask in the early stages of the planning process:

- What technical parameters must the procured item have?
- What are the quality differences for this item from different manufacturers?
- What are the specifics of working with each particular vendor?
- What would be the best purchase batch in terms of logistics?
- Are we buying a spare part or a spare part supply and installation service?
- Will the spare part from manufacturer X require more time and resources to replace and maintain than that from manufacturer Y?
- In the event of an accident interrupting production at supplier X, do we have a proven backup source of supply?
- How will these spare parts affect the performance and wear of the machine where they are installed?
- What is the total cost of ownership, considering the cost of supporting the procurement and further operation of equipment for each of the options?
- If we select a lower quality option, will this affect the motivation of maintenance service employees, resulting in the quality of their work dropping?

These are the types of questions to ask before the actual purchase requisition is placed because the reliability and efficiency of supply in the future will depend on the answers. In reality, when there is a need to buy something *yesterday*, there is no time to deal with all of these issues, and losses from delays can exceed the benefits of a detailed analysis of the situation and finding the best solution. Therefore, it is vital that all parties work together from the very moment the demand arises: engineers draw up lists of technical requirements

The earlier the buyers are involved in the planning process, the higher the chances of executing the purchase optimally from start to finish.

that will ensure the minimum required level of compliance while buyers search the market for available options, delivery, and payment terms. Only such joint efforts will allow for the effective assessment of the situation, the selection of the most suitable option, and the building of further procurement processes in an optimal way.

Procurement planning is not limited to demand planning. In business dictionaries, one can find a definition of *planning* as a basic management function that defines tasks and goals, draws up a strategy to achieve them, organizes and creates the necessary resources, implements processes, and monitors and directs activities in the necessary direction. With this in mind, procurement planning must include at least the following:

- Defining goals and objectives for procurement activities
- Allocating teams and resources required to achieve the goals
- Defining methods and tools to achieve the goals
- Executing planned activities

In many companies, the procurement function is housed within procurement budget planning. Though procurement is responsible for the execution of the procurement budget program and provides required data and forecasts for its drafting to internal clients, who plan their operational and CAPEX budget based on the inputs on expected market price changes, it is better for procurement not to actually own the budget nor be the budget controller, as this may create a conflict of interest. The procurement function provides a service to its internal clients, and the main task of procurement is to respond quickly and efficiently to requisitions and fulfill them while saving money. However, this is where tricky conflicts may arise. When procurement becomes the owner of the budget, it gets to mandate to the internal clients how much they can spend; for example, on maintenance services. In this situation, this means that procurement shall also be responsible for defining the required amount of services and to be able to do it, one needs to manage the whole maintenance cycle, which, in fact, is a technical department's responsibility. If buyers are entrusted with the function of budget control, there is a mixing of two responsibilities: the responsibility for budget execution and the responsibility for budget control. In other words, the one who controls the budget is the one who spends it, which also creates a conflict of interest. It is much more transparent when everyone does their job: procurement helps the budgeting process with market pricing forecasts, but internal clients own the budget, define what is the volume of products and services they need, and build their forecasts based on the pricing inputs obtained from procurement. When it comes to the actual purchase, procurement helps their internal clients get the best conditions and prices from the market. The finance department then controls budget execution by technical departments and procurement efficiency by tracking the savings.

PROCUREMENT CYCLE PLANNING

I often hear from procurement professionals that their internal clients usually do not care how much time the tender takes, where an attempt to speed up the procurement cycle can do more harm than good, but they do care that purchases are made on time. In the case of planning a procurement schedule, internal clients often ask what the timeline for a particular procurement procedure is and expect that it be as short as possible.

Let's clarify what "on time" really means for the client. In most cases, it means by a required deadline, *not* within a certain period of time. If so, then what difference does it make how much time a buyer spends on a tender as long as the delivery meets the deadline? And though oftentimes procurement policies directly define that the procurement procedure shall not take longer (or shorter) than X days, the time spent on procurement procedures should not interest the client at all. A better approach is where the procurement department maintains the database of contracted or forecasted delivery lead times for groups of goods and services, which also includes the time necessary for tendering and negotiations depending on the category complexity. If a purchase is given a deadline of four months or more because of complicated negotiations and longer supplier manufacturing times, the key thing is to make sure that the client is aware of this cumulative lead time, sees the step-by-step process, is confident that they will receive their goods and services when needed, and that the procurement will be conducted efficiently to help manage their budget.

Of course, this approach imposes certain requirements on the client to plan and submit a purchase requisition on time. It is one of the key responsibilities of internal clients in the procurement process, and it can even be measured with a key performance indicator (KPI)—for example, assessing the share of purchase requisitions created on time. It is important, especially in young organizations, for stakeholders to understand how their actions affect the overall result and keep them accountable. Great results cannot be achieved when expectations are made of each other, but there is no shared responsibility for the end result.

"The beauty of delivery starts with the purchase requisition." We once presented souvenirs with this inscription to our most engaged internal clients at the annual conference of the procurement department, where we once again discussed the strategy for developing the function and initiatives to improve interaction with internal clients. This inscription showed the gratitude we had for our internal clients for their effective collaboration and engagement in our team tasks.

DEMAND AND INVENTORY MANAGEMENT

Another popular question is whether a buyer needs to check with the client to see if it is *absolutely necessary* to buy a particular product or service and in exactly that amount. As we have previously discussed, procurement should not act as a budget controller, but challenging an ask from a client can make sense at times.

This is especially the case when it comes to safety stock. Yes, buying a little more than necessary is often a very useful practice and helps avoid unforeseen risks. But how much extra stock is enough? Where is the boundary beyond where excess inventory begins to negatively affect a company's financial results? Do we really need to buy what we ordered, or does the customer really need something else entirely? How do we get answers to these questions?

It would seem that the most dependable way to answer these questions is to rely on our own experience and the experience of colleagues. This is undoubtedly true, but there are other tools to test our assumptions and related decisions. In the case of determining the optimal level of safety stock, everything is relatively simple—here, the statistics of consumption and lead time will help. Perhaps the foreman at a production site says that he needs to have 200 liters of lubricant in reserve in order to be able to work efficiently. This is easy to check: you can calculate the optimal stock level, the optimal safety stock level, as well as the optimal order quantity, and even the optimal time to place it with the supplier. But in a situation where there are doubts as to what exactly the customer needs—for example, new equipment or improving the quality of service for the existing one—different scenarios are possible.

The very first thing a buyer should start with is to ask what exactly the problem is that needs to be solved. New equipment is purchased for the purpose of increasing productivity, improving product quality, or reducing the costs associated with operating existing facilities. But it may turn out that all these tasks can be solved without the purchase of additional equipment, just by improving the operating conditions of the existing equipment or replacing raw materials and components. A detailed study of a purchase order for equipment may instead turn it into a purchase of services for its maintenance. The important thing is to understand the core problem and offer not only obvious solutions but also to test hypotheses in related areas.

For many procurement departments, inventory management is a separate section of an effective cost management task book. There are two main types of approaches to material requirement planning: *deterministic* and *statistical*.

Deterministic planning is based solely on consumption forecast data: a certain quantity is needed by a certain date. It is used in cases when:

- Consumption statistics do not reflect trends in future needs (just because last month's consumption of bolts was 20 kilograms does not mean that the next month the same amount will be needed)
- The procured item has a high cost per unit and an unstable demand associated with one-time needs (for example, a large, expensive unit of a production assembly is serviced once a year, but it is not 100% clear in advance what long-wear spare parts might need to be replaced)

If these conditions exist, it is best to plan based on specific needs. However, exceptions do occur. For industrial companies, there are cases when certain unique units can be stored as safety stock for a long time—even at a very high cost—due to the high risks that would arise from a sudden breakdown and the loss of manufacturing output while waiting to replace them. It is important that such decisions are made after carrying out an assessment of the possible risks connected with not having replacements on hand.

Statistical planning is based on consumption history (for example, in situations where you can say with a high degree of certainty that during the next month, you will use approximately the same number of items as the previous month). This method of planning is used when future needs cannot be accurately calculated and depend on the influence of external factors: the sentiment of customers, the fulfillment of client orders, and the reliability of supply.

Statistical planning can be more complicated to set up but much easier to maintain and execute because you do not have to wait for client orders to create a procurement plan. With a certain level of accuracy, you can calculate the procurement volume forecast without having actual purchase requisitions. To calculate the optimal batch and time of purchase order placement, the economic order quantity (EOQ) is used. In this planning approach, it is critical to have a digital trail of every inventory transaction—the more frequently the data in IT systems and batch calculations are updated, the more accurate the consumption forecast and, therefore, the procurement orders will be. A basic model for calculating the EOQ is shown in Figure 7.1.

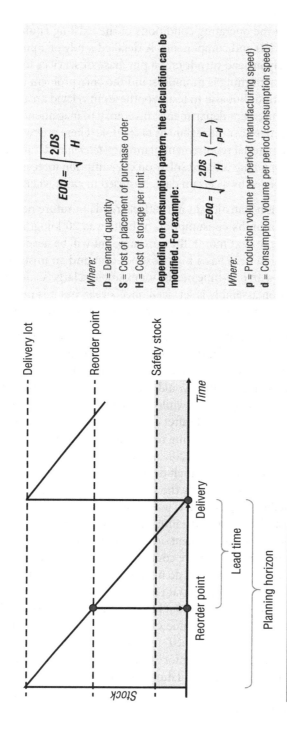

$$EOQ = \sqrt{\frac{2DS}{H}}$$

Where:

D = Demand quantity

S = Cost of placement of purchase order

H = Cost of storage per unit

Depending on consumption pattern, the calculation can be modified. For example:

$$EOQ = \sqrt{\left(\frac{2DS}{H}\right)\left(\frac{p}{p-d}\right)}$$

Where:

p = Production volume per period (manufacturing speed)

d = Consumption volume per period (consumption speed)

Figure 7.1   Economic order quantity and reorder point calculation.

The format of this book does not allow for an in-depth review of the various scenarios for calculating statistical models of inventory management. Fortunately, there are plenty of great books and articles on the subject. However, here are general, practical steps to improve the efficiency of inventory management:

1. Ensure a digital trace of all inventory operations is inputted into the company's electronic management systems; this is the only way to establish effective monitoring, automate calculations, and improve planning accuracy.

2. Set up reports that will help track inventory changes by category, group, and period; regularly monitor compliance with key planning milestones to help provide information quickly for both operational management and category strategy development purposes.

3. Organize and update inventory data online to ensure timely decision making regarding changing calculations and updating supply plans. Track and remove irrelevant requisitions from the IT system. Update deadlines in overdue documents, regardless of the reason for the delay—it does not matter why the delivery did not take place on time and may have shifted production plans; the important thing is to adjust the delivery plan for the newly updated requisition dates so that excess stock does not accumulate.

4. Where possible and where statistical planning makes sense, automate the calculation of procurement requisitions for all categories to eliminate manual operations as much as possible and reduce errors and process costs.

5. Automate the calculation of optimal inventory level, reorder point, and safety stock level for efficient supply management.

6. Monitor not only overdue deliveries but also premature deliveries because goods that arrive in the warehouse before the deadline set in the purchase order put a strain on working capital.

All of these activities will help to effectively maintain optimum inventory levels. Inventory management and maintenance of appropriate analytics are important areas of work and are best entrusted to dedicated specialists.

TECHNICAL SPECIFICATIONS

Buyers quite often encounter situations when the terms of reference for the procurement clearly or implicitly contain conditions that provide preferences for a predetermined supplier or manufacturer, making their selection a formality because it deliberately limits the possibility of a wider choice.

There may be many reasons why such a situation arises, including corruption or unscrupulous employees. However, many times this occurs because of simple convenience. Few people want to deal with something they are not completely sure about, something new that has yet to be figured out (which means an increased risk of mistakes), or something that forces employees to learn about new products (which means an increased workload)—all of which can occur when changing suppliers or contractors. A client has more confidence in a known brand or a historical supplier that can fulfill the order on time and at a high quality, so the client tries to find ways to justify that supplier's offer over others. Or, the specification of an item includes knowingly exaggerated requirements, which are an optional but pleasant bonus for the client. This can arise, for instance, when buying a specialized vehicle and adding additional requirements that do not affect performance and safety but make it more comfortable to use, such as a stereo system or special upholstery for the operator's seat. But how do you evaluate this extra convenience? What is necessary and what is unnecessary?

Bias in the preparation of technical specifications is not necessarily abuse on the part of the client. In the vast majority of cases, it boils down to a lack of understanding of the subject of the procurement, lack of time, little professional training, or the absence of qualified specialists on staff who are able to competently draw up the specifications and determine the optimal set of requirements. Of course, the corruption component cannot be discounted, but again, this is just one of the many possible reasons for drawing up biased terms of reference and not the main one.

One of the special competencies of procurement is to build the process of working with technical specifications in such a way that it is as structured and transparent as possible. Our task is to help the client's team create the best specifications possible. The following list of tools can help:

- **Drawing up standard technical specification templates**—the templates should contain a set of fields for entering the characteristics and requirements for the subject of the procurement. It works well to check templates with suppliers when you draw on external expertise or independent verification in order to exclude terms that limit competition from the technical specification. Try to work on the template without reference to a particular purchase but in general for the category, including the widest possible set of acceptable options.
- **Engaging external expertise to draw up or audit technical specifications**—there are a number of independent engineering companies

that provide such services. They should be selected based on the scope of the subject of the procurement and the industry.

- **Creating expert teams**—the potential and combined knowledge of employees is often not fully utilized within companies. The highest-quality technical specifications are always the result of teamwork that creates opportunities to discuss ideas, ask each other questions, and find the best solution. This is normal if there is a need to refine the terms of reference based on changes in the market during the procurement process. Optimal results are achieved through teamwork when the voices of different specialists are heard, and the decision-making process is not limited to one person or one department.

The following is a story from a telecommunications company in Eastern Europe that will give you a better understanding of the value of teamwork in drafting and refining technical specifications as part of developing a category strategy.

When the team started working on a data center development project, it seemed there was a need to build or rent additional space to house more servers. An analysis of the market and possible solutions for the construction of buildings was launched. At one point, in order to understand what exactly the requirements for the premises were, the procurement team began to analyze the characteristics of the equipment used in the data center. The team traveled to one of the data centers to inspect the equipment already in use. Onsite, they found that many of the server rack slots for housing processing units were empty. It seemed strange; there was free space, but why was it not being used? It turned out that through inertia, the technical service had ordered old equipment that was less efficient in power consumption than modern servers. Therefore, experts could not use the empty racks because the network voltage would not be able to bear the extra load.

After the procurement department completed its equipment review, it became clear that it was possible to increase the efficiency of the available space by selecting more modern equipment. Two significant consequences arose from the work carried out on the *data center buildings* category. First, there was no need for extra space after all, which saved the company a lot of money. Second, a completely different task was created—sourcing the right computing equipment. The head of the technical service who was responsible for the operation of the data center lost his job because he had failed to ensure the most efficient use of space and did not carry out timely modernization of the equipment.

This story allows us to draw some interesting conclusions. To get to the root cause of an issue, a systematic approach and attention to detail are important. The buyer does not need to know all the technical details in order to understand that something is wrong with the technical specification. The main thing is to communicate more with the market, take an interest in the topic, ask the right questions at the right time, immerse yourself in the peculiarities of the category, and perhaps involve several potential suppliers in the discussion of the specifications.

Conducting an analysis of the technical specifications and studying the experience of operating the subject of the procurement provides an opportunity to see what would otherwise be impossible if you blindly trusted the assurances of colleagues. Such revelations and strategic discoveries to save costs are not uncommon if you responsibly approach the issue of developing a category strategy in general, along with the technical specifications, in particular.

The story about the data center is interesting because procurement became a driver of technical development, but this is not the most ideal situation. Work progresses much better when time is set aside internally to work through strategic topics, important issues are discussed between various departments, consideration is given to the opinion of buyers on the optimal market and supplier strategy, and the opinions of technical services are sought as to which technologies are the most effective. In some cases, suppliers can also be involved in the development of solutions for category strategies, and there is little risk in this if the view of more than one partner is solicited and conclusions are synthesized on the basis of this information for the benefit of the client. As a result of this work, you will be closer to getting the perfect technical specification.

SELECTING SUPPLIERS AND MANAGING SUPPLIER RELATIONSHIPS

When it comes to making decisions about the selection of supply partners, the many regulations and procedures governing that process come to mind. The regulation of procurement and certain aspects of the evaluation of supplier proposals will be discussed in more detail in Chapter 9, but here we will analyze such issues as the evaluation and qualification of a potential counterparty and managing the relationship with the supplier throughout its life cycle.

Rodrigo Ferreira, who has held senior positions in the procurement functions of prominent global corporations, says that 70–80 percent of all supply problems occur because suppliers fail to meet their obligations. This is especially true for companies that do not manufacture the goods themselves but rather buy most of the components for their own products and services from the market. Often companies lack awareness as to how dependent they really are on the ability of suppliers to work efficiently.

In training sessions, procurement employees are taught how to select suppliers, prepare for negotiations, evaluate proposals, and then monitor contract execution. Afterward, they enthusiastically return to their desks only to realize that applying all these detailed tools to every deal is incredibly difficult. It is physically impossible to find the time to do it because even in medium-sized companies, there are too many suppliers and agreements for procurement employees to set aside a few hours for each of them to discuss partnership issues.

As with category classification, it is useful to allocate suppliers to different priority levels in order to focus resources on key cooperation issues and to predetermine a strategy for them, including the frequency and format of communication with a particular counterparty. Kralich's matrix, which was mentioned in Chapter 4, is suitable for determining a supplier strategy for a particular category, as is Kearney's *The Purchasing Chessboard*.[1] Other tools including Michael Porter's Five Forces Matrix, developed back in 1979, and the famous SWOT analysis[2] are still great for assessing supplier relationships.

It is worth noting that the process of evaluating suppliers is not one-sided. When we talk about procurement, we usually think that only the buyer chooses its counterparties, but that is not always the case.

Suppliers also choose who to work with and on what terms.

It is important to keep this in mind and apply methods of interaction that will satisfy both parties and motivate suppliers to develop their relationships with their customers.

Along with categories, suppliers also undergo segmentation—they are assigned to segments, each of which has its own approach to managing and building interactions. The methods of interaction will differ for suppliers of noncritical categories where there is a lot of competition and those who supply business-critical components that have high market value and a shortage of sources.

How you name your supplier segments is a matter of taste. There are various methodologies for segmenting. By and large, it is up to the buyer to decide how to segment them. For example, my colleagues and I used the methodology from the book *Supplier Relationship Management*,[3] which segments suppliers according to such criteria as performance (meeting the buyer's expectations on the key parameters of cooperation set for the supplier) and strategic potential (expert evaluation of opportunities to create added value for the client). As a result, each supplier fell into one of the segments depending on their performance and potential. Others suggest segmenting suppliers based on their spend and risk probability, and by risk, I mean the risk that is generated by the impact that the supplier has on their customer's business, both in terms of current supplies and future development of new products and services. The logic behind not making *spend* the main criteria for segmentation is that a supplier may have low spend, yet be very critical for business continuity, so when paying attention to spend only, one might miss important aspects of their relationship with the supply partner.

The boundaries between the segments are often blurred because the conditions of cooperation are not static—they can improve or worsen. It is much more important to have a clear difference between the segments that is accurately interpreted by all parties, creating the right expectations for all sides.

Let us see what the possible strategies of supplier relationship management are, depending on the importance of the supplier—be it in terms of criticality that may oftentimes account for spend or their strategic potential. As mentioned before, there are various approaches to defining supplier segments. I favor a relatively simple approach that is built based on the Kraljic Matrix that defines four main segments or groups of suppliers for relationship management, from most important to least important: strategic, critical, preferred, and transactional (see Figure 7.2):

Figure 7.2 Supplier segments based on the Kraljic Matrix approach.

1. **Strategic suppliers**—are partners that provide the most important supplies and are ready to invest in the development of their business with the client. They are truly valuable because this might lead to the creation of new products and services that both parties would benefit from. Cooperation, where a supplier is both important and involved, opens up the possibility of strategic partnerships or long-term agreements that can change the marketplace or create a competitive advantage, not only for the supplier but for the client. This group includes suppliers with impeccable performance who have the ability to create growth opportunities for the buyer's business. Forms of collaboration such as strategic partnerships and long-term agreements require significant investment on both sides but are definitely worth the impact that they can generate in the long term through sharing best practices and collaborative technologies. Suppliers in most cases do not single out one key customer, so regular communication is critical to maintaining the relationship. As a rule, there are only a few such suppliers, but their value is high, and the allocation of significant time and attention in this case is justified. When working with strategic suppliers, it is important to be able to find areas of mutually beneficial cooperation, additional sources of profit, motivation for joint development, and the identification of new business opportunities.

2. **Critical suppliers**—are important, but they might continually make mistakes or have chronic communication problems. This group includes suppliers who may bring innovative ideas to the buyer but also demonstrate average performance. On the buyer's side, it is important to constantly monitor such suppliers to stop repeated mistakes or obligation breaches and thus stabilize performance. It is important to periodically draw conclusions about the progress of cooperation and possible transfer of the supplier to another group or even an additional investment in relationship development if the supplier is important to the customer. It is worth defining joint goals, launching competency development programs, and providing the buyer's resources (e.g., a production floor for testing new products) to the supplier. If the supplier demonstrates a willingness to improve, it may be beneficial to invest time, money, and resources to help adjust the operational effectiveness of these suppliers in order to move them into the strategic group. If any of the critical suppliers are not performing up to expectations and do not improve over time, it is best to limit the cooperation whenever possible.

3. **Preferred suppliers**—are usually the suppliers that not only have a large impact but also perform well because their risk is low, be it supply continuity risk or performance risk. Maximize the value of the relationship with your supplier without an extra commitment. For you and these suppliers, the relationship is virtually problem-free, requires little resource involvement, and has the potential for innovation, which could eventually move the supplier into the strategic group. Frequent feedback is required to maintain effectiveness and develop the relationship.

4. **Transactional suppliers**—are generally considered to be average; they perform well, but they require support because changes in the market situation can shift them in either direction, they can either improve or fall out of your list of suppliers altogether. It is beneficial to monitor supplier performance and maintain the quality of interaction. Help the supplier to correct deficiencies while considering the positive results of cooperation. In the case where a supplier has persistent problems with delivery, cost, or quality, and efforts made to improve the situation have been unsuccessful, it is best to minimize or stop working with them altogether. The risks and costs of switching to other suppliers should be reduced by finding alternatives in a timely manner.

It is necessary to observe any changes in the supplier segment and make timely adjustments to the interaction models throughout the entire work life cycle of a supplier, as in fact, any supplier may either grow or demonstrate deterioration of their capabilities. These adjustments can range from minimizing the relationship and complete refusal of cooperation to providing additional privileges.

In order to allocate resources and time wisely, a buyer should compile a short list of suppliers that best meet the basic qualification requirements and analyze their capabilities and offerings in detail. It all depends on the needs of the buyer and what results they want to achieve in terms of competition and cost savings. Although there may be many suppliers found in the market, not every supplier is worth working with, and the short list of suppliers should include only those that are capable of meeting the requirements—or capable of developing enough to meet them in the future. A typical approach to vendor base management involves the following steps (see Figure 7.3).

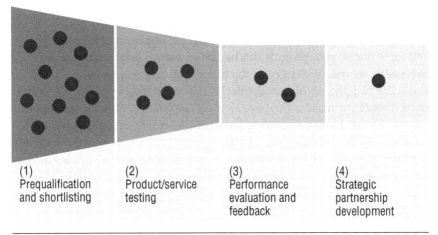

Figure 7.3   Basic approach to supplier base management

Prequalification and Shortlisting

In this stage, the buyer determines the capabilities of the supplier and its compliance with basic requirements, such as:

- Assessing production capacity
- Looking at their approaches to quality management
- Checking on the availability of innovative developments
- Studying remarks on cooperation from existing customers
- Conducting a reliability check
- Ensuring compliance with other requirements

Based on the information gathered, suppliers are ranked according to the buyer's requirements and qualification conditions. For example, the buyer can refuse to work with a supplier if it discovers that the latter is not paying its taxes.

The ability to apply certain supplier prequalification criteria also depends on the system of restrictions under which the buyer operates. For example, for state-owned companies, the application of certain prequalification conditions is complicated by a number of restrictive criteria imposed by public procurement laws. Nevertheless, here we are talking about generally accepted approaches, which are best practices, and the task of each company is to find ways to apply them in their processes as required. At the prequalification stage, it becomes clear which suppliers will move from the long list to the shortlist.

Product/Service Testing

Product testing is performed to fully qualify the supplier in critical categories, and for services, pilot projects can be run in a small area. Such tests will not necessarily be free of charge for the buyer, but they will make it possible to assess the compliance of the supplier to the requirements under real conditions in order to make a final decision on the qualifications of the supplier, proceed to the discussion of long-term commercial terms, and carry out the selection of the contractor for a certain period. At this stage, we are already working with a short-listed supplier. A formal audit of the supplier is performed at this stage, and a decision is made to start cooperating if the requirements are met. Agreements should be reached on terms that are acceptable to the parties.

Performance Evaluation and Feedback

Once cooperation begins, the buyer collects feedback from internal clients about the work of the supplier and conducts a benchmark assessment of the interaction according to a set of criteria, such as overall customer focus, the number of noncompliant deliveries, violations of contract terms, etc. Based on the results—which include both commercial conditions and an interaction assessment regarding the quality of products and services and how swiftly the supplier responds to client requests—a list of recommendations is drawn up for the supplier, or a joint action plan is agreed to in order to improve interaction processes. In the event that a number of issues are found with a supplier from the *transactional* segment, the parties will most likely not waste resources on a more detailed assessment, and the buyer will simply replace the supplier with another one.

Strategic Partnership Development

After evaluation and feedback, it becomes clear what direction the cooperation will take—toward deeper ties where perhaps alliances and joint ventures can be formed with strategic suppliers or into a wider divide where the supplier will return to the first stage. There can be scenarios where, after the evaluation of the cooperation history, the supplier is blacklisted due to significant violations of working conditions. Even at the stage of strategic partnership development, the process of interaction assessment is periodically repeated; there are reviews of KPIs, joint work results, audits, and feedback. The parties decide on further steps to improve interaction processes based on the outcomes of these reviews.

There is a widespread belief that strategic alliances should be formed with all suppliers in the strategic cluster and that such suppliers should be called nothing less than a "strategic partner." This is actually a misconception. A true stra-

Strategic partnership entails the joint development and conquest of markets in which both parties are willing to invest.

tegic partner is not a monopolist who dictates terms and conditions, nor an incumbent supplier with high spend who gives discounts every time, but rather a partner who helps a company develop its competitive advantage. A partnership does not mean painful codependence where one is always looking to escape.

It is difficult for a company to manage multiple strategic suppliers. Therefore, the term *strategic supplier* in the supplier segmentation matrix should not be confused with the concept of a *strategic partnership*. A strategic partnership is only truly strategic when you are able to invest sufficient time, resources, and attention into it.

KEY CHAPTER IDEAS

- There are special subprocesses within procurement processes where the overall methodology requires separate attention and management:
  - Emergency purchases
  - Planning and control of the procurement process and budget
  - Procurement cycle planning
  - Demand and inventory management
  - Technical specifications
  - Selecting suppliers and managing supplier relationships
- Emergency purchases are almost always disproportionately expensive compared to planned purchases. The main lever for reducing the volume of rush purchases is the quality and timeliness of planning processes for procurement needs, as well as constantly maintaining a sufficient level of safety stock and keeping the database of reliable suppliers up-to-date.
- Combining the functions of budget control and execution in procurement creates a conflict of interest and potential risks in budget management transparency.
- Managing procurement demand and inventory means critically assessing demand, constantly monitoring changes, keeping data up-to-date,

and systematizing information to ensure its reliability in the search for opportunities to optimize working capital and procurement costs.

- Technical specifications require separate attention and a methodology. The highest-quality specifications are created through cross-functional collaboration and external expertise, if necessary. This approach is more effective but requires additional investment of time and resources.
- Supplier base management involves analysis and classification of suppliers by such criteria as value/profit impact and supply risk, which also involves performance risks. It is important to invest enough time into the development of suppliers, depending on their importance. Draw up relationship development plans and carry out periodic audits for those suppliers that are in the most important segments for the buyer.

ENDNOTES

1. Source: Kearney. https://www.kearney.com/insights/books/the-purch asing-chessboard
2. SWOT analysis—a planning method based on identifying internal and external environmental factors affecting the organization and dividing them into four categories: strengths, weaknesses, opportunities, and threats.
3. Christian Schuh, Michael F. Strohmer, Stephen Easton, Mike Hales, Alenka Triplat, and A.T. Kearney. 2014. *Supplier Relationship Management.*

CHAPTER 8

PROCUREMENT RISKS: IDENTIFY AND MITIGATE

The sense of uncertainty in the world in March 2020 was unprecedented. The web was full of articles about the catastrophic effects of the COVID-19 pandemic on businesses—how it would affect the economy, where to find those few business opportunities that still existed, and how to escape from the oncoming deluge of cascading negative events. In various places, there were hysterical cries of "all is lost," "everybody's plotting against everyone else," and "what will happen now?" More uncertainty and heartache followed after Russia invaded Ukraine in February 2022 and started a full-scale war in my home country—something no one would have believed would have happened just a few months before. The feeling of irreparable disaster was imminent and unavoidable, and many businesses, including the largest steel manufacturers in the region, were at the epicenter of this violent military struggle.

The world was turned upside down. We had never been in situations like these before. It was hard to imagine that these events could really happen. Despite the abundance of warnings that a pandemic or a war was possible in today's globalized world, most were confident that they would not be affected. The majority of us were not ready for such turmoil. The thought that we had underestimated the importance of risk management kept going around constantly in my head as these events unfolded.

Nevertheless, after the initial shock to these historic events wore off, many came to their senses and began to restructure their approach, changing their attitude from panicky to *panic-analytical*, gradually coming to the understanding that even when a horror movie is happening in real life, there will be ways to minimize the harm and find alternative ways to supply what is needed.

Yes, forecasting is a thankless task. Yes, most of the time, we are just guessing because the same numbers can be interpreted in many ways, depending on the quality of inputs, number of unknowns, calculation formulas, assumptions, and the power of our imagination. When an unprecedented emergency strikes, we feel far more confident to face it if we have food in the fridge and some medicine in the cabinet. It is the same with company procurement and how its managers react in moments of crisis—"I wish I had known sooner where to put the safety net."

Indeed, these events led to many situations where forecasts and plans were unexpectedly disrupted. Along with that, there were other events that shook the markets, including the semiconductor shortage that led to an increase in the production time of computers and shut down the factories of major automakers[1] and the shortage of raw materials for the production of batteries.[2] More widely, the capabilities of manufacturers themselves were reduced because of the surge in demand for raw materials and components.

A host of other factors can cause supply chain disruptions, including natural disasters, industrial accidents, fires, strikes, poor quality control, unscrupulous partners and employees, etc. These risks can occur without warning and are more likely than we would like to believe. Assessing and predicting supply chain risks in general and procurement risks in particular allows you to have a contingency plan, even if in a pandemic or a war. It can significantly mitigate crisis management scenarios and save that most valuable resource—time.

Procurement is at the forefront in times of crisis. Like doctors during a pandemic and the military in a war, buyers and logisticians need to be on the front lines to keep the company running. Risks are often difficult to manage even in situations where you are mobile and can quickly pack up and go to a supplier to check on the quality and shipment of goods or find a new supplier if the previous one suddenly becomes unable to fulfill its obligations. Imagine, for example, that a supplier has had a production accident, and shipments have abruptly stopped. Under normal circumstances, you could quickly find several alternative supply options, go to those sites, audit the new suppliers instead of sending out long questionnaires and checking piles of supporting documents, and then choose the new supplier with few real issues. Now, imagine having to do this when you can't leave home or in the midst of a war. In these scenarios, you run the real risk of not receiving what you expected, so careful supplier quality and reliability checks become vital.

In addition to the increased burden of searching for and procuring urgently needed goods and services, there are unforeseen pressing tasks associated with saving all other supplies, optimizing transport routes, re-signing agreements, and changing payment schedules. There is no time to relax; the number of tasks for procurement services increases sharply during crises, and optimal decision making determines whether it will be possible to overcome an emergency.

Consider a scenario where a key supplier has a production accident. The buyers assessed possible risks ahead of time and foresaw this possibility, so they already have a ready-made agreement with another supplier in place. The moment supplies from the first supplier suddenly stop, purchases are promptly and painlessly switched to the other supplier. An ideal scenario, yes? In practice, of course, everything is a little more complicated, but it is much easier to switch to an alternative source of supply if everything has been thought out and worked out beforehand.

A few years ago, I went to see a friend of mine in Germany who lived near Hamburg. We decided to visit the nearby Airbus production facilities to observe their aircraft assembly workshops. During the visit, the company employees enthusiastically told us about the supply management system and the aircraft assembly process, as well as the complex logistics of delivering components from different parts of the world to the assembly shop. The A-320 is assembled at the main production site, but the components are brought in from across the world. The wings are assembled and brought in from the United Kingdom or Brazil, while almost all of the major units for the aircraft are sourced from other parts of the globe. It is cheaper for the company to maintain complex logistics than to create a localized full production cycle. The Airbus workshops are perfectly clean; in some places, there is soft music playing at the assembly line—they say this helps with concentration since aircraft assembly requires high precision. Oh, and there is *no* storage! None at all. All the components are delivered to the assembly site exactly when they are needed.

At the end of the tour, the guide told us an interesting story about how a breakdown in the supply of toilet parts temporarily halted the aircraft assembly processes of several manufacturers, including Airbus and Boeing. He said that the supply disruption happened when the loading operator at the manufacturer's warehouse accidentally drove into prepared pallets containing unique components and damaged the cargo. It goes without saying that the manufacturer had no safety stock—the just-in-time[3] supply approach simply did not provide for them. This resulted in several days of downtime throughout the supply chain until a new batch was produced. At the same time, the aircraft manufacturers could not continue aircraft assembly because it followed a strictly regulated order of operations, most of which were carried out manually and were subject to strict quality control checks after each step. Even though toilet supply parts are not a critical component of the plane, they still caused a significant disruption.[4]

Such stories illustrate how fragile even the most reliable supply chains can be. If you do not have a procurement risk mitigation plan in place, things can spiral out of control quickly.

Even the most reliable supply chains can be broken when the unforeseen occurs.

There are a number of specific risks in the procurement process that are typically relevant to any procurement organization, but there are also risks that are unique to specific types of organizations. Many factors influence the variety of risks: company size, the ability to distribute authority among different employees and their qualifications, the accounting approach, the ability to automate and integrate data from different IT systems, the maturity of processes, etc. This chapter will provide a general overview of possible risks and methods to minimize them, but a whole book is not enough to cover the topic. Here, we will discuss the most important considerations that can form the basis for building a holistic procurement risk management system.

There are many different models and methods for classifying risks. I offer a slightly simplified basic model that allows us to take immediate practical steps to identify and prevent procurement risks in any organization, regardless of size. I would distinguish six major procurement risk groups:

1. Markets and prices
2. Operational processes
3. Supplier and supply chain reliability
4. Business ethics and procurement malpractice
5. Information security
6. Knowledge and talent management

We will discuss knowledge and talent management in more detail in Chapter 11 and focus on the first five risk groups in this chapter. But first, let's think about a basic rule that holds true for the whole topic.

Any activity that seeks to reduce risk must work in such a way as to prevent it, not establish a fait accompli.

MARKETS AND PRICES

The cost of everything we buy depends on market conditions. Changes in quotas and raw material prices, supply and demand imbalances, mergers and acquisitions, new technologies, legislative developments, taxation systems, and regulatory requirements can all affect the purchase price of goods and services.

Everyone is familiar with the consequences of dramatic changes in the price of oil and other raw materials, but these are not the only examples.

Many people associated with the steel industry remember the acute short-age of graphite electrodes that are used in the steel-making process, which started in early 2018. This market has always been highly competitive and saturated with offers from a variety of manufacturers, and buyers had a number of supply options. At a certain point due to the introduction of steel industry reforms, China shut down a number of older and inefficient steel production facilities, which required them to switch a higher share of their steel production to an electric arc furnace method, which requires the use of graphite electrodes. The increase in demand for this type of electrode overwhelmed manufacturing capacity; thus, there became a shortage of the needle coke used in the graphite electrode manufacturing process. This led to a sharp increase in prices and a deficit in electrode production. The situ-ation turned 180 degrees for buyers. Whereas typically, buyers simply had to arrange tenders to choose a supplier and negotiate discounts, almost overnight, prices soared to ~10 times their original price, and manufacturers even started holding auctions to sell to the highest bidder.

It is difficult to level out or predict such risks because there are no accurate forecasts that can catch such developing market situations. However, this does not mean that forecasting is not worthwhile, only that it is not enough.

In addition to having alternative sources of supply and implementing a set of measures that will keep you afloat until a new solution is found, there is another proven method of managing market risk. This is to stipulate in agreements with your suppliers how you will work together in the event of unforeseen market changes. There should be formulas for price recalculation; conditions under which it is acceptable to cancel the contract and order from another supplier; methods of compensating for price differences through ad-ditional services, training, or other bonuses; temporary or permanent switch-ing to alternative products; and other possible scenarios.

Of course, if the terms of the contract are written in the buyer's favor—one could argue that unforeseen changes in market prices or the balance of supply and demand are entirely the supplier's problem. But is such an approach really applicable in every situation? Insisting on performance under force majeure circumstances can significantly weaken the supplier, leading to their loss as a source of supply in the future. The primary obligation of both the buyer and the supplier is to ensure that an adequate assessment of the situation and the commensurate actions of all parties involved are aimed at minimizing losses across the entire value chain and restoring or improving the business relationship. In the long run, working together and learning from this type of experience can be of far greater value than a contractual penalty.

OPERATIONAL PROCESSES

Another good friend of the Chief Procurement Officer (CPO) is the auditor because the proper process audit might uncover many hidden risks. An audit can help speed up deliveries, make the procurement process easier, and uncover serious operational risks, even regarding any changes that were going to be made to existing processes, since the possibility of unintended consequences could be uncovered. Here are the main operational risks to procurement:

- **Unauthorized purchases**—purchases that are not properly planned or agreed upon are likely to be excessive
- **Inconsistencies within a transaction**—or a violation in its sequencing caused by a lack of document conformity controls over the original terms of the transaction, such as price, agreed purchase quantities, or specifications.

Automation plays an important role in preventing unauthorized purchases. Today, with almost any accounting system, it is possible to set up procurement compliance controls with predefined rules and limits of acceptable deviations. However, in many organizations, such controls are still implemented not by automating process controls and going digital but by adding more approval levels to contracts, specifications, and purchase orders. There are even dedicated controllers who are required to check all purchase orders against the agreed-upon specifications. This method is far from a best practice, but it can be used as an interim measure if the procurement volume is large, there are many requisitions, and automation is still not in place.

A separate, particularly favorite topic of mine is the procurement department controlling the procurement budget. As discussed in Chapter 7, the responsibility of the procurement department should be limited to ensuring that purchase prices are in line with the budget, helping with forecasting, and drafting the budget, but in no way should it include the responsibilities of budget control or otherwise influencing how and on what the allocated funds should be spent. Procurement staff, although they may be knowledgeable in such matters, are not required to be experts in how many repairs should be planned for a given period or what the required capacity is of the substation that the electric grid operations department has decided to build.

Perhaps these statements may seem strange. After all, when discussing the topic of category strategies and demand management, we are talking about the need for the procurement department to take an interest in the justification of procurement volumes—sometimes even questioning them, making clarifications in terms of technical specifications, and proposing alternatives.

Yes, all this is true, but there is no contradiction here. You just need to distinguish between *control* and *collaboration*. Taking an active role and helping manage costs by suggesting optimal solutions and alternatives is not the same as being a supervisor of the budget or technical specifications. The principle is simple: it is not a good idea to shift budget controls to the procurement function because the function has not been organized to carry out this role. The right solution is to make the necessary structural changes and separate the procurement and budget control functions.

There are many examples of companies that have abandoned the classic meaning of a budget. Rather than being a fixed plan, a budget is a guideline that is determined for the year ahead and considers only the information and events that have occurred or are known at the time of its formation. When planning a budget, we try to guess what will happen tomorrow or a year from now. Taking into account that most companies prepare next year's budget in September or October and data for it are prepared in July or August or even earlier, it turns out that we are trying to predict not just the future year but 15–20 months ahead.

The consequences of not being able to modify the original budget when it makes sense to do so can lead to substantial losses. Here is an example to consider. In the middle of a fiscal year, there is an opportunity to buy, at a very favorable price, a batch of goods that is constantly used in production and does not have an expiration date. And the price is so good that buying the entire volume a year in advance, even taking into account the cost of storage and the opportunity cost of money, is more profitable than deferring the purchase. But it turns out that there is no budget for such a purchase. What will be the result if you do not make this purchase? Clearly, you will still buy that volume later, but you will overpay for it. The optimal solution in this situation would be to allow for over-budget spend to save money.

As you can see, things can change at any time. But does this mean that budget planning, like the budget, is not needed? Not at all. Planning is absolutely necessary—be that for spend discipline or benchmarks. However, it is necessary to treat the budget as a reference point that can be managed and amended as required depending on how situations develop internally and externally.

Another typical example of process inefficiency is when companies carry out mass contracting at the end of the year for the next year as part of the budgeting cycle. This approach might make some sense for companies that are regulated by public procurement law, but for the private sector, it makes absolutely no sense. First, closing all the contracts in a short period of time greatly increases the workload on employees. The heightened stress level can lead to mistakes. Second, such an approach does nothing to improve the efficiency of procurement and can seriously undermine the organization's ability to get a better deal. The most successful negotiations are not rushed, so you are doing a disservice to think you can successfully qualitatively analyze and negotiate hundreds or even thousands of deals with partners within two or three months. The best that can be achieved under such conditions is mechanical execution and low-quality deals that were concluded in a hurry using formal procedures with no assessment of their long-term impact on the business and with a high risk of execution failures in the event of unexpected changes in the market.

The same can be said about fixed timeline ordering campaigns, where internal clients are requested to create all purchase requisitions within a certain period of time. Here, procurement lives under the illusion that fixing requisitions for a certain period and having a strict deadline by which all purchase orders in the company must be created *en masse* and transferred to the procurement department ensures the efficiency and timeliness of procurement activities. While this approach might work for some, it has far more significant disadvantages than advantages, in particular:

- Directly—and always negatively—affects the average inventory level because the demand is fixed for a long time ahead, and if a planning error is detected, it will be impossible to undo. This increases the risk of creating obsolete stock because of the change in demand over time and the inability of the procurement process to ensure flexibility of supply when it is really needed.
- Increases workload and creates inefficiencies in the procurement process—instead of working within framework agreements under which a requisition can be placed at any time as soon as the need arises, buyers conduct many repeated small tenders and enter into a large number of contracts for one-time deliveries, often with the same counterparties several times a year. This negates the opportunity to benefit from pooling procurement volumes, increases the burden on the function, requires more head count, and reduces the effectiveness of each purchase transaction.

It makes a lot of sense to eliminate end-of-year contracting campaigns and fixed monthly purchase orders. It is far better to switch to rolling planning and daily updates of procurement requisitions in your planning system and to replace contracting deadlines with on-time delivery targets. This may be hard if current business processes are not flexible, but it just takes some time and a little bit of effort to implement this approach, which is actually much easier to maintain both for internal clients and for procurement.

Sometimes, short-term planning means that procurement cannot meet delivery deadlines because the procurement cycle is longer than expected or requisitions are created too late, leading to emergency procurement and increased workloads. Instead of running small orders that seem to be more accurate, people end up doing more transactions and having more stress from the need to constantly run transactional activities. However, if buyers have a framework agreement ready for items that are always in demand, placing an order with a supplier after the next month's requisition pops up only takes a matter of hours. To deal with emergency requisitions, it is worth adding automated planning cycle controls at some point. If the client tried to raise a requisition with a delivery date that was earlier than the defined delivery cycle time, the buyer would have to confirm that it was possible for the supplier to fulfill the earlier delivery date.

SUPPLIER AND SUPPLY CHAIN RELIABILITY

Supply chain disruptions are not always the fault of suppliers. In many cases, buyers themselves cause problems by implementing inconvenient processes or by arranging interactions in such a way that compliance creates supply chain bottlenecks. Here is a simple example from my own experience several years ago that served as a lesson for our team.

One of the companies in our group began to have interruptions in the supply of spare parts for repairs at remote locations. Deliveries were made directly by suppliers, bypassing our company's central warehouses. This process, which did not involve the central warehouse in any way, was implemented to improve delivery times and eliminate unnecessary costs—and it showed good results. Before implementation, we analyzed the situation to determine the categories in which such deliveries were possible and where the average batch size and historical delivery statistics allowed for this approach. We liked the direct and timely deliveries on short notice, so we decided to go further in the direction of reducing the average inventory level and began to make orders more often and for smaller batches under the framework agreement. However, as a result, there was a failure in supply brought on by us. The suppliers were not ready and could not rearrange the logistics for smaller deliveries in time. Some shipments became too small to be delivered using their own transport, so they had to involve carriers and logistics aggregating platforms, which led to additional time and cost. The disruption would have been avoided if we had coordinated with our suppliers in advance.

Needless to say, this is a relatively simple situation that might have been predicted. But oftentimes, we are too busy with something more urgent or important. Therefore, it is best to have a checklist of predefined groups of risks that should be reviewed when developing or updating supply processes. The groups of risks under consideration can be divided into four main subgroups:

1. **Reliability of the supplier base**—includes an assessment of supplier reliability in the most critical categories, including an audit of production, logistics, and financial capabilities.
2. **Reliability of logistics and infrastructure**—consider the geographical location of suppliers, the availability of transport infrastructure, the network of service companies that provide logistics support, etc. This can also include risks associated with the presence or absence of technical and human resources.
3. **Geopolitics**—this definition includes situations with complete closure of borders, the imposition of sanctions, and other restrictions between countries. Moreover, restrictions associated with the administrative features of governance in different regions are also quite real.
4. **Information management**—includes management of information flows and documentation in the supply process.

Having listed the possible groups of supply chain reliability risks, here are some methods to manage or at least minimize them:

- **Supplier qualification programs**—should include a detailed check of the supplier's financial condition, credit history, tax discipline, and compliance with the law. Today, there are many open data sources that can help gather the necessary information.
- **Audit and supplier development programs**—work with your suppliers to create an action plan to improve reliability, supply discipline, quality, assortment, etc. Many companies have separate departments where employees receive special training to conduct supplier audits, and there are specialized organizations that provide services in this area.
- **Finding alternative sources of supply and transportation**—as well as scenarios for switching to them if necessary. This requires an understanding of the market and often cooperation with several suppliers for the same items in order to provide two or more existing sources of supply. This method may be difficult to apply in companies that operate under public procurement regulations, but even so, the law does not limit the buyer in any way in terms of understanding the market and establishing communications with a wide range of suppliers that can be used for emergency procurement when necessary.

- **Joint stock management**—work with suppliers of spare parts, materials, and equipment on the creation of safety stocks and their timely replenishment. This method can increase your partner's costs, which, most likely, the supplier will try to compensate for through price increases and hidden charges. Therefore, one must be precise as to what level of safety stock is necessary—establish it only for those positions where a supply disruption caused by unforeseen events can lead to an output decrease or complete production stoppage.
- **Procurement alliances**—combine the purchasing volumes of disparate buyers to obtain special conditions in comparison to the market, as well as to ensure alternative supply sources. Procurement alliances are common in a number of industries. In the automotive industry, for example, auto parts dealers have been uniting in purchasing alliances for decades, and cooperation programs help even small companies get direct contracts with manufacturers, special terms, and even the ability to use one another's logistics infrastructure. There are also numerous examples of airline alliances that allow their members to use partner companies' aircraft in case of shortages or breakdowns of their own aircraft.
- **Technology development and process digitalization**—we will talk more about information availability and digitalization of procurement processes in Chapter 10.
- **Talent management and motivation systems**—play the same strategic role as supplier relationship management systems. We will discuss the important aspects of procurement team development and the competency matrix in more detail in Chapter 11.
- **Implementation of measures to impose penalties on counterparties in case of a breach of obligations**—we will discuss this method of improving the discipline and reliability of supply next.

Claims Against Suppliers

It would seem simple and obvious—if you violate your obligations and do not rectify the situation in time, you face a claim. But in fact, this traditional and rather formalized bureaucratic process has several organizational pitfalls.

Making a claim is an extreme measure that is only used if it is not possible to settle a disagreement or receive compensation for losses from violations through a pre-claim procedure. Raising a claim is a bad signal to all participants involved. After all, the emergence of a claim indicates that an effective relationship was not built and the partner is not reliable. But if all other efforts have failed, pressing a claim becomes inevitable.

The reality is that companies are often unable to track down all violations in an efficient and timely manner, and even if they do, they are unable to apply the necessary penalties expeditiously. Claims are also not issued even when the grounds to do so are strong, the company has a capable legal department, and all the facts point to the buyer being right. This happens because of one of three reasons:

1. There is no time or no one to take care of it
2. The violation is for a negligible amount of money
3. The buyer takes pity on the supplier

For example, a supplier is overdue in supplying a small number of spare parts. The buyer decides that it is not significant enough and not worth the paperwork, especially if there is no shortage on the buyer's side and enough time for the missing batch to be delivered. Lack of time, people, and other urgent tasks can cause such claims to get lost in the flow of other business issues. As a result, most of the small claims are simply not pressed by buyers. However, the total sum of these small amounts over a year can become substantial.

Systematic violations, even for small transactions, are sufficient reasons to press claims or refuse to cooperate with the supplier at all. Discipline in performing obligations is a mutual responsibility of both suppliers and buyers. You should not expect disciplined behavior from suppliers if you violate payment deadlines or paperwork yourself. But if you fulfill your obligations and the other party does not, the imposition of penalties must follow.

The following story depicts a very common situation. A supplier bails out a buyer by providing an urgent delivery, allowing a deferral in payment, or by overlooking the buyer's poor paperwork. This causes the buyer to feel that they have no moral right to make a claim against this supplier, so even when the occasion calls for it, the buyer lets them off. It is fair to say that this does make sense sometimes in order to maintain a mutually beneficial partnership. The problem is that the feeling of being owed something can drag on for a disproportionately long period of time until the benefits from long-standing assistance become many times less than the damage that this supplier is causing by frequent disruptions in delivery or poor product quality. The loyalty of the parties to each other must be carefully nurtured because you never know when the situation may arise that you need your partner's help. But the opposite holds true as well. You need to be on equal footing, and there should be no misuse of each other's goodwill.

The leverage of financial penalties must be brought to bear when audits and joint action programs that are aimed at improving the quality of cooperation do not work. Nothing encourages discipline like the possibility of monetary loss. Those supplier discounts can be devalued by poor delivery discipline and other irregularities. Such losses can be quantified even if they do not directly affect the client's production of the finished product, and there is no visible loss because the product got to the market in time (e.g., the repair service had to postpone work because of a lack of spare parts; wages were spent on contractors to cover staff down time; or the production line had to be rearranged to reduce the output of the finished product). Every disruption has a price.

Writing the phrase—"the buyer takes pity on the supplier"—made me think perhaps my perception and experiences were deceiving me. Maybe most organizations do not really have this problem? It seemed to me that my views lacked evidence; therefore, I decided to involve my procurement community network in testing this hypothesis. In May 2020, I sent a questionnaire to my fellow procurement managers in order to determine which factors most influence our decisions to submit or not to submit a claim. One of the questions read as follows: "What do you think are the main reasons that violations go unaddressed?" The respondents could choose one or more reasons that they thought were valid (see Table 8.1 for results). Note that the responses to the survey did not depend on the size of the company, the industry, or the amount of annual purchases. It turns out that this does not matter at all—the problems are the same everywhere.

The most common responses are the negligible amounts lost through violations and a lack of resources to make the claim. This is something to think about. It is quite possible that over the course of a year, a substantial amount of loss is accumulated on minor violations. It is not difficult to calculate because the contract price for violations is often already defined. And it is just as

Table 8.1 Survey results of reasons for not submitting claims against suppliers (May 2020).

#	Answer (Reasoning) Option	Number of Answers
1	Small cost—losses are insignificant for us and do not affect key performance indicators	24
2	No resources or time to deal with the claim	21
3	Empathy for suppliers by our employees	13
4	Very complicated procedure of claims processing, billing, and approval	13
5	The human factor—mistakes, inattention	12
6	Lack of automation	11
7	Exclusive supplier, world's only producer	1

possible that adding the resources needed to customize the claims process will pay off fairly quickly by preventing losses and/or being properly compensated for them.

The next most frequently mentioned reasons are sympathy for suppliers and the complicated procedure of claims processing, billing, and approval. Interestingly, there was an additional question on the questionnaire about possible excessive sympathy for suppliers on the part of procurement officers. It read, "In your opinion, how likely do you think it is for procurement staff to be lenient to or feel sorry for suppliers? (e.g., the supplier has previously helped you in difficult situations, and therefore, you feel indebted)." In the overall survey, 13 of 24 respondents who answered that particular question had sympathy for suppliers. This shows we cannot dismiss the human factor in procurement, which is not only the source of errors but also of consciously or unconsciously ignoring the need to follow your own rules that were laid down in the contract. The complicated claims process is also a thought-provoking response because we have basically created processes that cannot be used effectively.

Segregating responsibility for operations is a simple method to reduce the risk of excessive personal involvement on the part of employees. You can simply separate the claims staff from the rest of the procurement function—as is often done in large companies—or automate the claims calculation and compensation process, eliminating manual operations as much as possible. Even if you cannot automate everything, standard calculations and templates can be put into auto-production mode. Employees who communicate directly with vendor company representatives will find it easier to maintain a productive relationship with them because they will be put outside the claims process and will not have to make excuses for the harsh actions or decisions being taken by another part of the company. And this will be even more the case if the claim is automatically issued by a soulless IT system.

It is important to note that you cannot correct discipline and ensure effective deliveries simply by issuing claims only—this measure cannot be regarded as a panacea. Claims are a last resort, and counterparties must be sure that if all other measures to remedy the situation have not succeeded, this step will be taken. Quite often, issuing a claim is the beginning of the end of a trust-based partnership. The constant application of harsh punitive measures on employees and suppliers simply means that you do not have an effective procurement organization. Discipline is likely to be maintained, but in a critical situation, this approach can have serious consequences because it leaves no room for creativity and out-of-the-box solutions.

BUSINESS ETHICS AND PROCUREMENT MALPRACTICE

Procurement is an area with a large number of potential risks; among them are violations of business ethics for the purpose of illicit enrichment. Often, people think this is a *substantial* risk in the profession, but it is a belief mostly held by those outside of procurement. In my experience, this risk is no more common in purchasing than it is in sales, manufacturing, or even the top management of companies.

"Our buyers are thieves!"—the manager and owner of a small business once told me angrily. "Really? And why is that?" I asked perplexedly. It is an interesting juxtaposition: *us* and *them*. It sounds like the *procurement* division is part of some other company with different principles, cultures, and approaches. There is a company—and there is something called *procurement* operating by itself. And they steal.

I can say with confidence that if someone steals in a company, it has nothing to do with a particular function; instead, it is about the company itself and its managers. Stealing is a systemic phenomenon. Procurement does not operate in a vacuum; someone or something allows them to do it. In addition, theft can be encouraged by excessive oversight procedures. A paradox? Not at all.

Management practices based solely on strict rules, threats, and excessive control, but which do not use trust and motivation for professional growth, provoke fear and block the desire to do anything useful.

The main reason why excessive oversight is not effective is because it puts employees in a position where they just need to work well enough not to *break the rules*. This is an important demotivator—being afraid of breaking the rules is far from being motivated to experiment, develop, and implement truly innovative solutions. There can be controls for anything and everything; controls can be cross-checked with others, but if there is no balance of factors that motivate staff to do their job professionally, honestly, and transparently, abuses are bound to happen. Ask yourself the following questions:

1. Why do people come to work for your company or procurement department?
2. What does your company offer employees?
3. What is it about your organization's culture that supports honesty, openness, trust, and accountability for results?

4. What makes your procurement people proud of their work?
5. Why should your procurement team want to work with integrity?
6. Why might there be a risk of abuse in the first place? What factors contribute to this? What is countering them?
7. Who is on the team: those who see procurement as a profession and vocation, those who want to make a difference, those who do not understand how and why they ended up in this function, or perhaps, those who want to be told clearly what to do and are not asked many questions?
8. Do you trust your team to make important decisions? Are they required to make independent decisions and take responsibility for them—or does the leader always make all the decisions because they trust no one else?
9. How do you deal with mistakes? Even the most professional and honest people make them. Do you punish without looking into it—or do you get involved and help solve the problem?
10. What do you want to spend your time on: compiling hundreds of pages of procedures that no one is able to finish reading or creating value?

Controls must be in place, and intentional violations must be punished. But first, you need to be able to answer the previously listed questions.

I believe that when building procurement processes, it is necessary to proceed from the presumption that if the process itself is built poorly, risks are bound to occur. If the process is built transparently and soundly, the probability of these types of risks is low—both with respect to errors in processing documents and corrupt practices. When it comes to risk management, everything is important—from the interaction between process participants to the organization's talent management system.

When it comes to preventing corruption, I would spend a lot of time picking the right team first rather than focusing on stringent control procedures. Controls will not stop someone who intends to steal something from their employer because there will always be loopholes, even if you have harsh penalties or a strict system of controls in place. Most of the time, employees with a penchant for underhanded enrichment will not concern themselves with improving category strategies but rather with circumventing controls. Managers will go on endless hunts for wrongdoers instead of trusting employees and relying on their decisions.

It is important to establish rules in the organization and openly publicize your policy regarding potential violations of business ethics and abuse.

Receiving gifts from counterparties, participating in various events organized by partners, and hospitality expenses should be regulated, and the limits of what is acceptable should become a guideline for employees as part of the corporate culture. Be prepared to openly discuss suspicious cases and the limits of what is acceptable in business ethics. And, of course—*trust, but verify.*

Steve Albrecht's *Fraud Triangle*[5] theory stipulates that there are three main factors in any act of fraud, and the absence of any one of them increases the likelihood that the violation will not occur (see Figure 8.1):

- **Factor 1: Pressure or motive**—the person must have a reason to break the rules. Examples can be family problems, a need for extra money, a difficult life situation, pressure from the environment, or an addiction (e.g., gambling).
- **Factor 2: Opportunity for fraud**—typically, weaknesses in internal controls, as well as poor corporate culture and discipline, create favorable conditions for violations. If an organization does not fight against fraud, it means that it supports it.

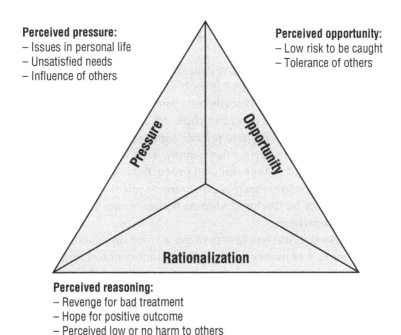

Perceived pressure:
- Issues in personal life
- Unsatisfied needs
- Influence of others

Perceived opportunity:
- Low risk to be caught
- Tolerance of others

Perceived reasoning:
- Revenge for bad treatment
- Hope for positive outcome
- Perceived low or no harm to others

Figure 8.1 "The Fraud Triangle" by Steve Albrecht.

- **Factor 3: Rationalization**—every person generally understands what is *good* and what is *bad*. A person may believe that they don't get paid enough for the amount of work that they do for the company (even if previously they agreed to these conditions voluntarily), or they convince themselves that they will commit this violation *just once and no more*, and believe that this lets them off the hook.

It is useless to fight against possible violations by control methods alone; only a set of measures works—which includes, at a minimum:

- Building a culture that does not tolerate violations of ethical business principles or interpersonal communication
- Ensuring you have an adequate system of controls in place
- Creating a motivation system that will provide employees with opportunities for self-fulfillment based on a fair assessment of their performance

INFORMATION SECURITY

Every procurement professional should understand what this concept encompasses and what measures should be taken in the organization to ensure information security and integrity.

Information security is a sensitive issue. When making decisions in this area, it is important not to go to extremes by blocking access to everyone and everything. You need to be sufficiently transparent to both internal clients and suppliers because that will determine how effectively you can interact with them. For example, it is helpful to provide suppliers with data and consumption forecasts for the materials they supply. This will help those suppliers better predict demand so they can plan production and deliveries. However, some of this information—such as procurement prices—is strictly confidential and should not be disclosed to third parties, much less to any supplier, under any circumstances.

Procurement is a function that manages a company's money, and it is often a large amount of money. How aware are buyers of warding off phishing techniques and data spoofing so that access to sensitive information remains secure? What methods are in place to transmit data securely? What checks should be performed when a letter that has been signed and stamped by an existing supplier suddenly arrives, informing them of a change in bank details? How will the employees act upon receiving such a letter, and what will they do first: change the data for payments in the company's accounting system or call the supplier's authorized employee to make sure that they really sent the letter? Companies should have procedures in place to answer these types of questions.

It is best to consult specialists to put a detailed plan in place for information security risk management. If your company does not yet have an information security specialist on staff and you are not one yourself, you should consider hiring one or engaging a consultant. It is also vital to educate the procurement team on the importance of ensuring that information security is an important aspect of procurement management.

Here are a few basic principles that usually guide me in determining the levels of access to certain procurement information for different categories of company employees:

1. *All employees who influence procurement decisions in accordance with their authority should have access to purchasing information.* If an employee is a representative of the ordering department and is involved in selecting a counterparty for a particular category, they do not need to have access to the entire procurement database or lists of suppliers and transactions.

2. *Employees with potential or existing conflicts of interest must disclose them to their supervisors.* The manager must ensure that the employee's business activities and decisions do not pose a conflict of interest and, if necessary, reassign responsibilities or even transfer the employee to another department.

3. *The legal requirements for handling confidential information must be established.* Employees handling sensitive information must sign a confidentiality agreement making it clear that the transfer of information to a third party is not permitted.

PROCUREMENT RISK MITIGATION

For successful risk management, it is important to regularly monitor and identify possible risks and the probability of them coming to fruition. At the top level, all control procedures can be divided into three main groups: before-the-fact, during-the-fact, and after-the-fact.

Before-the-Fact Controls

Before-the-fact control procedures ensure that measures are implemented before risk events occur. The tools of preventive controls are budgets, plans, forecasts, and policies/procedures/instructions. All of these tools are designed to predict a negative event and keep it from happening. A budget helps control the overspending of allocated funds, a plan serves to predict the timing of projects or other tasks, and forecasts can include everything from currency exchange rates to weather forecasts in the regions through which your logistics routes pass. Today, there are various online solutions that help companies predict the risks of working within specific regions and with specific suppliers. Even DHL offers its own service in this area. Using its resources, it has developed a system that automatically analyzes supply chain risks in a given geography—from weather and natural phenomena to political instability.[6]

During-the-Fact Controls

These procedures provide the implementation of controls during the execution of process steps or a specific operation. The tools for this type of operational control are quality control, schedules, and authorization limits. A very simple example could be if you try to enter information into the IT system about the receipt of goods with a date that differs from the electronic waybill, the system will block such an attempt. Similar controls are used in an automated payment management system; links are set up between electronic documents in the transaction chain where each subsequent document must match the previous one through a set of key attributes. The quality control procedure is organically *embedded* into the procurement process and is carried out in parallel with other operations, such as logistics. It is a prerequisite for the transfer of ownership, delivery acceptance, and payment settlement once the goods have arrived at the buyer's warehouse. Rolling quality controls can screen out substandard goods or raw materials from the conveyor, thereby preventing time and resources from being wasted on substandard products. In mining operations, such controls—with the help of special equipment— help identify impurities or foreign objects in the ore before it enters the crushing equipment. Budget limits will help alert against overspending but do not always prevent it because a shortage of funds can be detected only in the process; for example, if the IT system has set a limit on the planned expenditure for a particular project and that limit is breached.

After-the-Fact Controls

Such procedures ensure that controls are performed after an operation has been completed, an event has occurred, or a process step has been carried out. It is impossible to prevent an event that has taken place with after-the-fact controls, but it is possible to avoid its recurrence in the future. This group of controls can include audits and periodic performance reports.

The value of such controls lies in gathering and systematizing information about what has gone wrong in the past and what violations have been identified. Then, based on this information, it is possible to take actions that will help eliminate similar risks in the future. It should also be remembered that in many cases, the nature of the risk is such that it cannot be controlled before or at the time of occurrence; for instance, accidents and unpredictable breakdowns, breaches of processes or established procedures, and breaches of delivery deadlines without warning. An event that has occurred in the past usually cannot be corrected, but it is almost always possible to identify deviations, learn a lesson, and use the information gained to introduce preventive controls.

Audits or periodic benchmarking reports on key indicators help identify deviations from standard processes or suspicious transactions and under-achievement of targets, quality, timeliness, or completeness of deliverables. Based on this, policies and procedures and other types of control settings can be reviewed and adapted to prevent identified process violations.

At SAP,[7] employees can independently order any item or gadget worth up to approximately $500 from a catalog of available items for purchase without the approval of a manager or controller—the request is automatically sent to procurement. The limit was first set at $200, then $300, and later raised to $500. Of course, there were fears that the lack of control would have a negative impact on costs and that staff would buy things they could do without. However, this did not happen, and the individual irregularities identified by means of post-checking through special reports did not cause any significant losses. At the same time, the employees remained satisfied with this process, and the procurement service did not have to administer every small order.

Segregation of duties is an additional tool for process control and is widely used in the auditing environment. In essence, all key decisions in the process should depend on several people because when operations are concentrated in the hands of one person, the risk of violations increases. A common company practice where the same person cannot prepare a contract and also sign it is a clear example of segregation of duties. Procurement and contract signing or contractor selection decisions are also usually carried out by different people. The buyer, who is responsible for drawing up the contract and placing purchase orders, should not have the authority of the stock manager to record the receipt of materials or services in the system, as this creates the risk of improper transactions and accounting for failed deliveries. Segregation of powers can be explored in more detail as part of the audit of business processes.

Perhaps one of the most underappreciated aspects of risk control in procurement is *reputational and disclosure risk control*. Sometimes, the most innocuous events can have far-reaching consequences. Reputational risks are negative events that badly affect stakeholders' relationships and their willingness to cooperate constructively and support each other in future activities. The main problem is that we cannot know how our partners will react to this or that event. Often, the greatest damage to a company's reputation is caused by financial abuse, fraud, lack of transparency in work and processes, environmental damage, poor quality of products and services, and high staff turnover.

How does the procurement service affect these risks, and how can they influence the effectiveness of procurement and cost efficiency? In procurement, such risks are often realized due to a lack of coordinated teamwork and agreements and unclear rules about what is acceptable and what is not. For example, if a company does not clearly spell out that it will not work with tax dodgers, exploiters of child labor, and polluters, then the consequences can range from the unpleasant need to explain yourself to your company to a possible criminal investigation.

One day, one of our departments needed to purchase a special storage unit. Without consulting procurement, the internal client researched the market and arranged delivery after ensuring the buy was within the limit allowed for small purchases. The counterparty was not checked for compliance with company policies and reputational risks. Subsequently, it turned out that the supplier was not the manufacturer of these products, even though it described itself as such. And worse yet, it turned out that the company was engaged in money laundering. As a result, a small purchase grew into an entire criminal case.

Here is another cautionary tale. To better communicate to the supplier exactly what needed to be delivered, an employee of the procurement function sent the supplier the text of a contract with another supplier for similar goods without involving procurement, having previously blacked out the sensitive information using the text highlight color function in MS Word. A misunderstanding of the basics of document handling, coupled with good intentions and a lack of knowledge of how to handle text applications, led to all the information from the contract becoming available to the third party. Revealing blacked-out text in a Word document is two mouse clicks away. This resulted in the divulging of trade secrets, ruined relationships with the former supplier, and a court case.

If we think that such blatant and ridiculous mistakes can happen in any company except ours, then we are greatly mistaken—even qualified employees sometimes mistakenly send documents to the wrong place or act illogically. The most common reason for this is a lack of awareness and clear criteria for what is acceptable and what is not. And sometimes people just aren't paying attention for various reasons.

There are times when you are tempted to take advantage of information that happens to fall into your hands, for good or ill. A colleague of mine, the ex-CPO of a major technology company, shared the following case.

> One day, I was negotiating the purchase of some equipment. We were in our company's office, and the vendor needed to print off some sheets. He was given a network printer to connect to, but instead of printing several sheets, he accidentally sent a whole document to the e-mail address of one of our company employees. The situation was interesting. We had information at our disposal that I could have benefited from—the documents contained data and calculations of the supplier's marginal position. Nevertheless, with a heavy heart, I asked the system administrators to find and delete the file without trying to use it in any way.

Admirers of tough negotiations will probably be dismissive of this decision. In fact, what happened was exactly what was supposed to happen in a situation where business ethics, trust, and the expectation of long-term successful cooperation are more valuable than a short-term victory in negotiations over a particular shipment. Had my acquaintance behaved differently, the whole relationship between the two companies would have been destroyed in an instant.

It is impossible to foresee every single risk, just as it is impossible to write a control procedure for every scenario. But what you can do is start to track and systematize potential and existing risks, openly discuss them with employees, explain the consequences, and deal with cases. This creates a culture of collaboration, mutually controlling decisions, and the ability to identify risks without having to read through lengthy regulations. Business ethics must be a fundamental part of procurement work.

KEY CHAPTER IDEAS

- Risk assessment and mitigation is a prerequisite for effective procurement management.

- Risk tolerance and the lack of a systematic approach to risk assessment will limit the ability to improve process transparency and test innovative solutions. Risk progression by area helps make faster decisions when testing new types of products. For example, testing spare parts in aviation is a highly sensitive issue, and detailed risk assessment matrices for each category of spare parts or materials help make the right decisions.
- Any risk can become real and significant. It all depends on the relationship of factors such as time, circumstances, product criticality, and scale. A fire at a sole vendor's production facility or a phishing scam to swap payment details are far more real than they may seem.
- Based on the moment the risk happens, risk control methods can be divided into the following conditional groups:
  - *Before-the-fact* (preventive): measures aimed at preventing the risk and reducing the likelihood of its realization.
  - *During-the-fact* (or simultaneous): control activities that are carried out in parallel with the main steps of the process and duplicate or verify them.
  - *After-the-fact* (post-controls): checking the compliance of the operations performed and their consistency after the process has been completed and the purchase has been made.
- Segregation of duties between the participants of the process is an effective way to control responsibilities and operational risks.
- Analyzing the experience that an organization gains in situations where risks materialize is a valuable source of information for creating tools to protect and manage risks in the future.
- For each risk, it is worth your time to develop a procedure for addressing it or a scenario for dealing with the risk when it materializes. You should not put off dealing with risks because you *think* they are unlikely to occur. Things can change at any moment. Do not wait for the next crisis; start preparing for it today.
- Business ethics have a significant influence on procurement effectiveness. Their basic principles should be clearly defined and fixed in place.

ENDNOTES

1. "Timeline: Causes of the global semiconductor shortage." SupplyChain, January 11, 2023. www.supplychaindigital.com.
2. The Commodity Boom Is Starting to Push Battery Prices Higher. Bloomberg, November 4, 2021. www.bloomberg.com.

3. Just-in-time—a method of organizing deliveries when goods arrive from a supplier at the exact time when they are needed. In some cases, delivery can bypass the warehouse and go directly to the production line or to the store shelf.

4. First toilets, now engines: Aircraft supply chain can't keep pace with demand. Supply Chain Dive, October 30, 2018. www.supplychaindive .com.

5. The Fraud Triangle Revisited. Research Gate, April 2016, Security Journal 29(2): pp. 107–121. www.researchgate.net.

6. DHL originally launched Resilience360 (www.resilience360.dhl.com). It is now available as Everstream Analytics (www.everstream.ai).

7. SAP company is a producer of business process management software with headquarters in Germany. Case provided at an open SAP event.

CHAPTER 9

PROCUREMENT POLICIES: YOUR RULES TO PLAY

Whenever it comes to regulations, and especially procurement regulations, I am reminded of a scene from an old movie. I can't remember its title, but in it, a candidate is being interviewed for a management position. At one point, they bring a cart into the room with piles of papers half as tall as the man and say, "These are our policies and procedures. If you can turn them into something coherent, you're hired." Unfortunately, for many companies, the presence of a mass of unconnected policies, instructions, procedures, regulations, and directives is the reality of our digital age. The task of studying, understanding, and memorizing all these documents is beyond the physical capabilities of an ordinary person.

Procurement regulation may seem like a straightforward topic. Regulations are a necessity, especially for organizations where procurement is regulated by the government. The first thing employees do in any situation is look at the relevant policies and procedures. Regulations are a guide, a protection against violations, a remedy against errors, and an independent paper referee in case of need. But when you ask a group of procurement professionals whether procurement rules are a help or a hindrance, the mood among the audience usually noticeably drops. After delving into the subject a little deeper, you realize that procurement regulations perform quite well as a control, a protection, a source of rules for audits, and even as a set of penalties, but no one has ever called it an assistant that makes work easier. This is not because all regulations are poorly drafted but because these documents are perceived as a set of restrictions. Of course, all regulations are rules, and rules are, in essence, restrictions.

This awareness naturally arouses negative emotions. After all, it is uncomfortable and boring to grasp the control procedures and dry definitions, to segregate responsibilities, to learn what can and cannot be done, to evaluate whether proposals should be done this way or that way, and to demand that the supplier submit a proposal by a nonnegotiable deadline. Many employees resent this approach because compliance with procedures requires a particular set of steps that they do not perceive as useful or valuable. Purchasing managers and staff sometimes complain that regulations, especially in the case of government-regulated procurement, impose completely meaningless restrictions and do not help them make effective decisions. It's safe to say that most buyers have heard indignant clients complain about the complexity and sluggishness of their procedures.

But let us look at it from the other side. Nothing good comes from the absence of rules. Without rules, you do not know what is acceptable and what is not, how to act in this or that situation, how to control the quality of the process, or what to focus on in your daily work. I admit that for small companies, it is not reasonable to write out all procedures. This works well when the team has a 100% understanding of what's going on, all participants are interchangeable, and there are no external reasons or stakeholders who would insist on some special requirements to control risks in procurement. But once an organization expands to a scale where you no longer know everyone personally and cannot control every transaction, having at least basic rules and guidelines is a pressing need.

It is also true that there are few people in an organization who are truly interested and have the time to carefully read procurement policies and procedures from beginning to end. Regulations are often long, complicated, and uninteresting. The motivation to study them is completely absent. And if no one reads the policies, are they even needed? Will the rules that are laid out be followed? What should you do if regulations are needed? How do you make sure that most of the employees who are affected by the policy's requirements are aware of their contents and comply with the rules they establish?

PROCUREMENT POLICY OBJECTIVES

To begin, it is necessary to define what the regulation is trying to achieve. What exactly is it for? Who will use it? What level of detail is needed? What key performance indicators (KPIs) and control procedures will determine whether a particular policy or procedure is effective?

The answers to these questions depend on many factors and even on the culture of the organization. I would highlight the main objectives of procurement regulations as follows:

- Define the base high-level processes
- Establish controls in the procurement process

- Define decision-making powers and responsibilities
- Provide flexibility in the procurement process

It may seem that the last point contradicts the previous ones. How can flexibility coexist with the other objectives of the regulations without conflicting with them? The point is that flexibility does not mean the absence of rules.

The disadvantage of policies that are too rigid is that if you try to prescribe them to every nuance of daily procurement work, employees do not need or try to make independent decisions. For an organization where the procurement function is undeveloped and there are doubts about employee qualification, perhaps this approach is justified. You do not have to think too much; just open the policy or procedure and act in the prescribed manner. However, this approach has a huge disadvantage because the lack of the need to think means that employees will not look for ways to interact more effectively and achieve better results.

Before drafting a regulation, a good step is to interview everyone involved in the process to find out how it works. You should not rely only on your own experience; a good working policy is always a team effort. The most common mistake in drafting policies and procedures is an overly detailed description of operational processes and controls. The lower the qualifications of employees and the less transparent the company's culture and processes in general, the more detailed the procurement regulations tend to become. However, the result is that the document becomes bloated and unreadable/unusable.

A procurement policy or regulation should only give direction and set the overarching rules and limitations (the *upper bar* of the most necessary controls) while not limiting opportunities to find additional levers to reduce costs or improve processes. Here is my approach to drafting a procurement policy, which I have tested in practice several times. To begin, I will list what tasks should be performed by the document:

1. *Guiding principles*—support fair competition, set procurement consolidation rules, and create the criteria for justification of procurement spend
2. *Spend management approach*—which purchases in the company are managed centrally and which can be made by various departments independently
3. *Governance*—how decisions are made, who is authorized to make procurement decisions, and what it depends on; for example, if the spend amount exceeds a certain value or falls within a critical category or project, the decision must be confirmed by a senior executive

4. *Operating model*—how responsibility for managing certain procurement categories is determined, which units are involved in the procurement process, and how they interact

5. *Performance management*—what are the key strategic performance indicators and the approach to performance management in procurement operations

Procedures Supporting the Policy

A regulation or procurement policy is a top-level set of rules and guidelines, not an instruction for creating documents in an IT system. Everything that reaches the level of an operational process becomes a separate procedure or an instruction—one topic, one document. It is unnecessary to overload the policy with details; it is far better to provide references to more detailed operational documents. When certain aspects of operational processes are described in various small documents, you can update them more often and with more flexibility when needed without revising the main policy document. The result is a kind of construction kit, the individual blocks of which can be used when necessary. Of course, in the case of breaking down the policy into smaller documents, care must also be taken to ensure that they are all collected in a single repository and are supported with an easy-to-use search function so that one can find the information they need.

For example, if you can simply agree with your colleagues on the format in which you analyze vendor proposals and not worry that someone will use a different format, use it the way you have agreed and do not create a procedure out of it or automate the corresponding forms in your IT systems. When it is set up in a digital system, there is no need to have several pages of regulations to describe template contents and format—it just works the way it was set up. In general, even the most detailed templates do not guarantee quality data inputs because there will always be someone who will respond with *not applicable* or leave the field blank to a question that needs a detailed answer. On a policy level, a procedure can be limited to a simple sentence: "The format of document X is determined by the settings of the procurement IT system." Most likely, no changes can be made to the forms in the company's IT systems without the agreement of the owners of these forms, so you can be sure that they are always up-to-date and correct.

There is no need to try to foresee in the main procurement policy document all the situations that can arise throughout the procurement cycle. It is not only impossible to predict all market developments or supplier behaviors, but it is probably even harmful to the business. Under rapidly changing external circumstances, standard procedures can only be prescribed for a limited number of the most common scenarios. This means that it is impossible to build an effective interaction process if it is based on rigid rules and procedures that cannot be adapted when common sense requires a different solution.

It is worth mentioning that in public procurement settings, it is customary to have strict regulations. Overly detailed rules are due to the need to control, in detail, the work quality of procurement employees in public organizations. This is due not only to the fact that state-owned companies must account for how taxpayer money is spent but also because, unfortunately, there are often not enough qualified employees working in the procurement departments of these firms.

Some of you reading these lines may think that I am denigrating the experience and skills of all the people who make their careers in public procurement. Indeed, there are high-class professionals everywhere, and no big entity can function without highly professional staff with a deep knowledge of their subject, regardless of the form of ownership. Procurement professionals who are working in the government sector must have the ability to understand all the legislation and do their job so as not to create problems for themselves or their employers. This is an area where you need to skillfully maneuver between the requirements of the law and the need to squeeze the maximum out of inflexible procedures to get good results out of procurement. Many state-owned companies implement advanced e-procurement solutions, have highly effective control systems, and demonstrate excellent workflow discipline.

But consider the thousands of smaller state concerns scattered all over the country, in smaller cities, towns, and even villages. Very often, procurement there is performed by people who have no training and no opportunity to receive any. Public procurement regulation is, among other things, an attempt to compensate for the lack of competence of large groups of civil servants by imposing strict procurement regulations. The restrictions are designed to ensure that people with even the lowest qualifications can mechanically follow the procedures and thus ensure operational procurement efficiency (e.g., select the minimum required quantity of proposals, allow suppliers a strictly allocated time for their preparation, process the results by the deadline, correctly draw up the contract and reporting documents, etc.). The situation is truly difficult. This does not cancel the responsibility of the heads of these entities to create a system in which the quality and transparency of procurement and the competencies of the procurement teams are constantly enhanced. Unfortunately, today, competency development in state company procurement often does not mean improving the effectiveness of procurement by implementing a category management approach, changing the performance evaluation system, or introducing tools to work with data or automation. Rather, it involves training in strict adherence to the letter of the law, a violation of which may lead to administrative and even criminal charges.

I believe that a system that does not allow for deviations from regulations when it makes sense to do so cannot be effective. The market situation changes faster than regulations, so it is important to leave room for swift adaptation (e.g., an additional round of negotiations might be required even after a tender is underway). Obviously, the procedures and decision making for regulated and unregulated procurement will be different.

Government procurement regulations can be thought of as a balance between the shortcomings of personnel management and best practices. Often, when it comes to building an effective procurement organization in state-owned entities, the roots of the problem are with the stakeholders who lack interest in the subject because the state, as a primary owner of the enterprise, is a rather abstract concept. Oftentimes, they lack a development strategy and clear targets, as their primary task is to support the government processes, not generate revenues or create new products and services. It is also not very clear who the stakeholders are who are interested in the final results of their improvements. And if no one is clearly interested, why bother? When drafting procurement regulations for such enterprises, it is vital to answer the same basic question: What are the purpose and main objectives of this document?

STRUCTURING THE POLICY DOCUMENT

There is a popular rule in procurement policies that is found nearly everywhere, from public procurement laws to the procurement policies of many private companies. It states that during sourcing, a certain minimum number of bids from different suppliers must be solicited. Usually, a minimum of three bids is required for a tender to be valid. Let us consider a hypothetical but very plausible situation. Suppose the regulations say:

- What the minimum number of acceptable proposals is
- Who has the right to decide on the purchase
- Who is a member of the tender committee
- What are the terms of the procurement procedure
- What documents must be drawn up to approve the purchase

However, the rules say nothing about:

- How exactly to evaluate bids
- What to do if there is only one supplier in the market

- What to do if it is possible to collect many more bids than the minimum required by the regulations
- What to do if the implementation of certain requirements prescribed by the regulations could adversely affect the outcome of the procurement

For example, there is a short-term reduction in prices in the market with a small window of opportunity to make a purchase, but the regulated timing of the tender does not allow for a prompt purchase to be made. Most likely, the employee working with the relevant document will automatically trigger an associative series:

regulation → rule → restriction → violation → punishment

Therefore, the thought process likely to follow would be:

- I need to follow the procedures so I don't break any rules
- I need to find any three proposals to comply with the procedures
- Among the three proposals I find, I need to select the lowest-priced one

It is worth paying attention to the fact that according to this hypothetical regulation, it is not the *best* three proposals that must be found, just *any* three—since nowhere in the rules does it say that they must be the best. It also does not say that if there are 12 suppliers in the market, you must first select the best among them and allow at least three of all those who qualify to participate in the tender.

I use this example to show that the policies should include not only what you cannot do but also what you can and should do. It is important not to neglect such sections when laying out the policy's goals, as well as the meanings and logic of the rules contained within it. You can use the following list of questions to draw up the final purpose and contents of the policy:

1. What is the purpose of this or that procedure? Why was it introduced in the first place?
2. What are the differences between the different types of procedures/methods of procurement? In which situations is it recommended to use one or another approach: either a request for quotations (RFQ), a tender, or conducting negotiations?
3. In what cases are exceptions possible? Who decides on them: the buyer herself, a group of people, or a manager?
4. Who is authorized to approve the choice of supplier? Who is authorized to make the final decision in the selection process?

5. What is a hard rule, and what is a recommendation—which will improve the quality of the final result? Which provisions in the regulations are at the discretion of the buyer and are not mandatory?

6. Is there anything that prevails over standard policy regulations (e.g., a category strategy)?

Let's go back to the policy of having a minimum of three bids. On the one hand, this rule is quite reasonable. It is important that the necessary minimum effort be made to make the best procurement decision, and in this sense, the rule is justified. But on the other hand, how can this rule help to achieve the best results? How can we motivate participants in the procurement process to make more than just the minimum effort required by the regulations? The following are possible methods to address these challenges:

- **Provide a description of the target outcome.** What would be considered an acceptable or excellent procurement outcome? What exactly is the buyer responsible for in this process?

- **Utilize a procurement performance evaluation system.** What are the main goals and objectives of the procurement? Do they include ensuring the transparency of procedures or ensuring their effectiveness? Or both?

- **Establish procurement process control points.** At what stages and how exactly is the procurement process controlled? At what point may negotiations be held? How are the prices in the protocol checked for compliance with the prices in the contract concluded on its basis? Who is authorized to make decisions when disputes arise?

- **Prepare a description of the logic of existing business processes.** Business processes should not interfere with the order in which regulatory requirements are stipulated. Sometimes this can be difficult to ensure. For example, the regulations may require a tender for the selection of a supplier only if there is a requisition from an internal client. However, the internal client may not be able to formalize documents in advance due to the lengthy process for approving procurement budgets. Such situations are quite common, and such controls in the regulations are aimed at avoiding uncoordinated or unreasonable costs, although in practice, they cause excessive bureaucracy and protracted processes. The approach can be changed without risking a loss of time and money for the parties involved. For example, agree that holding a tender does not mean an obligation to place a purchase order immediately. Based on the results of the tender, you can conclude a conditional framework contract, inform the supplier about your indicative procurement plans if you do not yet have all internal approvals at the time of signing the contract, and place orders as the need arises and all internal approvals are obtained.

- **Ensure proper and timely communication.** It is important to make sure that the key players in the process are aware of the rules that are in place and that new employees who join the team receive as much information as those who have been there for a long time. You can put together a great and detailed policy, but if communication is poor, there is no guarantee that stakeholders will know about it. Sure, you can appeal to the fact that *ignorance of the policy is no excuse*, and *it is the employee's responsibility to know the regulations*, but when you find out that the *rule* is not enforced or is not even known and therefore not enforced, it may be too late. Effective communication is a natural part of the regulatory process, and the task of the authors of the regulations is to ensure that it reaches all those who interact with it and to make sure that stakeholders are informed at all times.

The main intention of regulations should not be to impose penalties but rather to be a tool to make processes more efficient and facilitate sound decision making. It becomes a tool of punishment in extreme cases when all of the more effective methods of maintaining order have not worked. Ultimately, regulations should ensure transparency and controllability of the processes, as well as secure the optimal level of procurement costs. No single policy or regulation is an effective management tool by itself—the system will be effective if the regulation is supported by additional tools, such as the previously listed methods. In the following sections, I propose a list of key provisions that should be reflected in the procurement policy of any company.

Guiding Principles

This includes both general principles and principles for individual cost categories. For example, it is important to put *in writing* procurement strategic priorities; base principles, such as integrity and compliance with external and internal policies; and the basic approach to managing procurement spend.

In order to avoid situations where purchases of the same category are split up over a short period of time, appropriate limitations and procurement consolidation principles should be defined. Procurement spend consolidation may be done by the following groups, sometimes incorporating more than one consolidation factor:

- *Location*—at the level of several production sites or divisions located in one region
- *Function*—within a functional unit (department/division)
- *Timing*—consolidation once a week, once a month, or once a quarter, depending on expediency
- *Category*—consolidation of the entire volume of goods/services/work that fall into one category

There are a number of technocratic but necessary provisions that are also part of guiding principles. These include:

- *Conflicts of interest*—define what would be considered unacceptable in terms of conflicts of interest in your organization; for example, affiliation of bidders with employees of your company or with each other. Describe the rules of interaction and business ethics, how they should be monitored, and what liability is imposed on participants in the procurement process in case of a violation of these provisions. Pay special attention to the responsibility for controlling the execution of contracts; in other words, in which cases is procurement responsible, in which cases are the internal clients responsible, and how the performance of the parties is monitored.
- *Confidentiality*—determine what information is confidential and how exactly the organization manages and protects confidential procurement information; basically, who has access to it, how this information is shared between participants in the procurement process, under what conditions can the information be disclosed to officials, and how the process is documented.
- *Conflict resolution*—sometimes mistakes are made in the procurement process, or participants are dissatisfied with the results for a variety of reasons. Determine who in the organization will handle such cases, how decisions about resolving conflicts are made, and how feedback is provided. Over time, the communication channel through which suppliers and clients can submit their complaints may generate a lot of insights that will drive process improvement programs.

Spend Categories

Policy may define key categories by their purpose, source of funding, or degree of consolidation. The detailed category management approach is better to keep as a separate procedure since there are many details to this process that may make the overarching procurement policy too heavy. However, it is worth mentioning in the policy what the category management principles and regulations are and lay out the differences in the procurement processes for the various groups of spend.

Spend allocation means that procurement categories are divided into direct and indirect goods and services:

- *Direct*: goods and services/works that are directly used as part of the final product (good or service) that the company produces. For example, direct purchases include raw materials.
- *Indirect*: inventories and services/works that the company purchases to support operations or development, such as insurance services, maintenance of administrative facilities, repair of production equipment and spare parts, and investments—the benefits of which are expected in the future.

An *accounting and financing approach* means that spend is sorted as operating (OPEX) or capital (CAPEX) expenditures:

- OPEX: the direct and indirect purchase of goods/work/services, which are financed from the current budget to support operating activities
- CAPEX: the indirect purchase of goods/works/services, the financing of which is carried out with a view to the future

For this classification, it does not matter whether the material is used in the production of the final product or not; what matters is the source from which this purchase is financed.

Degree of consolidation means that the purchases are divided into:

- Fully centralized (consolidated)
- Partially centralized
- Decentralized

This classification is not always applicable and depends on how procurement is organized in a given company. Some categories are procured centrally; the entire annual demand is consolidated, then the procurement department conducts a single procurement procedure, selects the source of supply, and enters into a supply contract for the entire volume at once. Partially centralized purchasing may occur when, for example, in the category *metalware*, there are large and small subcategories. The procurement service coordinates the largest part of the costs, but the company allows the units to buy small batches of nuts and bolts on their own at the nearest store using the corporate credit card. In this scenario, the procurement service determines the sources of supply for only part of the category. Another example is a company that has several production sites; for some of them, the procurement service performs centralized purchasing, and the rest is procured in a decentralized way. As you may have already guessed, the decentralized part is unconsolidated procurement.

What exactly belongs to each of the aforementioned categories, whether to define such categories in your company, and whether it affects the choice of procurement rules depends on how you structure your work.

Governance

The regulations should determine the governance principles and decision-making authority in the organization within certain procurement categories. For instance, what the procurement service is responsible for, what can be procured independently by all other units (in which cases the involvement of the procurement service is required even for decentralized categories), who is authorized to confirm tender decisions, and how authorization limits are defined.

It is important to critically assess decision-making and approval processes and levels of authority. You may find that the approval process is redundant and that senior managers are essentially just repeating the signoffs that have been carried out by their subordinates—and usually for a very trivial reason. If your organization has the problem of excessive approvals, analyze what value is brought by the actions of each of those signing off on a decision, and openly discuss the authority and feasibility of the participation of certain specialists in the chain—what exactly do they do? Consider what might happen if you exclude this or that level of clearance.

Operating Model

This section includes a description of the main overarching stages of the procurement process and the essential requirements for each of the stages:

- What the basis is for initiating the procurement
- How the decision to buy and enter into a contract is confirmed
- What the roles and responsibilities are of the participants in the procurement process (client, buyer, authorized representatives, suppliers, etc.)

The procurement policy should not normally describe all of the details of procurement processes—that is the task of dedicated procedures and manuals that supplement the procurement policy. Yet, it should define the set of key activities in the procurement process and their guiding principles as related to supplier selection and market offerings evaluation. Major parts of procurement processes usually covered by the policy include:

- *Supplier selection methods*—this part defines applicable ways of supplier selection, the base rules, and exceptions to the rules. There are several types of supplier selection methods:
  - ▫ *Tender*—a multistage procurement procedure. At each stage, participants whose proposals do not meet the requirements or do not pass the qualification requirements are eliminated. A tender necessarily includes a negotiation stage. It is used for the largest/most significant purchases or the procurement of complex and unique goods/services.
  - ▫ *RFQ*—a procedure that does not necessarily involve negotiations and generally has less stringent requirements than a tender. It is typically used for categories where there is a well-developed supplier market, there are enough bids, and the subject of procurement is not complexly configured or has no unique requirements.
  - ▫ *Reverse auction*—an RFQ with a price reduction. This can be conducted as a separate procurement procedure or as a separate stage of the tender. After selecting all suppliers and their proposed goods/services that meet the qualifications and technical requirements criteria, a reverse auction may be conducted where the bidder who offers the lowest price wins. Reverse auctions are often used for the procurement of commodities since the specifications are mostly standard regardless of the origin of the raw materials, purchases are made in large batches, and the markets are competitive.
  - ▫ *Single-source procurement*—a procedure that does not imply any competitive bidding but is carried out by negotiation only, being applied in situations where there is only one technically qualified supplier available.

The rules of procurement procedures should, on the one hand, give sufficient tools and time to the buyers to conduct quality analysis and negotiations and, on the other hand, ensure that all participants are treated equally and given enough time and information to prepare a quality proposal. For each type of supplier selection procedure, it is important to provide not only rules and a sequence of steps but also deadlines. The minimum time required for the preparation of proposals by the participants before the tender moves to the proposal analysis stage is an important condition that gives an opportunity to even the starting position for all participants.

I am against setting a maximum time frame for the supplier selection procedure. You can often find internal clients demanding that procurement procedures be carried out quickly. But such restrictions not only do not help to improve spend efficiency but also go against common sense. Sometimes the entire process, including several rounds of negotiations, can take several months, and that is as it should be. The focus of the request should not be on getting things done *quickly* because, in most cases, that would mean *poorly*. Rather, the focus should be on getting the entire procurement done by the required deadline, which is a very different approach. In order to make the purchase on time, you can start to perform some tasks before the tender starts, such as preliminary requests for information, specification clarifications, building forecasts, etc. However, setting a maximum time frame for the tender committee to agree on the results of the tender is an effective measure that ensures that operational processes are not delayed. It is important to agree on the rules in advance so that they do not come as a surprise to anyone.

It is good practice to define communication rules. For example, if one of the bidders has asked for a clarification that other participants have not, all the bidders should receive the same answer without revealing the identity of the competitor who asked the original question. If someone has asked for and been given a deadline extension for preparing a proposal, the same extension must be offered to all. This applies also to those who have already submitted proposals since they might be able to improve them.

Providing a roadmap of the key steps in the competitive bidding process will create transparency in the tender's timeline for clients and suppliers. The roadmap should include all key events, including the planned number of tender rounds, negotiations and internal discussions, the stages of paperwork, and much more, up to the receipt of goods or services. With a clear roadmap in hand, those involved in the process are sure to have fewer doubts about the adequacy of the proposed timelines for the procurement procedures, even if they are significant.

- *Guidelines for the evaluation of supplier offerings*—one can choose the most acceptable offer in several ways: by price, by a set of evaluation criteria, by the total cost of ownership, or by compliance with the technical specifications. Which method is optimal depends on the specifics of the category and the information at your disposal. Consider assigning a percentage weight to the individual components of the proposal. One of the purposes of this approach is to structure the work and feedback to the bidders. By referencing the formula, it is easier to explain why the cheapest proposal did not win the tender. But, as stated before, this is more of an attempt to hide behind the calculation than a real evaluation.

If there is no data to estimate the total cost of ownership or to estimate losses or benefits, it is not a good idea to come up with how much weight a particular component should have. In this case, it is better to decide on price and payment terms by calculating the present value of the capital invested in the purchase. And, of course, it is worth determining as accurately as possible the potential gains or losses in each case.

- *Supplier relationship management principles*—the approach to supplier relationship management might be the subject of a separate policy, but the main procurement regulation document should define at least the key principles, such as the approach to supplier segmentation and key supplier interaction rules, and also reference supplier interaction models and the performance management approach.
- *Negotiation guidance*—it is important to determine when negotiations are recommended, whether certain categories of employees or internal clients are allowed to take part, how the negotiating team is determined, what powers they have, whether they can make decisions regarding certain material conditions of the future deal or whether additional approval is required, etc. Note that the negotiation process should be as flexible as possible. You should not put too many restrictions on it, but the procurement rules should define the authority of negotiators and support the negotiation process.

For example, direct negotiations with bidders by members of the tender committee, clients, and even company managers without the involvement of the responsible procurement officer should be banned. A client or manager may think that they can help if they quickly call back a supplier's manager and clarify this or that issue, and indeed, this can sometimes be helpful. However, in an effective team, the actions of all participants in the negotiation must be coordinated. Otherwise, the chances of missing essential details or handing out seemingly useless, but in reality, important information to the counterparty increase, which will ultimately affect the course of the negotiation. There is no need to regulate the negotiation process in too much detail, but reasonable rules for interaction within it should be clearly defined. One should not hope that all participants in the process guess on their own what would be best for a particular purchase. Such things should be discussed in detail; otherwise, each participant is likely to have their own idea of how the process should go, and that is a direct path to conflicts.

- *Contracting*—it is good practice to implement a separate policy on contract work, which describes the rules for various types of contracts, from procurement and sales to insurance and finance. The topic of contracting is broad and includes many aspects. Within the basic procurement regulations, it is worth paying attention to topics such as the contract drafting process and allocation of responsibilities, approvals, registration, and copying of the contract onto IT systems; responsibility for contract tracking and closing; conditions and retention periods for original documents and electronic versions; and regulating access to contract texts for various participants in the procurement process.

- *Commercial settlements*—this group of provisions regulates various aspects of the financial settlements between the parties and defines the events that will be considered binding for the client. For example, this is the point at which it is possible to send a formal confirmation to a supplier that they have won the tender and are awarded a contract; usually, this is the moment when the tender protocol is agreed to by all the participants of the tender committee. In addition, recommendations are determined on the optimal payment conditions of the contract.

Performance Management

The procurement policy shall also define what the key strategic performance indicators are and the approach to performance management in procurement operations. While operational KPIs may fluctuate and their list may be updated quite often, the list of strategic objectives will remain relatively stable and worth making part of the policy.

For convenience, all of the aforementioned levels of procurement policy from this chapter are shown in Figure 9.1.

Regulations should impose rules, but they should not limit the ability to make effective decisions or stifle the common sense and creativity of the participants in the process. It is important to remember that regulations are necessary in order to build and support effective processes, not to hinder their constant improvement. The market is constantly changing, so procurement regulations themselves should evolve accordingly. Even if you have to make changes to your procurement policy every six months because of changing

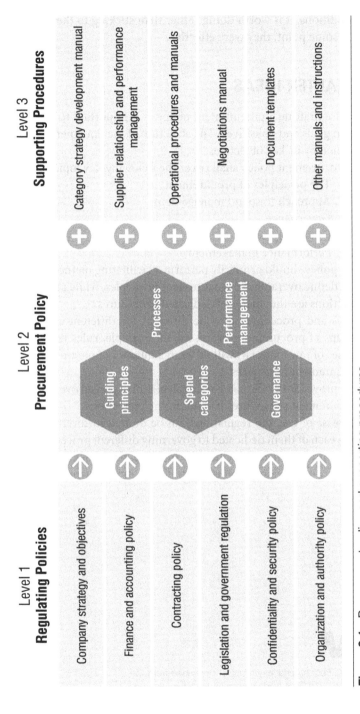

Figure 9.1 Procurement policy and supporting procedures.

Level 1
Regulating Policies

Company strategy and objectives

Finance and accounting policy

Contracting policy

Legislation and government regulation

Confidentiality and security policy

Organization and authority policy

Level 2
Procurement Policy

Guiding principles

Processes

Spend categories

Performance management

Governance

Level 3
Supporting Procedures

Category strategy development manual

Supplier relationship and performance management

Operational procedures and manuals

Negotiations manual

Document templates

Other manuals and instructions

market conditions, it is worth doing rather than sticking to the old rules just because, at some point, they were effective.

KEY CHAPTER IDEAS

- Before drafting a procurement policy, it is important to determine its main goals and objectives. The structure of the document is primarily defined by its key objectives.
- A procurement policy shall cover the following key topics:
  - The principles of procurement
  - Approach to spend management
  - Governance
  - Operating model
  - Performance management
- The policy should primarily perform a facilitating methodological role and define overarching procurement principles, while process control functions are the matter of dedicated procedures.
- Rules and procedures may be different for different categories and groups of procurement processes; for example, rules regulating purchases of raw materials will differ in a number of parameters from the procurement of services.
- The provisions of the category strategies may prevail over the standard procurement procedures laid out in the regulations.
- For ease of use, the regulations can be drafted in several documents, with each of them dedicated to governing different processes or aspects of the procurement activities, for instance, tendering rules, the methodology of developing category strategies, inventory management, etc.

CHAPTER **10**

DIGITALIZATION CAN'T
WAIT ANY LONGER

WHY DIGITIZE?

Procurement digitalization is one of the hottest topics in the profession. We have long ago entered the digital era, and without the use of appropriate technologies, it is simply impossible to achieve efficiencies at the level of the world's best companies. Today, the terms *digitalization* and *digital* are the key buzzwords for driving procurement improvement.

Digital solutions provide transparency of information about procurement spend and enable analytics for decision making. Back in 2019, my colleagues and I did a little analysis. We concluded that, in our case, two-stage electronic bidding yielded an average of 4–6 percent in additional savings compared to bidding without IT systems at the first stage of the supplier selection process and an additional 10–12 percent in savings at the second stage of bidding when information about the best current offer is available to all bidders. Nowadays, the variety of solutions is vast, covering not only the procure-to-pay cycle but offering more advanced tools in strategic sourcing, contract and supplier relationship management, and even category strategy development powered by AI.

Digital technologies are developing swiftly, and it is absolutely necessary to embrace the opportunities that they offer. Otherwise, losses in the speed and efficiency of the processes may become so critical that a company may not be able to catch up. Instead, those benefits will be reaped by those who began large-scale digital initiatives at an earlier stage. However, this does not mean it is necessary to abandon all existing nondigital tools at once or to implement the most advanced and expensive solutions without any thought. Your company may not need all of them today. The case for digitizing procurement depends on the strategic objectives, cost structure, and size of the company.

The larger the organization, the more difficult it is to manage processes, so the more automation the better. Without dedicated IT applications, it is impossible to keep track of hundreds or even thousands of contracts and deals, negotiation terms, and an array of analytics.

Digitalization and automation tools are used to achieve the following objectives:

- **Reduce process cost**—by automating individual operations or process steps and optimizing workload and process and lead times
- **Increase reliability of operations**—by reducing human mistakes and ensuring consistency in transactions
- **Improve process transparency**—by enabling digital analytics

As an example, let us consider administering a procurement contract. Figure 10.1 shows a diagram of the connections between the various blocks of a procurement process data map and how a contract and all the documents that supplement the contract are connected.

To draw up a contract, as well as ensure the subsequent monitoring of its performance and the correct configuration of the links between the documents, at a minimum, you will need to keep records of the following information:

- **Supplier register**—the counterparty's registration number, name, address, contact and banking data
- **Contract validity dates**—the period during which the document is valid, which will help to keep track of the approaching expiration date of the contract
- **Contract identification number**—unique contract identifier, which will be used both by the buyer and the supplier
- **Contract subject**—a brief description of the subject of the contract and assignment of the contract to a certain category group (hardware, bearings, light fixtures, office supplies, repair services, etc.)
- **Technical specifications**—lists of goods and services to be supplied under the contract and their technical specifications, required certificates, and other types of documents that must be provided with delivery
- **Contract value and price of goods and services**—both the total estimated value of the contract and the prices of specific items of goods or services to be delivered under the contract
- **Delivery basis**—terms on which delivery will be made (delivery to the buyer's warehouse, pick up at the supplier's, etc., applicable Incoterms[1])
- **Terms of payment**—payment terms and conditions, the share of advanced payment, and required supporting documentation

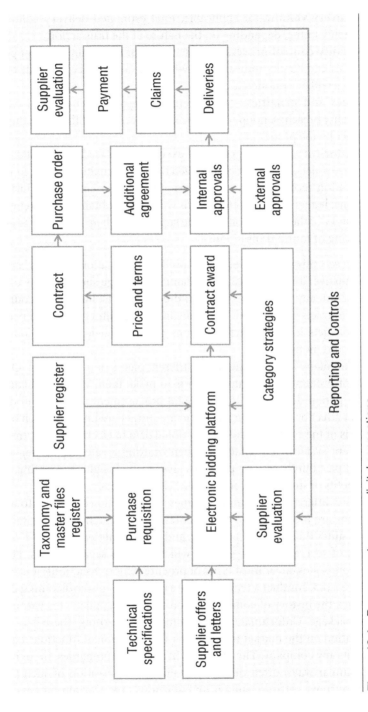

Figure 10.1 Procurement process digital connections.

- **Delivery volume**—if applicable, total estimated delivery volume or batch volume, depending on the nature of the transaction
- **Quality control process**—a description of the quality control procedures and quality indicators by which the acceptance of goods or services will be conducted
- **Fines and penalties**—the structure of applied penalties in case of quality breaches, nonperformance, or improper fulfillment of the contract by the parties
- **Historical records on contract execution**—placed and fulfilled purchase orders, payments, past applied fines and penalties, critical communication records, links to minutes of the tender committee, justifications, letters of intent, etc., which will help to obtain a comprehensive history of the interaction with the supplier and help to adjust the structuring of future transactions

As you can see, this is a considerable amount of information, and this list is far from exhaustive. It is still possible to manually manage such an array of data when the company has dozens or a hundred contracts, but once a couple of hundred contracts are reached, a reliable digital repository is needed because information gets lost, contract violations go unnoticed, and the company loses time and money.

There are many links among these different pieces of information. One of the tasks of procurement digitalization is to make them visible and connect them to a parent document. In the digital procurement database, all documents that affect or depend on a particular contract are linked to each other.

Analysis of the contracts and transactional data in electronic procurement management systems is a vital tool when drafting a category strategy. The analysis of past purchases and practices gives many insights for getting additional benefits or improving cooperation with suppliers.

There are different views among business digitalization experts as to which IT solutions are more suitable for procurement: comprehensive digital procurement suites that cover all processes and functionalities or a *digital toolkit* consisting of several systems, each of which handles separate tasks. Digital procurement suites cover most types of procurement transactions: it is possible to place a bid, conduct a tender, create a contract, register incoming documents, track the history of communication with the supplier, etc., within one software package. Unfortunately, at the time of this writing, there is no universal solution on the market that handles all procurement functions equally well and fits any company. The processes in different companies, though they work in similar ways, often differ in detail, and the creation of such a universal all-purpose software suite is an enormous task. Certain process steps need separate solutions for automation (for example, organizing and accounting for the results of supplier audits, goods and services quality management systems, purchased equipment efficiency, and savings accounting). The main functionality of integrated solutions for procurement today is the automation of the procure-to-pay cycle to process purchase requisitions, orders, contracts and payments, request for proposals and tenders, reporting, and, less frequently, supplier sourcing and claims management. Separate solutions are also needed for auxiliary processes such as the evaluation of the total cost of ownership, audits and risk management, development of category strategies, process analytics, supplier relationship management (SRM), and project management.

From the very beginning of my work in procurement, I have been involved in the automation and the selection of IT solutions. During this time, I have accumulated much experience in procurement digitalization. This allows me to say that using several IT solutions in the procurement process is not only okay but is, in fact, the *optimal* approach.

Complex solution suites are much more difficult and expensive to develop and maintain after implementation. When it is necessary to tweak a process in one place, it often entails a whole chain of system improvements in several other places. None of the solutions that looked great in demos and presentations done by sales managers actually covered all of the required functionality. More than once, we were disappointed when it turned out that our understanding of the required level of detail in the data or process was different from that of the software developers. It seemed as though we spoke the same language, yet the understanding of the process details and how exactly the data were processed always seemed different. Sometimes we ended up with complex solutions that were simply not used because they were impossible to adjust to the evolving real processes. This is neither good nor bad. Developers try to create a truly universal solution with functionality that is needed by a majority of their clients, but if you are in the group of customers who have some special needs, it might become a problem to adjust the software to those needs. All in all, we have learned a few important lessons:

1. **You need to test the solution with your own hands.** Never trust demo presentations made by salespeople. We asked for testing access and then checked what the system could do and how its real functionality coincided with the picture that the seller was trying to put in our heads.

2. **Keep the standard configuration of the digital software solution as much as possible.** Understand how the system is configured and take that into account when designing your processes. It may seem strange

that processes should be adjusted to an IT system—in the end, we buy expensive systems to support our processes. However, the reality is that (a) oftentimes, the existing process is not as smooth as it may seem, and (b) it is always more costly to customize IT solutions. Complex connections in the system will be harder to maintain in the future, so try to keep it simple whenever possible.

3. **Never expect too much from any system.** No system is going to be perfect, so lowering super-high expectations is a good idea. Be ready to pay more for additional software customizations, which should be considered in the budget of a potential digitalization project in advance.

If a company decides to use different IT solutions for specific tasks (for example, electronic tenders are handled in one system, contracts are maintained in another, and demand management and procurement planning in a third), it is ideal to set up a landscape where all of these systems are integrated with each other and qualitatively perform the work for which they are designed. If there is a small task, then create a *bot* that will carry it out. Here it is important not to go overboard with the number of solutions and buttons to push. Too many ways to perform the same task can cause confusion if one person has to use a dozen IT applications at once. To avoid this it is better to group applications by functionality and take into account the distribution of roles in the organization. If the IT solution brings obvious improvements, but the current segregation of responsibilities in the organization conflicts with the way the future ideal processes in the IT system are built, you need to reallocate roles and responsibilities and possibly even change the organizational structure as needed.

At a conference held in 2018, colleagues from procurement at ECOLAB told us that their company was simultaneously running 47(!) separate installations of enterprise resource planning (ERP) systems at 50 production sites. Truly, this is a monumental task for procurement to pull all the demand data together. However, this effort has paid off. As an example, they managed to reduce the time to calculate On Time In Full (OTIF)[2] from two weeks to a few days by integrating some systems, cleaning up databases, and setting up additional digital solutions, like data collection bots. It is acceptable to use several systems as long as there is smooth integration between them, and additional stand-alone digital solutions may be required to meet this purpose.

Figure 10.2 displays an example from my own experience where five different solutions were used simultaneously to support the procurement process.

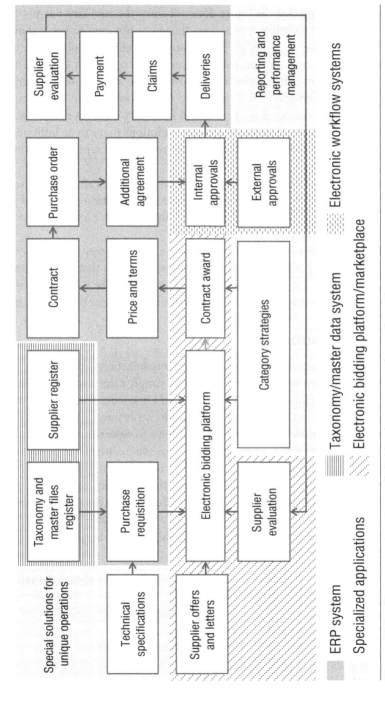

Figure 10.2 Procurement systems digital landscape sample configuration.

It is worth noting that the figure does not show the auxiliary narrow-purpose systems used to support processes that were not core to procurement. These included, for example, an online store for selling obsolete inventory and a separate system for approving prices of materials and equipment in the specifications of construction contractors. These systems were integrated with the ERP system and pulled or pushed data between them on taxonomy classification, current purchase prices, and inventory stock levels. A separate block not shown is the process robotization solutions that can be built on top of any of the IT systems being used in procurement and replace or optimize human labor in routine operations.

A few years ago I was thinking about how to structure a strategy for developing digital solutions in procurement. I ended up creating a pyramid of procurement functionality that required digital support, with each block needing its own digitalization plan (see Figure 10.3).

This pyramid does not necessarily cover all procurement aspects, but it is a good starting point to be supplemented with blocks that are relevant to your organization. Let us take a closer look at each of the five blocks of the pyramid, as well as the challenges that automation may pose for each of them.

Block 1: Capabilities

Managing knowledge and information in an organization is not an easy task. People come and go, move around, and often simply forget important things. Every manager is familiar with the problem of knowledge transfer and information continuity in the organization. How do we ensure that previous work is not lost and that new employees do not have to research a category from scratch or lose leverage in a negotiation because someone forgot to pass over important information? Dependence on the knowledge of specific employees is a significant risk for an organization. Since the organization cannot remove the risk of depending on the talent of individual employees to draw conclusions, make decisions, and negotiate, it should make *knowledge continuity* imperative. The range of applications of digital solutions to address this issue can be determined by answering the following questions:

- How exactly are knowledge and past-experience insights systematized, recorded, and accumulated?
- How is knowledge and information transferred between different employees and teams?
- How easy is it to find the right document or report?
- How do managers determine that their employees' competencies are sufficient?

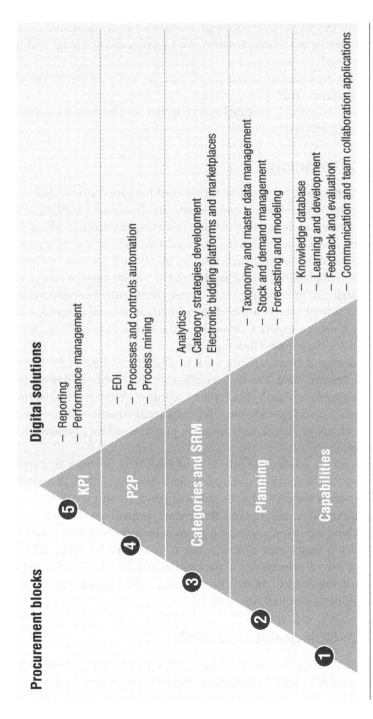

Figure 10.3   Digital procurement functionality pyramid.

- How exactly are training programs for employees designed?
- Is there a loss of effectiveness due to a lack of knowledge and information?
- How is performance monitored and the achieved results calculated and recognized?
- How is feedback provided and collected, and how are its results processed and systematized?

Block 2: Planning

In many companies, it is the responsibility of the procurement staff to consolidate information about demand—there are dedicated specialists or planning departments whose tasks include collecting information about future purchasing needs. The collection of this information can also be automated. ERP systems allow for real-time updates of demand forecasts without the involvement of planning specialists. Instead of writing letters to the procurement department or e-mailing requisitions, clients enter their orders into an automated system, which consolidates all updates to total demand with the inventory balance, forecasts demand for the future at prescribed intervals, and calculates the required order quantity.

This functional block will not work successfully without tools to manage basic procurement data. Key data include records of purchased items (materials, equipment, services), registration records of counterparties (suppliers, banks, insurance companies, etc.), organizational structures data (roles, authorities, storage locations, etc.), contracts, purchase orders, payments, invoice details, and more.

Managing the quality and relevance of these data becomes an important issue when the number of purchased items reaches several thousand and purchase orders are placed by the hundreds since there is a risk of duplicate entries and incorrect descriptions that distort demand data. Such a situation is fraught with the risk of purchasing goods of inadequate quality or not meeting the client's needs, making a payment using incorrect or irrelevant details of the supplier, etc. The quality of data and information is the key to accurate analytics on the history and structure of costs, trends of past periods, as well as the plotting of adequate forecasts.

Block 3: Categories and SRM

To manage the supplier base, it is important not only to have their complete register but also to keep a relationship history by recording data on deliveries, submitted offers, contracts, orders, delivery failures, contract violations, claims, qualification and audit results, negotiations history, etc. Accumulation of this information helps to build optimal cooperation conditions, improve analytics and market forecasts, ensure consistency in negotiations, and establish a long-term partnership.

Another component of this functional block is the management of supplier selection procedures. Electronic tenders and auctions no longer surprise anyone today. The market offers many solutions for companies of any size and with any purchasing volume. Transferring communications with suppliers from e-mail to a digital space where every step or change in the initial offer is recorded is a definite advantage. Though not all tenders can be effectively conducted through electronic platforms, a common database of procurement procedures containing the history of submitted bids will ensure the transparency of the process and greatly assist in building an analytics database and the development of category strategies.

Block 4: Procure to Pay

The procurement process is full of routine operations, from amending a contract by changing payment details or extending its term to paying invoices for purchased goods or services. Today, there are many solutions for automating such operations: digital recognition and registration of invoices, e-signatures and electronic document management, automation of controls and notification of suspicious transactions, electronic data interchange (EDI), and drafting of claims for contracts in which delivery terms or quality were violated. And this list could go on and on.

All this helps to significantly speed up the procurement process, drastically reduce the number of risks, avoid potential errors when creating documents manually, and increase customer focus within the procurement process by setting up automatic notifications of key events in the process for stakeholders. The main condition is to record all steps of the process in the electronic system. Even if it's not very clear today exactly how accumulating information electronically will help in the future, it's important to start doing it as soon as possible. Over time, it will certainly give you new opportunities to streamline processes and improve procurement performance.

Many solutions that are actively used in online sales—such as chatbots—can also be successfully applied to procurement. Such solutions make it much easier to find necessary information, improve communication between procurement departments and their internal clients and suppliers, and make the process more understandable for all participants.

Process mining[3] solutions have developed dramatically in recent years. This is a useful tool that allows businesses to analyze processes and determine whether they comply with an ideal scenario. When we first applied process mining to analyze purchase orders, we learned that there were more than 30,000 ways to create a purchase order, even though it consisted of only about 10 actions of pressing keys and entering data into the system (quantity, delivery date, payment terms, number of approvals, delivery terms, etc.). We initially assumed that we had several hundred ways to create a purchase order, but the reality turned out to be more complex than we had imagined. The data on the number of clicks in the process and possible deviations in the standard sequence of steps for creating a purchase order was hard to analyze, but with the help of process mining, we were able to do it and find the blind spots. Later we transferred this practice to other processes, making it easier to find inefficiencies and risks. For the analysis of the most routine operational processes and for making forecasts, such technology solutions are very useful. Here were some of our achievements made possible thanks to process analytics:

- Modeling processes and forecasting the reliability of supplier performance added three percent to our OTIF indicator
- Determining the optimal procurement procedure for an electronic bidding platform reduced prices in certain categories by an average of three percent
- Optimizing the loading of scrap trucks reduced the number of underutilized vehicles by half

Block 5: Key Performance Indicators (KPIs)

Transparency in reporting of operational results is essential for achieving strategic objectives. Without digital tools to process data online and calculate KPIs in real time, these are hard to monitor.

It is important to calculate actual performance live when the data are up-to-date. If KPIs are worked out manually and the calculation for the past month or week appears two weeks after the end of the performance period, it is likely that such an indicator no longer has value. This is because the opportunity is lost to react early enough to correct a bad situation.

It is important to answer these and similar questions to determine your digitalization plan for the KPI and performance assessment block:

- Should the KPIs be available as a report that requires manual processing or as a ready-made dashboard of indicators that can be monitored in real time?
- Do you need to forecast performance indicators?
- How often do you need to track them? Who will be able to access the performance dashboards?

KPIs and performance monitoring include operational reports that are necessary for daily work: how many receipts for goods are expected, how many invoices are in the works, what are the amounts of bills that need to be paid, and how many advance payments have accumulated for which goods or services have not yet been received. These and many other data points are needed to support everyday decision making, so it is important to ensure that they are available online and up-to-date.

JUSTIFICATION OF SPEND FOR DIGITAL SOLUTIONS

I often heard from peers in procurement that it was difficult to get funding to automate procurement processes. IT solutions cost money—oftentimes a lot. That is why many executives want answers to this important question: how do we calculate the return on investment (ROI) on digitalization and justify the cost of implementing new IT solutions in the procurement process?

Today, investing in sales digitalization has become a natural process driven by client feedback. If a company has a poor online sales platform that does not offer well-developed functionality and auxiliary services, such as order monitoring, payment processing, or even financing and insurance, it directly affects customer satisfaction. With procurement, however, the story is different. Often, internal clients and suppliers cannot escape suboptimal procurement processes because they simply cannot change the providers of these services. At the same time, company management may believe that most procurement automation initiatives just serve the convenience of procurement employees, so incurring these costs may be perceived as an unnecessary luxury expense. This is an easy trap to fall into. I propose to get out of it by using this equation:

$$Convenience = user\ satisfaction = no\ useless\ actions =$$
$$speed + accuracy = efficiency = better\ results$$

There is a direct link between *convenience* and *better results*. Our job is to identify exactly what convenience affects and set those metrics as a goal. But how do you identify those metrics that can justify automating procurement? The impact of IT solutions may be either direct or indirect:

- *Direct impact*—expressed directly in monetary terms through improved process costs, reduced number of mistakes, and shorter process lead times
- *Indirect impact*—expressed as benefits in the form of better convenience and improved user satisfaction, not only for the procurement team but for all process stakeholders

The value of implementing IT solutions is almost always at the intersection of these direct and indirect effects, which can affect not only the processes of procurement but also related functions.

Identifying the monetary effects of automation can be challenging. Procurement savings due to a well-run electronic tender may or may not be because of an IT system. By and large, many things can be done without implementing complex digital processes, but the difference in the speed and accuracy of processes and the completeness and reliability of results, especially when you have many tenders, is a critical parameter of process efficiency. A procurement IT system should clearly benefit the tender process, but how much weight to give the system is up for debate.

Remember the claims management example in Chapter 8. The benefits are obvious when a system—independently and without human intervention—issues claims to counterparties immediately upon violation, obtaining additional revenue through the payment of penalties. However, it is short-sighted to implement such functionality for just the sake of making additional revenue from claims. The main purpose of automating the process of controlling contract violations and issuing claims is to reduce the number of violations *before* they happen and to improve supplier discipline through a soulless IT system that acts ruthlessly in situations where people tend to get emotional.

In turn, improving delivery quality and discipline means reducing the cost of handling returns and claims, as well as getting the benefits from the purchase on schedule or in a shorter time frame by ensuring that the product or service arrives on time and without complications. For example, if an organization has delivery delays averaging 15–20 days and the IT system can address the problem, the company may well be able to bring its products or deliverables to market earlier and earn its profits sooner. You can calculate the average value of existing delays, estimate losses from them, and make that value justify the ROI of an IT solution that will help solve all or part of your supply chain management problems.

Such effects are not always achieved solely due to the IT system, but without it, the benefits can be much more difficult to achieve or be delayed. Often, a digital tool complements other solutions, without which the process would not create the desired effect on its own. To assess and identify such effects, it helps to map—in as detailed a way as possible—the process or part of the process that is to be optimized using a digital solution. The map should indicate all steps, actions, and relationships and highlight gaps that automation is meant to close. Next, a list is made of all the improvements that will be identified, and it is determined which aspect of the procurement process they affect: speed, flexibility, quality, accuracy, transparency, costs, etc.

The next step is to calculate the effect. In some cases, the effect will be direct. For example, speeding up delivery gets a product to market sooner and allows the earlier realization of profit. The difference in the value of the money generated by speeding up market entry will be the end effect of the chain. In other cases, the effects may be indirect. For example, when automating reporting, the report itself will not instigate action or qualitative change but can be used to make better decisions in a shorter period of time.

Let us look at an example where some purchases are transferred from a centralized procurement process to direct purchases by the client via an online store. This is done *without* the involvement of procurement resources (people), but transparency and control of the process are still maintained. This change allows minor repairs to be completed more quickly since there is no time-consuming process of creating and approving requisitions and waiting, say, 30 days for standard contractual delivery. In addition, paper consumption is reduced, and company warehouse workers have less overtime because the goods are delivered by the supplier directly to the client. Chances are the engineer, who previously spent several hours a week ordering material according to a standard process, has saved time and, instead of doing routine operational tasks in the system, has worked to reduce the production equipment's electricity consumption. We may not learn about this indirect effect because the connection is remote, but we should not deny the benefit.

The list of possible tangible and intangible or direct and indirect effects from the introduction of digital solutions is endless because they can be found in the most unexpected areas. Nevertheless, as a sample, I have put together a list of some of the most typical areas to search for such effects (see Table 10.1).

Table 10.1   Areas of the effects of digital solutions implementation.

Direct Impacts	Indirect Impacts
• Reduction of process lead time • Increased accuracy of transactions and data • Optimization of workload • Reduction of head count • Additional cost savings • Working capital improvement • Reduction of process and cost losses • Increased productivity • Improvement of contractual obligations execution, etc.	• Improved decision making • Increased stakeholder/client satisfaction • Improved end-user experience • Faster new employee onboarding and adaptation • Improved knowledge and information sharing • Time savings • Transparent performance data, etc.

WHY IS DIGITALIZATION NOT TAKING ROOT?

Yes, it happens; a company has spent lots of money implementing a modern IT system, but there are no obvious positive effects. There may be four main reasons for this:

1. Stakeholders are uninformed or untrained
2. Employees do not understand the purpose and value
3. The organization retains the option to work without the use of an IT system
4. The selected solution is not tailored to business needs

Together or separately, all of these reasons can lead to a waste of effort, money, and time. But this does not mean that the situation cannot be corrected, even when the new system is already running. It is important to be aware of potential mishaps in advance and always allow for the possibility that the system will not be used exactly as desired or planned. Methods to prevent or correct such situations exist, of course, and I will describe them later on, but one must also remember another condition without which success will be difficult to achieve: if halfway through the implementation of a digital solution it has become clear that the situation has changed, critical errors were made, or even that it is not needed anymore, it is better to stop the implementation, admit failure, go back a few steps and try again or find another solution.

If the solution does not meet expectations, there is a high chance that costs that were already incurred during implementation will only increase in the future, leading to even greater losses.

So, let us look at ways to fix possible bad scenarios. In a way, these words will complement the section on change management in Chapter 3 because implementing new digital applications is also a change that causes anxiety among its users.

As usual, everything is simple and complex at the same time. The simplicity is that the solution, by and large, is obvious: implement training programs, teach, demonstrate, explain the value, encourage the most active users, and share the picture of the future (ideal) state of the finished system.

But here's the problem. In large organizations, getting a high level of engagement in the learning process from the beginning is extremely difficult.

People are busy, distracted, or think that the change will not affect them. Therefore, they do not read the change announcements and manuals or, at least, do not read them completely. This happens not only because of skepticism but because they are simply overwhelmed with information and other daily tasks.

Whether training in large or small groups, I have found that the inclusion of gaming and competitive elements makes a big difference in success. For example, getting points for completing tasks makes the training way more engaging than just reading boring manuals and listening to a lecture—the format facilitates learning from each other the things that may not appear in manuals but were discovered by users while they were testing different options. How exactly to conduct training—face-to-face or online—is a secondary decision, especially after a global pandemic. Practical tasks and repeating the training two or three times to reinforce it are mandatory procedures.

The meaning of the changes should be conveyed to the target audience. Inform people about the changes through all possible communication channels, repeat the messages, and talk about the benefits and expected value from the implementation of the solution—not only for the company but also for the employees themselves. Be honest—oftentimes, change implementation will require more effort and discipline, so talk about it and name the difficulties that the organization is going to face. It is necessary to create an atmosphere of truly positive change that can be trusted.

In addition, it is important to create a sense that the change is irreversible. This can only be achieved if, in addition to broadcasting the information, organizational measures are taken that make it impossible to return to old practices. For example, you can forget about automation if an electronic document management system is introduced in a company, but managers continue to accept documents on paper. Of course, you cannot go to extremes at the implementation stage while everyone is trying to adapt, otherwise important processes may be disrupted, but no matter the difficulties, you should not retreat to the old practices.

The feeling that everything takes a little longer and may not be as convenient as it was before cannot be avoided. Development and change are almost never comfortable—they always involve abandoning old habits—and sometimes not only the bad ones. After a while, if the new solution gets the job done, people forget the way it was before and get used to the new practice. A well-rehearsed transition, where time and attention are given to users and their feedback and the change implementation team acts cohesively, helps accelerate the process.

KEY CHAPTER IDEAS

- Digital solutions in procurement are powerful tools that will optimize the cost of the procurement process, identify and eliminate losses, improve operational efficiency, and, thereby, reduce the cost of purchases.
- The effects of process automation can be direct and indirect, and the value expressed in cost savings is created at the junction between the two.
- When making decisions about digitalization, it is important to start with the systematization of data and information. How exactly are information and data accumulated and organized? Is it possible to benefit from them? After answering these questions, it will become clearer which direction to take next.
- The procurement function development strategy should be complemented by a digitalization strategy for procurement, which will determine the target state of procurement process digitalization from a short- and long-term perspective. The digitalization strategy should be updated regularly, considering developments in IT solutions.
- If halfway through the implementation of an IT solution, it becomes clear that the situation has changed, that it is no longer required, or that critical errors have been made, it is better to suspend the project and reconsider the solution to prevent an even greater loss of resources.
- Implementation of digital solutions, like any organizational or process change, requires change management, a communication plan, training programs, and rehearsals of the transition to the new process before the actual go-live of the implemented software.

ENDNOTES

1. Incoterms (International commercial terms) is a set of international rules in a dictionary format that establishes the basic terms of world trade.
2. OTIF (On Time In Full) is a measure of the timeliness and completeness of deliveries.
3. Process mining (process analytics) is the common name for a technology that is used to analyze, model, and optimize business processes.

CHAPTER 11

THE PROCUREMENT TEAM: WHO ARE ALL THESE PEOPLE?

PROCUREMENT SKILL SET AND TEAM DEVELOPMENT

In this chapter, we will discuss the desired skills of the procurement team and building effective teamwork. The topic of procurement specialist skills and the requirements for candidates who apply for procurement roles is multifaceted and has been well-researched. On the one hand, there is the view that ideal procurement candidates have an economic or technical background, are good with numbers, and have excellent communication skills. It is hard to argue that a potential candidate should meet this set of expectations, but in practice, it is not always so. I am a living example of this. I recall one amusing incident where a colleague and I were interviewing a candidate for the position of senior procurement manager who had a degree in philology. The colleague did not know about my degree in philology and was concerned that a person with such a degree would not be suitable for us, despite all of his experience. You should have seen his face when I told him about my educational background.

At my undergraduate university, I majored in philology with a specialty in English. I worked as an interpreter for 3 years before I became a procurement officer and, later, a manager of a large procurement team. Of course, as I progressed along my career track, I studied and upgraded my skills, took a special business course in finance, and eventually received my MBA. However, I became the head of a procurement function well before I started getting more qualification degrees. Did my lack of an economics degree make things more difficult? More likely yes than no. Did my background as a philologist help me? Definitely yes! Knowing English helped me communicate and collaborate more effectively with foreign partners and allowed me to access more English-language books and professional articles to study procurement more deeply. Working in procurement without a business background was difficult only at first. I had to figure out what procurement management consisted of, what to pay attention to, and what the best practices in procurement were in general. This took a lot of time and effort and it meant educating myself on the fly in high-stress situations.

Of course, I realize that my situation is somewhat special, but it is certainly not unique. In my circle, there is a Chief Executive Officer (CEO) of a finance company with a degree in medicine and a Chief Financial Officer who has a finance degree but is also a celebrity pastry chef. Our stories show it is possible to become a professional in any field, even without the targeted education at the start. Rising up the ranks of the procurement function is about opportunity, persistence, and perseverance while also closing the knowledge gap through additional qualifications or a second degree. Truly understanding a subject does not come without some kind of education, either on the job or via the classroom. You have to study all the time, and in order to know your subject really well, you have to love what you're doing. It does not matter what education you begin with or even what career; what is important is where you *end up* with your qualifications and whether you are ready to invest time and effort to further educate yourself.

There is a place in procurement for many different skills and specialties. *Purchasing*, especially in large companies, requires not only skill in sourcing, data analysis, calculations, and the development of category books but also in communicating effectively, building teamwork, and improving processes. All of this requires abstract thinking skills and competencies that are similar to the typical skill set of someone with a humanities degree, not necessarily an engineer or a mathematician. The most effective teams are those with a wide range of competencies that complement each other. If a candidate has the right background from the start, that is certainly a plus, but its absence is certainly not a barrier.

The following list describes the common responsibilities of a procurement professional:

- Analyzing supplier proposals, procurement demand, inventories, and specifications
- Sourcing (searching for suppliers)
- Drafting requests for information/proposals
- Developing category strategies
- Evaluating, qualifying, and auditing suppliers
- Assessing procurement options, savings, and total cost of ownership
- Preparing and conducting negotiations
- Drawing up contracts

- Placing purchase orders
- Processing accounting documents and payments
- Forecasting prices and the market situation
- Assessing supply risk

So, what should a professional buyer know and be able to do? Let's take a formal approach and consider a set of basic skills that a buyer or procurement manager should have. To begin with, here is a list of professional skills (or hard skills[1] as they are oftentimes called):

- Knowledge of computer programs and office applications
- Analytical skills, including basic reporting automation skills
- Statistics and data analysis methods
- Data validation, analysis, and reasoning
- Understanding legal aspects of procurement
- Understanding accounting and taxation principles
- Drafting business letters
- Managing projects and change
- Knowledge of foreign languages
- Understanding the financial aspects of procurement
- Understanding supply chain logistics flows

Depending on the specifics of the company, the characteristics of its business processes, and the level of the job itself, a whole range of additional skills may be required, such as knowledge of certain IT systems or the ability to prepare special documentation. The listed skills, as in any other profession, will require different levels of proficiency. For example, a category management team leader does not need to log documents into the accounting system, while a back-office specialist who processes invoices does not need to understand all the details of developing a category strategy. It is important for a Chief Procurement Officer (CPO) to be able to navigate demand forecasting techniques, but they do not have to spend time creating purchase order documents in the accounting system. Similarly, one category may require skills for reading technical drawings, and another may not. When making requirements for candidates in terms of education and skills, it is important to decide on a reasonable minimum that is required. Sometimes setting excessive requirements may result in good candidates not responding or being overlooked. On the other hand, personal qualities (or soft skills)[2] are no less important:

- Communication skills (including negotiating and presenting)
- Emotional intelligence

- Critical thinking
- Ability to find common ground with most colleagues and peers
- Honesty, integrity, openness, and respect for others
- Client centricity
- Self-organization, task setting, and prioritization
- Effective time management
- Planning and goal setting
- Reflection; the ability to ask for and give feedback
- Tactical and strategic thinking
- Teamwork, organizational, and entrepreneurial skills

The skills listed here also require varying degrees of proficiency, depending on the organizational role of the employee and their area of responsibility. Nevertheless, I would put the ability to communicate effectively as the most important. The job of a buyer requires a lot of communication. Google does not know everything about suppliers, and the ability to get missing information quickly and efficiently is an essential skill for those who want to know and do not hesitate to ask a lot of questions. It is important not only to talk but also to effectively listen to the other side, use arguments appropriate to the situation, and present your point of view—you cannot use a computer screen as a barrier to stop communicating with people.

In order to determine which competencies need to be developed in procurement, you can use a matrix that will list these skills and the required level of proficiency depending on the organizational structure, role, or area of responsibility. An example of such a matrix is shown in Table 11.1. I will not describe a fully exhaustive competency matrix here because such a document requires individual development within a particular company, but this can be used as a starting template for you to draft and adapt your own procurement competency matrix.

The structure, roles, and levels will vary from organization to organization, and the set of competencies itself may be detailed or more general. There is no single standardized assessment of what is considered a basic or advanced level of competence. Nevertheless, it can be defined for a particular procurement organization. For example, when we talk about the necessary skills for *procurement planning*, we can introduce the following qualifications.

1. Entry Level

Knows:

- Standard functions of MS Office (Word, Excel, PowerPoint, Access)
- Basic questions for conducting an interview with an internal client

Table 11.1 Procurement competency matrix template example: levels of competencies depending on the organizational role.

Organizational Group	Professional Competency	Competency Level						
		Intern	Specialist	Manager	Senior Manager	Department manager	Category Manager	CPO
Category Management	Procurement planning	—	—	3	4	4	3	4
	Category strategy development	—	—	3	4	4	3	4
	Supplier selection and contracting	—	—	2	3	4	2	4
	Supplier relationship management	—	—	3	4	4	3	4
	[. . .]	—	—	—	—	—	—	—
Operational Procurement	Procurement planning	—	1	3	4	4	—	—
	Category strategy development	—	1	2	4	4	—	—
	Supplier selection and contracting	—	2	3	3	4	—	—
	Supplier relationship management	—	2	4	4	4	—	—
	[. . .]	—	—	—	—	—	—	—
Project Office	Methodological support for procurement	1	—	3	4	4	—	—
	Procurement planning	1	—	2	3	3	—	—
	Category strategy development	1	—	3	4	4	—	—
	Supplier selection and contracting	1	—	2	3	3	—	—
	Supplier relationship management	1	—	3	4	4	—	—
	[. . .]	—	—	—	—	—	—	—

Legend: The levels of proficiency
1 = entry level; 2 = basic; 3 = intermediate; 4 = expert.

- The rules and time limits for conducting procurement procedures
- How to use digital accounting systems, generate reports, and upload data

Is proficient in:

- Conducting interviews with internal clients and managing the data collection process
- Instructing colleagues and internal clients on process rules and lead times
- Preparing periodic reports

2. Basic Level

Knows:

- Advanced functionality of MS Office
- Sources of information for factor analysis
- Demand forecasting techniques

Is proficient in:

- Analyzing large amounts of data using standard office applications
- Assessing changes in the volume of consumption based on the dynamics of influencing factors
- Building supply-demand plans
- Planning the schedule of a procurement
- Analyzing procurement plan fulfillment

3. Intermediate Level

Knows:

- Resource planning methods and requirements
- Methodology for calculating the economic effects of procurement initiatives
- Advanced settings and functionality of software applications

Is proficient in:

- The determination of the factors affecting the volume of consumption in a category
- The evaluation of resource requirements
- The calculation and planning of economic effects in procurement
- The use of advanced functionality of software applications

4. Advanced/Expert Level

Knows:

- Principles of procurement plan development
- Influencing market factors

Is proficient in:

- Building the procurement plan
- Assessing the market
- Conducting negotiations

All competency levels are described in a similar way. Such documents are not created to break everything down into the smallest detail but to set general guidelines. Excessive detail can often do more harm than good—it imposes a framework and reduces flexibility.

In my experience, I have had cases where an employee jumped from the role of a trainee straight into a category manager. The competency matrix should not become an obstacle to talent development and prohibit such moves, but it can help to guide employees by giving them an understanding of which skills need to be improved in order to move to the next level. The matrix can thus become the basis for building up training programs and career tracks.

The competency matrix can be used to formulate a career development track in any function, depending on the employee's career expectations and their own potential. A vertical career development is the most common; for example, from back-office specialist to analyst, from analyst to category manager, etc. In practice, career paths in procurement are much more interesting. Vertical, horizontal, diagonal, and zig-zag paths are normal. It is possible to go from being a specialist in the back-office department to a leader on the reporting team, and from there to the project office, then onward to engage in the implementation of strategic initiatives, followed by work as a category manager or moving immediately to the head of a procurement team, and then to CPO, and finally to CEO. With a certain confluence of talents, performance, opportunities, and circumstances, it is possible to *fly over* several stages at once. The main thing is to do your job well and not become obsessed with set competency matrix limits.

The competency matrix can also be used to select candidates and assess their skills in a more formalized way. It can serve as the basis when building professional development and appraisal programs for employees and procurement managers, as well as performance evaluations and professional development feedback.

Do not overlook horizontal career development opportunities in procurement, such as the rotation of specialists between different categories and functions within procurement departments or short (1–2 months) placements in related functions. This includes reciprocal placements between procurement employees and the IT department, the internal audit department, and security service employees, as well as the financial function and production units. These placements can be very beneficial. In addition to bringing cross-functional teams together by developing personal relationships between the participants, additional experience is gained by observing the processes performed by other functions from within.

Rotation allows the expansion of competencies by working with different markets and vendor groups, processes, and tasks. The frequency of such rotations can vary and depends on the complexity of the tasks and categories for which the specialist is responsible. It is important that this happens at a frequency that satisfies both the employee and the business—if rotations are too frequent, they can have a negative impact on relationships with suppliers. The optimal period for rotations is once every 2–3 years. For many categories, where the understanding of technical specifications is important, it can be much longer without running the risk of losing interest or development opportunities. Rather, the opposite is true—the more immersion in the subject, the higher the expertise and value of the specialists themselves.

Skills development should be linked to the personal qualities of the employee. For example, a person may have the potential for analytical thinking and be great at working with data and information but not be able to negotiate effectively. People with different skills at the same high level are very rare, so it is better to be realistic in the search for talent. It is much more practical and useful to unite people with different competencies into teams where they complement each other. I have come across different team configurations; some of the category managers dealt with analytics and negotiations, while someone else worked in tandem with an analyst. The distribution of skills and roles depends on the complexity of tasks, the specifics of categories and processes, the availability of necessary resources and available competencies, personal abilities, and the peculiarities of how specific people interact with each other. Taking into account these influencing factors, a team is formed with a common task whose participants complement each other's competencies and skills.

The professionalization of procurement is one of the most important tasks for a business. The competency matrix as a whole should correspond to the strategic tasks of the business and, accordingly, the procurement function.

The skills and professionalism of employees in this function directly affect procurement costs. You cannot expect people without special training to know how to prepare for and conduct successful negotiations, draft requests and analyze proposals, or read market indicators and use them to make decisions. In a situation where there is no systematic procurement education, it is likely that most procurement employees will not work in accordance with best practices but rather with what they learned from their colleagues and predecessors.

According to the Center for Advanced Professional Studies (CAPS) research data,[3] companies spend between 0.6 and 1.4 percent of the total cost of the function on procurement training. According to the same study, procurement departments account for between 0.5 and 3.1 percent of a company's total head count, depending on the industry. In the last decade, more and more strategic areas of procurement work—such as project activities and the development of category strategies, which require specific skills—have been allocated to separate streams. According to CAPS, the number of employees whose role is *strategic* accounts for more than half of the total number of procurement employees. Several factors have led to this redistribution:

- **Focus on strategic priorities**—finding new sources of profit, implementing new technologies, developing partnerships, establishing category work, and achieving savings
- **Automation and standardization of operations**—implementation of operational improvements and increased transparency of procurement processes
- **Increased expectations of the function**—as a profit center and source of strategic initiatives rather than a cost-control center

All of this entails a pressing need for capabilities development. When it comes to finding employees for the procurement department, the first problem we face is that candidates, especially young university graduates, have little idea what exactly working in the procurement department involves and what the best practices in this area are. Procurement training mostly happens in the workplace and through separate training programs in areas such as developing category strategies, data analysis, basics of financial decision making, performance management and negotiations, social responsibility, and business sustainability.

Fortunately, the situation is gradually changing, thanks to a general increase in interest in the topic of procurement and investment by companies in their own training programs. Concurrently, more universities have started offering education programs that include specific procurement topics rather than wide and oftentimes quite abstract supply chain management subjects. Consequently, a more or less universal understanding of what procurement is all about is starting to take hold. Many firms are also developing their *own procurement schools*, and employees of the function have access to quality educational materials to develop their professional competencies right within the company. There are also private procurement training programs and courses on the market in various languages. Fortunately, today, it is much easier to find a suitable training program and a qualified trainer than it was ten years ago, although the supply is still limited.

In addition to training programs, a good practice in competence development is participating in industry conferences, organizing seminars, and having sessions within the company where people can share their experiences. Encouraging the participation of procurement employees in such events will help with their career development. In addition to valuable information from speakers, conferences provide an opportunity to develop a network of professional contacts. These relationships with colleagues from other companies allow us to share experiences and useful practices and get advice on how to handle nonstandard or difficult situations.

Experts in the field of talent management often stress that it is not necessary today to learn a specialty by going into higher education because knowledge becomes obsolete very quickly. Rather, it is to discover *how to learn*. I share this view. It is more important than ever to learn quickly, abandon old approaches in favor of new ones, constantly monitor changes, and be able to adapt them quickly to your own situation. Learning is a continuous activity.

TEAMWORK AND MOTIVATION IN PROCUREMENT

The motivation system in procurement consists of several components— and material motivation is far from being the main one. Money is certainly important, but salary and bonuses are not the only anchors that retain talented employees.

Building a motivation system is a serious professional topic that should be studied in detail by any manager before proposing one or another method of motivation in any functional area. I do not intend to describe here the methods or approaches to bonuses, teamwork, or goal setting—entire volumes have already been written about those topics. However, despite the large number of existing techniques, this area is still problematic, especially for companies where the pursuit of results often eclipses the needs of real people—namely, the employees. The following are three components of an effective motivation system, along with my recommendations for each of them.

1. Goal-Setting

- **Goals should be ambitious and even a little intimidating.** When goals are too easy, there is no incentive to develop; we do not feel the value of the bonus that awaits us at the end—it is too easy to achieve. I had a case where the manager who was responsible for obsolete inventory and processed waste sales was also the one who set the year's target. The figure was already a bit of a reach, but I suggested doubling the amount of sales. At first, there was consternation. But the results at the end of the year showed that the volume of sales increased not just twice, but by three times. When it is not completely clear how to achieve sky-high goals, bold and unconventional ideas often arise in the course of work.

- **Do not set too many goals or key performance indicators (KPIs).** Human resources management professionals say that no more than five goals should be set if you wish to retain focus and keep them in memory. Table 11.2 shows an example of a procurement KPI matrix, which can easily be adapted to your company. Different objectives can be included in the matrix depending on which areas of the function are the most important or problematic at the moment.

  The matrix example shown in the table reflects only upper-level goals and objectives. To achieve them, it is necessary to monitor many other indicators: market prices, lead times in warehouses, feedback from clients, etc. The latter can even be a goal in its own right, such as: *Achieve a minimum client satisfaction score of 3.5 out of 5 in the current year.* Procurement professionals undoubtedly have to deal with a lot of issues and track a lot more metrics than are listed in the table. Nevertheless, this does not mean that all of them should be included in the KPI matrix and influence material motivation. The indicators line up in a chain and influence each other directly or indirectly, but only those that reflect the final strategic goals get into the matrix. I gave a sample set of procurement strategic and operational indicators in Chapter 1.

Table 11.2 Sample procurement KPI matrix.

#	Sample KPI	Type	Front Office	Middle Office	Back Office	Project Office	Description
				Approximate KPI Weight Allocation Between Procurement Groups (%)			
1	Procurement Savings	• Team KPI—for all functions • Team KPI—for category group • Individual—for individual specialists	40	30	10	30	Strategic KPI: may be assigned to the whole procurement function as a team goal or to specific category teams or individuals
2	OTIF (On Time In Full) Deliveries	• Team KPI—for category group • Individual—for individual specialists	15	30	40	N/A	Operational KPI: OTIF is usually an important indicator for internal clients. OTIF formula is developed considering process configuration at a specific entity
3	Working Capital (WC)	• Team KPI—for all functions • Team KPI—for category group	5	10	10	N/A	Procurement influences WC through payment terms and applied inventory management practices
4	Process Lead-Time	• Team KPI—for category group • Individual—for individual specialists	N/A	10	20	N/A	Depends on the area of responsibility and seniority, e.g., the category manager would be responsible for lead times within their category
5	Continuous Improvement Program Implementation	• Team KPI—for all functions • Team KPI—for category group • Individual—for individual specialists	40	20	20	70	Managers would be responsible for the whole program, while individual teams would be held accountable for their respective projects
	Total Weight		100	100	100	100	

2. Material Motivation

- **Salary levels should be market-based.** This is an obvious consideration; if good employees constantly think they are underpaid, they are unlikely to stay for long. Perhaps excessively talented employees are not needed to keep the business afloat, but if the goals are ambitious, the skill level of the team must match them.

- **Motivation through bonus reduction or other negative sanctions does *not* work.** There is too much risk of a team hiding real problems and their failures for fear of a salary reduction or other repercussions. Only some kind of addition to what employees are already receiving can truly motivate, not the taking away of what is already there. Potential loss provokes fear and anxiety about one's future without motivating breakthrough ideas or inspiring confidence. Sanctions as punishment for violations are possible, but it has nothing to do with the goal-setting system.

- **Annual bonuses work better than quarterly or monthly bonuses.** I like financial incentive systems that include a time-deferred bonus. Cash bonuses can be seen as accountability to the overall company's financial results. It gives a sense of satisfaction and an incentive to put in more effort than you would just by receiving a paycheck. I have come across different approaches in my career, and even when I was told, "We deliver results that are evaluated once a month, and we want that to be reflected immediately in the monthly bonus," it turned out that annual planning worked better. There is no reason to tie bonuses to monthly or quarterly results, and it is better to consider long-term objectives rather than closing monthly or quarterly reports.

- **Remuneration should reflect the amount of effort required to achieve the goals.** If results exceed expectations, the bonus should be commensurate with the goal and adjusted upward as such. The *prize* for success should be tangible. It is not uncommon in professional procurement circles to discuss the topic of the company sharing successes in achieving savings with its employees. There are even suggestions that a portion of the savings should be put into the employee's paycheck. However, I am not a supporter of this idea. A simple example using the two notional categories of automotive repair supplies and coal purchases shows why. In the first category, there are thousands of items and lots of operational work, suppliers, clients, and, therefore, hundreds of issues that need to be addressed. In coal procurement, the challenges are different—it is a commodity that industrial and energy companies buy in large quantities for huge sums. Nevertheless, the number of terms, as well as the types of coal that a particular company buys, can be counted on the fingers of one hand. The employees who work in these categories have to spend vastly different amounts of time and effort to get one dollar in savings for the company. Therefore, the base amount for reward calculation should not be the category spend value or amount of savings but the value of the employees themselves, that is, their salary, to which a certain percentage is added based on the actual results achieved.

3. Nonmaterial Motivation

- **Eighty percent of success comes from nonmaterial motivation.** Shared values in the team, ambitious goals, interesting tasks, a supportive environment, development opportunities, constant feedback, attention to the needs of employees, a client-oriented attitude toward each other, team sessions and informal events, commendations, and honor boards—all of these are excellent motivators. Nonmaterial motivation creates a sense of belonging to something progressive and grand, in which you can find a purpose and benefits for yourself personally. It drives creativity while spurring the interest and desire to stay and develop together with a team of professionals. Strong teams develop newcomers and naturally squeeze out those who do not share common values or are destined to fail.

KEY CHAPTER IDEAS

- You do not need to have a specialized education to be a good buyer, but this does not mean that there is no need to constantly study and develop your professional knowledge in this area. Education in financial, technical, and economic specialties will be a plus.
- Procurement costs should be managed by trained professionals. A specially compiled competency matrix will help to manage the competencies of these professionals.
- The competency matrix can be used to structure possible career paths between different roles within and outside of the procurement function.
- Motivation through punishment does not work—instead of motivating, it creates anxiety and fear of loss, leaving no space for creativity and engagement.

- Material motivation is not the main incentive driver for high performance. The content of the tasks, the reward system, and the general atmosphere of the team are much more important.

ENDNOTES

1. Professional or hard skills are competencies that can be taught and measured. Acquiring these skills simply takes knowledge and instruction. The skills can be checked; for example, by means of an exam.
2. Personal qualities or soft skills are universal competencies that are difficult to measure with quantitative indicators. Soft skills are largely determined by a person's character and are acquired with experience; for example, the ability to work in a team, communicate well, or handle stress.
3. The Metrics of Supply Management (avg. data for 2021, 2022). CAPS Research.

CHAPTER 12

PROCUREMENT OF THE FUTURE: DREAMS AND REALITY

Procurement is being shaped both by its past and by present-day trends, with sustainable development, social responsibility, digital technologies, and professionalization being among the most important. The history of procurement and its current trends can be shown in Figure 12.1. Historically, procurement has been mostly about operational efficiency and basic savings, but that has changed rapidly, and new expectations and challenges are emerging. We will talk about the main ones in this chapter, as well as discuss what to expect in the development of procurement in the near future and what to pay attention to today.

AUTOMATION VERSUS DIGITALIZATION: WHAT'S THE DIFFERENCE?

Procurement is increasingly occupying a prominent place in overall company strategy. This is a natural development—both the company's operational efficiency and costs depend on the professional management of supplies, as well as the ability to continuously provide the business with necessary materials, goods, and services and to gain access to new technologies and supplier infrastructure, which today are increasingly becoming an extension of the client's core business.

Today, almost all companies are involved in transformation processes to one degree or another. Digitalization is proceeding at a rapid pace, and more and more interesting solutions are appearing for procurement as well. This is especially true for supply risk management, planning, logistics, price analysis, e-procurement, and even automated algorithms for preparing for negotiations and developing category strategies.

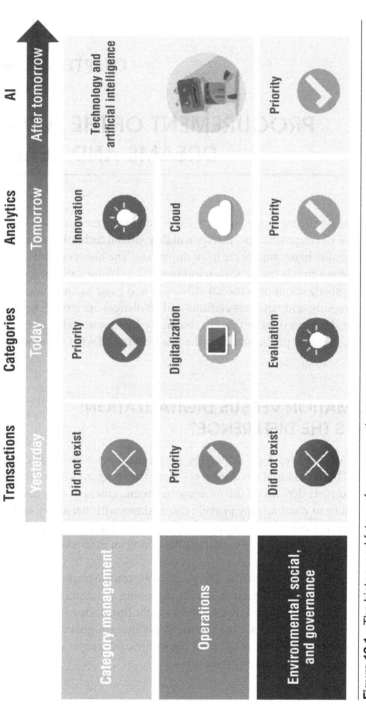

Figure 12.1   The history and future of procurement.

It is necessary to understand that digitalization is not the same as automation. In recent years, the world of procurement has come a long way in terms of automating and robotizing routine operations. Today, the main trend in digital procurement is the creation of smart systems that help not just to automate routine processes, but also to make the right decisions, develop category books, and facilitate the negotiation process.

Change is happening right now, and it is important to be part of it. There are already many opportunities for digital collaboration (for example, systems anticipating demand and automatically sending requests for proposals to suppliers, analyzing them, and making sourcing recommendations). Process analytics technology helps find bottlenecks in processes and data and focuses on closing any important gaps, while digital marketplaces are creating new ecosystems, displacing competitive sourcing, and making procurement much more efficient.

A lot of information on this topic is already available in the professional community. It makes no sense to list specific digital procurement solutions here because the situation on this front is changing rapidly. Therefore, the information may become irrelevant tomorrow.

It is my hope that in the near future, buyers will no longer need to create orders manually or do analytics using Excel (yes, a lot of companies still do that!). In about a decade or so, simple and inexpensive solutions will be available that will replace human labor in those areas, and even small and medium-sized companies will be able to afford them, provided they have databases that they can trust. Electronic bidding systems, with the help of self-learning algorithms, can independently conduct even multistage tenders without the participation of a buyer in accordance with the conditions laid out in an electronic category book.

The Internet of Things, blockchain, artificial intelligence, cloud solutions, mobile technology, platforms, and virtual reality all offer inspiring possibilities. Imagine that in a few years, buyers sitting in negotiations will know exactly all the details of the terms and negotiation alternatives of the other side, thanks to the fact that smart algorithms will calculate and analyze in five minutes the supplier's work history with all their clients—and thanks to blockchain technology, information about irregularities and shortcomings in the cooperation process will not be hidden. Such prospects are super enticing. Yet, there is a *but*; the supplier will also know absolutely everything about the buyer, and therein lies the great challenge for all market participants.

I am certain that the digital future of procurement will be exciting. Operational management tasks will become much simpler, and by increasing the quality of analytics and the speed of processes and innovation, solutions will become central. Is this not the real strategic role of the procurement function—to create value, not just ensure that operational processes are working?

At the moment, however, investment in digital procurement is still a controversial topic. In many companies, progress on digital procurement solutions has been slow. A lag in regulation and legislation and a lack of bold investments in technology are all contributing factors. For example, not all companies are willing to transfer their data to cloud-based applications, even those with legally enforceable privacy agreements and robust security infrastructure. It's important that the risks of data breaches or abuse are addressed not by prohibitions but by finding solutions. If a company understands that the risk is high and there is no solution yet, you can still take advantage of the new capabilities of the process *as is* and, in parallel, introduce additional control measures or reporting indicators that help identify risks quickly before an incident occurs. The idea here is to take advantage of cloud-based applications while also guaranteeing the safety of your data.

PROCUREMENT AND BUSINESS SUSTAINABILITY

The future is not coming to everyone at the same pace. When I say that the operational processes of procurement will be automated in 10 years, I mean that solutions for this will be available. Of course, not everyone will take advantage of them right away. The understanding of the importance of professional procurement management has taken decades to evolve, and for many companies, that day has still not dawned.

The pace of change implementation depends on the speed of development of a particular company and the processes around it, on the readiness of owners to invest time and resources in the development of technology and progressive solutions, and, of course, on the return of these solutions for a particular business. The idea that the most flexible and strongest will survive still holds true—those who take advantage of new opportunities in time will get an undoubted competitive advantage in the form of a more effective procurement and cost management system and larger market share.

Today, there is a rethinking of the function's core objectives and a redefinition of expectations surrounding it. Operational efficiency is not being relegated to the background. It is simply considered the norm—procurement processes must be reliable, transparent, and align with strategic objectives, and the development of category strategies is a standard practice.

Next-level objectives lie in the areas of innovation,
sustainable business development, partnerships, new
sources of revenue, and social responsibility.

Meeting these next-level objectives affects company market valuation and indicators such as total shareholder return (TSR)[1] and corporate social responsibility (CSR)[2] are closely linked in today's reality. The world is moving toward in-depth collaborations and performance assessment—not within a specific function or a single process but across the entire business and all of the functions that are involved in these processes. Metrics that are used to assess social responsibility have a direct impact on the market's assessment of the business and the company's financial results. They are no longer indicators that can be ignored.

We are still far behind in areas such as *green procurement*[3] and the development of small suppliers, including those representing special categories or minorities. In some countries, for example, governments impose quota requirements on purchases from local companies or businesses that are owned or run by women. Such steps often look controversial because they can be viewed as impeding free competition. Nevertheless, the issue is relevant, and regulators that are imposing these conditions have good reasons for doing so. Often, small businesses that have great potential but lack the resources to grow can greatly benefit from the fact that these regulations force large companies to pay attention to them and allow them to take part in bidding, thereby opening up revenue opportunities. Too often, many small companies are screened out—not through competition, but because they are eclipsed by the size of large, developed suppliers. And, of course, for a small company, the task of figuring out how to become a supplier to this or that well-known company can turn into a complicated quest. Therefore, these regulations do promote market development and competition in the long run, regardless of the mixed feelings they provoke at first.

In many countries, environmental issues and supply chain impacts are regulated by law, and failure to comply with these regulations can lead to financial losses. Conversely, being proactive can lead to significant savings and preferential treatment in taxes and benefits. Today, in many developing economies, environmental issues are simply not a significant topic for most companies, but the situation is changing rapidly. It is turning into an issue of cost that must be managed not only by finding new ways to recycle industrial waste, for example, but also by finding ways not to create this waste in the first place. Green procurement, small business development, and participation in charitable social projects are becoming important parts of the environmental, social, and governance (ESG) agenda,[4] which directly affects how the market values companies.

It is wise to think about how the choice of supplier or the subject of procurement is built into the ESG agenda in advance—at the moment when the decision to purchase equipment or a vehicle is made. How will its emissions affect the environment? Is it possible to properly dispose of waste from the production process? Should we buy lubricants in plastic or metal containers, and what will then happen to the containers in which these substances have been purchased? The answers to these types of questions affect the total cost of ownership, and if it is possible to digitize the evaluation of this impact, the resulting values should be taken into account when making a decision.

Large companies play an important role not only in national economies but also in helping address global social problems. Apple demands that all participants in its supply chain—from the main producer of devices to the final carrier—undergo thorough audits to confirm that they do not employ illegal labor. The problem of slavery and child labor in certain industries, including hazardous ones, is a huge issue for the planet, and how major companies structure their purchases and supply chains will determine whether this problem will be solved. So far, there are very few companies like Apple with sufficient resources to conduct such comprehensive controls. Such audits are long and expensive, which also means a potential increase in the price of the final product for the company's customers. As long as the requirement to conduct such audits is not mandatory, businesses will not invest in solving humanity's problems, even though they contribute to the sources of these problems through the pursuit of rare raw materials and low prices. The solution here is to start doing small things that are affordable for your business at the moment, learning how to create real impact and growing your social responsibility capabilities along the way.

We cannot know the future, but being flexible and prepared for anything is the number 1 procurement competency of the future.

Procurement professionals should be tasked to aid in business development, including the effective integration of procurement cost management during mergers and acquisitions.

The emergence of joint ventures (JVs) often comes out of an idea arising at the intersection of the procurement and sales functions of the two companies forming the JV—for example, the creation of a product that is in demand in the market, a change in approach to service offerings, and joint research projects. Such ideas come about not only through communication between the leaders of those enterprises, but even more so, they grow out of the daily tasks of securing sources of supply on the one hand and finding sales channels or synergy opportunities on the other. When Severstal acquired another iron ore business, the procurement, IT, and finance departments were the first to start the process of operationally integrating the enterprise with the holding company. As part of the sale of a production site, procurement specialists were also actively involved in creating and implementing a divestment plan for the asset.

When companies evaluate the creation of a joint venture, an assessment is made of procurement processes, the potential for synergies in the categories, and the benefits of procurement integration. Integration does not necessarily mean centralization of management, but it is important to determine in advance how processes will work during the transition period to assess potential and support business continuity.

A separate topic is the creation of new businesses. Procurement connects companies with suppliers along with their ideas and resources. Providing a client's production facilities to test a supplier's new product can create long-term benefits for both parties and provide a competitive advantage to the buyer for a certain period of time while the new technology is not yet available to the rest of the market. The ability to listen carefully to each other and look not only for immediate benefits but also to spot opportunities with long-term potential can create entirely new products and even entire businesses. Such companies as Vodafone, Sanofi, and Airbus have been supporting special accelerator spaces for supplier development for many years. More and more companies are actively attracting startups, testing new solutions, and providing opportunities for joint development—and procurement specialists are largely the driving force behind this.

KEY CHAPTER IDEAS

- The main trends in procurement in recent years—automation, the potential of analytical solutions, and robotization—have moved into the realm of the everyday. At the same time, ensuring the efficiency of operational procurement processes is an important part, but not the main task, of function development. The challenges of ensuring the reliability of the entire supply chain, creating ecosystems to develop partnerships, and ESG concepts within a social responsibility and business sustainability agenda are pressing issues for procurement professionals.

- The main competence of procurement specialists in the future will be the ability to adapt quickly to changing circumstances and new risks in order to find opportunities for the elaboration and implementation of new technologies and business development.
- Procurement departments can and must play a key role in developing new revenue streams for the company through sourcing ideas and forming collaborations with suppliers, as well as actively managing the cost base and sources of supply while ensuring they are transparent, legitimate, and environmentally friendly.

ENDNOTES

1. Total shareholder return (TSR) is a financial metric for assessing business performance.
2. Corporate social responsibility (CSR) is the business practice of including environmental and social policies with economic goals and functions.
3. Green procurement is a system that works in compliance with environmental criteria for purchased goods and services; for example, tracking the impact of purchases on pollution, making decisions about the environmentally friendly disposal of items at the end of their life, increasing the share of waste recycling, increasing the share of renewable resources and raw materials, etc.
4. The ESG (environmental, social, and governance) agenda is a concept of sustainable development. It calls for an increase in activities that contribute to ecology and environmental protection, social sphere and charity, corporate management, and corporate responsibility.

CHAPTER **13**

WHAT'S NEXT? TURNING THEORY INTO PRACTICE

WHAT THEY DON'T WRITE ABOUT IN BOOKS

Standardized processes and centralized functions in organizations do not mean that everything runs smoothly. Any company, any team, is a living entity in which changes are constantly occurring—people move, management practices fluctuate, external and internal environment requirements change, and many of the decisions of past generations of managers are forgotten, become irrelevant, or are called into question.

Practices that worked yesterday may not work today; new people come in with their own vision of *how to do things better*, and the details must be renegotiated with them. You cannot expect people to work like robots and execute exactly what is spelled out in regulations or considered a best practice. There will always be different levels of involvement, competence, communication abilities, and decision making to connect concepts and work out appropriate ways to collaborate. Even though one client is willing to get involved and help, another, even in advanced organizations where high-end solutions are implemented, may expect limited service and no support from procurement. One buyer may be great at negotiating and building effective interactions with clients and suppliers, while another may not be capable of it.

Does this mean that everything described in this book will not work in practice? Not at all. I just want to remind my readers that reality is always more complex than what we imagine it to be.

The truth is that no organization is perfect, even if books are written about them and they are held up as examples.

You cannot expect every idea you have about improving the procurement process to be immediately shared by your team and business partners. You will have to constantly adapt approaches to people and the organization, *sell* your ideas, look for new methods, improve models, and consider the many factors that facilitate or hinder the implementation of any initiative.

HOW TO JUSTIFY INVESTMENT IN THE PROCUREMENT FUNCTION

I often get questions about how to justify investments in the development of the procurement function. Of course, the most obvious answer is to estimate the effect of those transformation changes. For example, there are measurable effects like money and delivery speed, and there are non-measurable ones like customer satisfaction. And yet, it is okay that not everything can be measured. But what if an evaluation is still required when there is no measurable value? How do you evaluate something that cannot be counted? What are the effects? How do you evaluate procurement processes and the feelings and impressions of procurement employees? Here are a few thoughts on the subject:

- **Account for any feelings that may affect the bottom line**—this translates into engagement level, quality of operations, work coordination by project teams, and increased motivation to implement new ideas. You can introduce a change in interaction with one unit as an experiment, then evaluate the results and build a case for replicating the practice companywide.
- **Answer the question "Why?"**—if you see the need, start the transformation of a function with the basics, and then move on to a higher level of strategy so that the results of the change are clearer to those around you. First, clean up the data and the warehouse, and if necessary, ask for money to do it. If there is a problem with timely deliveries, even if it is not only rooted in procurement, optimize this basic process first and then move on to strategic partnerships and advanced models of cooperation with suppliers to get additional measurable effects. Some things can be done in parallel, but the general advice is to go from the simple to the complex.
- **Sign off on the promised results**—to get approval to invest in a function or IT system, you need to identify what you are ready to promise as the results. The rigor of this process depends on company culture, but quality communication and the ability of competent managers to

justify their proposals/decisions go a long way. If you meet resistance, do not rush to blame someone for their lack of understanding. Perhaps you need to justify your numbers and find answers to questions in a different way.

Investments in the development of the function can be divided into the following areas:

- **Supporting the overall development strategy of the company**—what exactly is the contribution of the procurement team? What is needed to achieve the desired results? What investment in the function is required for this? Is it possible to achieve the same result in the required time frame without additional investment?
- **Employee and client satisfaction**—assess the current level of service and determine what it should be in order to meet the expectations of stakeholders.
- **New sources of revenue and new lines of business**—this topic is about innovation and is particularly interesting. But if the basic processes do not work or just barely work, there will be no room for innovation. Stakeholders are unlikely to believe that procurement can become a new source of revenue or allocate the necessary resources for *next-level* initiatives if the underlying processes are working poorly.

I also get a number of questions about consultants. Is it worth engaging them, and what should they do? What results should we expect? I know many examples of successful engagements, but there are many other examples where the client claims, "We could have done it ourselves and even better." In my experience, this claim is often a fallacy. If your expectations of consultants are that they will come and do everything for you, then it is simply not worth inviting them in the first place. Even if the outcome of their work is clear and the client is satisfied, it will most likely not last. The reason is that if the client team does not work together with the consultant to find solutions, the outcome will not be accepted by the client's team as their own. External consultants bring expertise and knowledge from various industries where they have executed projects, different perspectives, and a deeper understanding of possible ramifications of the change—that is their main value. However, the best results are achieved by mixed teams when company employees and consultants work together, and the representative of the client company, not the consultant, is responsible for the final resulting outcome and *takes ownership*. When hiring consultants, it is important to remember that the result of their work will be better and more durable if the consultancy team becomes an extension of the client team.

HOW TO ENSURE THE CHANGES TAKE HOLD

So, we have implemented the changes, but how do we make sure they take hold and are sustainable? Here are a few basic principles that help to root the changes for the long term.

1. Build a Critical Mass of Supporters

It is not necessary for 100 percent of employees to believe in and act on qualitative change for it to happen. Of course, it would be ideal for the whole organization to get behind the changes and attempt to achieve the best result. In reality, it is never like that. There are always people who do not share the vision, do not believe in it, are not competent enough to change, have change fatigue, or simply do not want to get involved. The good news is that you only need about 10–20 percent of the total number of employees to support the change in order to achieve a sufficient critical mass that will pull the entire organization along. The example of quality change and engagement that these people will set will leave no other option than for the majority to fall in line behind them. Over time, this backbone will expand, and those who do not support the new approaches and values will naturally leave the organization or change their role or attitude. If there is a critical mass of people who share a common course of development, the team will gradually clear the holdouts, and newcomers will join with their more experienced colleagues to add new ideas to the development plan.

2. Create a Competence Center in the Organization

Project and methodological offices are the custodians of the organization's knowledge. They record its history, ensure the preservation of information, facilitate the qualitative adaptation of new team members, and transfer the knowledge to future generations of employees who will continue to develop the concepts that were created earlier. It is the Competence Center that is responsible for drafting training and adaptation programs for new employees, consolidating the most useful and valuable things that the organization has developed and implemented, monitoring the effectiveness of the implementation of any initiatives and projects, and providing a methodological basis and support for skills development.

3. Develop a Culture of Action and Open Discussion

If you implement category strategies but do not show interest in the results, then, like any other innovation that does not have a specific *client*, it will eventually turn into a useless appendage and simply stop being implemented. Automation will not protect you from inaction. You can accumulate a lot of useful data and never use it; you can write great category strategies and never use them, too. It is important to develop a culture where there is no room for unnecessary actions. Everything that is done should bring value, and it is important to recognize this value and to be interested in the results of innovations. The interest of managers should not be limited to a formal report on the work performed. Their participation in the work of the team is vital because the manager develops the ideas of employees, uses their administrative resources to implement them, eliminates possible organizational and bureaucratic obstacles, and as a leader, inspires the team to seek new avenues for achievement.

4. Ensure Continuity

This is a task not only for the Competence Center but even more so for leaders at any level. It is these people who ask the right questions, determine the organization's development strategy, select people, and form the team. Starting a change initiative from scratch every time is a recipe for disaster. Creating an atmosphere where knowledge within the organization will be transferred, supplemented, and developed regardless of generational change is a key to success.

5. Implement Data-Driven Solutions

When decisions are supported by data, they are more reliable and more likely to be trusted. We can rely as much as we want on intuition and even talk our colleagues into doing something because we think it will be better, but if the decision is tested with real data or the result has a measurable value, the goal of the change becomes clearer and easier to accept. Data helps to test and confirm hypotheses. Often our assumptions can be just guesses that do not hold up in practice. We should be wary of relying too much on our experience and intuition, although completely abandoning them is not good either and creates the risk of missing important details. When you know that a decision works, but the data do not support it, there is always the possibility that the problem is in the data itself. Decisions should be based on data, but if data are missing or unreliable, that is not an excuse to do nothing. It is important to use all available, reliable information, but be careful not to get lost in the weeds or get bogged down with double-checking. Otherwise, there is a risk of *analysis paralysis* where there is only a research study conducted all the time, followed by no action.

6. Focus on Results, Not Titles

One often comes across the view that functions that are not directly involved in the production of the final product—be it equipment or banking services—should move from the category of *service functions* to that of *business partners*. A lot has been written about this topic, but in the end, we are just talking about labels. There is nothing wrong with being a service function. The emergence of alternative terms is an attempt to get away from the negative connotations that the phrase *service function* evokes. When it comes to interaction within an organization, all functions are, in some sense, service functions in relation to each other. It is not the words that matter but how the functions and people interact. But it is worth acknowledging that the quality of this interaction is sometimes determined by words, so call it what you like best. The main thing is not to forget about mutual support, common goals, and organizational *well-being*.

7. Set Encouraging Key Performance Indicators (KPIs)

There are inspiring goals that may be a little scary—and there are goals that may be not only uninspiring but demotivating. Discussing goals with the team and testing them, in reality, are important prerequisites for an effective motivation system. KPIs should motivate development and growth, while any bonus or motivation should be in addition to already market-competitive working conditions. It is not the threat to cut pay that keeps people motivated. It is the opportunity to learn, develop, and grow a career in a supportive environment and gain more than the base salary that keeps employees motivated to do more and better.

8. Explain the Change

When change is necessary, there is often little time to tell the whole organization about it. Meetings, newsletters, and news feeds are all working tools that must be used to get your message across. In my experience, we have held open demo days where all functions presented their development plans during the active change period. These were organized in an open space or during internal conferences where any employee could come and freely discuss their opinions on development plans for functions or changes that have already been implemented. The whole company announces the day and time when this or that function is holding an *open house*. A stand is prepared, real or online, and information is posted on all of the major changes and initiatives that have already been implemented or are planned. The speaker gives a short presentation on this list, explaining the goals and details of the change(s), and then anyone can ask questions or give comments. Such events are another opportunity and occasion for communication in an open and relaxed format through which stakeholders can learn new things and share their opinions. It is important that such a discussion does not turn into a formal meeting; the key point is to reduce the degree of stuffiness. During the discussions we had, everyone was given the opportunity to ask questions and give feedback on our experiments, which we were constantly undertaking—not all of which were easy and successful. Direct feedback is sobering. We may be wasting time on things that are not really required by those for whom they are intended. Employees may not understand the value of change to themselves and, as a result, may not support it. The sense of irreversibility of change comes when it is expected—when it has a stakeholder or a client, whether it be company management or a foreman on the shop floor. However, for this to happen, both sides have to agree on expectations. The structure of the demo-day agenda can be built around the function development strategy (if it is described), key indicators, or upon requests from related functions. Here is a list of possible items for such an agenda:

- Measures aimed at improving the speed and transparency of the procurement process
- Quality of technical specifications: client requirements and standardization approach
- Development of strategic partnerships: status and plans
- Digitalization: everything connected to IT in procurement and related processes
- Changing approaches to setting KPIs and service levels or defining future performance management setup
- Data standardization and information management
- Development of procurement-related capabilities among stakeholders and suppliers

Discussing change should not only take place internally but externally as well. Recognition from colleagues from other companies helps to make sure your team creates something of value, which increases the level of motivation and cultivates a sense of belonging to something meaningful.

9. Ensure Stakeholder Support

Top management and other stakeholders' support of any transformation or change is the key success factor. A lack of interest in outcomes on the part of management and clients is a frequent problem, but this does not mean that the situation is hopeless. Rather, it opens the door for the procurement service to carry out an educational campaign—to convey ideas about effective procurement cost management. You can perceive a lack of support as a demotivating factor, or you can perceive it as a challenge and an opportunity to create a new model of procurement. Consider it an opportunity to test your abilities in practice!

Management interest in change may have to be created.

Do not expect management's eyes to open on their own and suddenly ask you to *fix things*. Perhaps your organization is incapable of making the request, managers are unaware that the work of the procurement department can be much more effective, or the owner of the company is the government, which has no particular stakeholder. The difference between state-owned and private companies is that state-owned companies think mostly in terms of procedures and regulations, while private companies think mostly in terms of results. But this does not mean that a state-owned company cannot learn to think in terms of results, just that such transformations may well need to happen from the bottom up instead of the top down.

Managers, suppliers, and buyers see the situation from their bell towers— multiple expectations and tasks coming in from all sides, the frenetic pace of life, market challenges, customer demands, lack of time, etc. However, improvements are possible everywhere, and sometimes a lack of interest is actually a lack of awareness.

10. Lead Team-Building Sessions to Drive Change

When I say *team-building sessions*, I do not mean events involving climbing trees, displaying athletic prowess, or having dinner and drinks together, although such activities are useful, too—in the right situation. A team session is a strategic meeting where, in a creative atmosphere, participants can disconnect from daily tasks and think through strategic goals, make a development plan, and agree on how they will interact with each other. When we decided to spin off the procurement back office at Severstal, we did not start to model future processes with a narrow management team or assemble a working group that would restructure all the processes—these groups appeared at a later stage. Our first step was to hold a large design session, which was attended by about 40 employees of the procurement department, all of them of different ranks. Over two days of work with facilitators, we created a transition model, drew up basic processes, and outlined priority steps. The first tangible changes were implemented within 90 days of the session. Without this session, it would have taken months to map out processes, let alone implement changes.

11. Manage Expectations

If, during the first stage of change, some indicators are expected to worsen, it is worth honestly telling the team, managers, and clients and agreeing in advance on expectations and at what point the indicators are expected to stabilize. At the beginning of my career in procurement, I was appointed manager of the fuel, spare parts, and fleet maintenance category. The first thing I encountered was a complete halt in the purchase of all spare parts for motor vehicles in the company, where about 1,300 specialized vehicles and passenger cars were on shift every day. The procurement of spare parts was stopped by my manager—and the company CEO (Chief Executive Officer) and maintenance department management knew why. Up to this point, we had not dealt with this category systematically, and the first analysis of data showed that our warehouses were full of spare parts. We had lost track of the inventory, so we were not sure what we really had in stock. At the same time, we had 200 suppliers servicing 28 geographically dispersed units and paid an average price of 20–30 percent above the market rate. Despite this decision being sanctioned by management, the heads of the transport departments were hostile to the move, even though there was no shortage of spare parts. This period was a real emotional hell for me: every morning at seven o'clock, the mechanics of all 28 locations started calling me to ask when the procurement of spare parts would resume. Some especially active ones started to come to the central office in Kyiv without warning to *deal* with me. No amount of communication, warnings, or announcements could make them understand. They simply refused to listen and were not interested at all in dealing with the mess in their warehouses. Moreover, some of them had a vested interest in working with one supplier or another, and they took as a personal affront the prospect of terminating contracts with them. Yes, it was hard, but at the same time, very interesting. We ended up going to every warehouse to perform an inventory count, and then we terminated all contracts and signed new ones. There were only a dozen new contracts introduced, and they were all with companies that had provided understandable terms of service and undertook to organize delivery to several locations at market prices. The situation got better after a few months, but we had to endure a real siege and the heat of emotions from our internal clients, who were very unhappy. However, the company executives understood why we had taken these actions and supported us.

12. Develop Nonstop

The future has already arrived; the main thing now is to keep up with it. Technology is developing rapidly, and tomorrow, many professions will become irrelevant, but what about procurement in practice? Where are procurement organizations headed, and what should you do to avoid getting lost? Even if your current procurement organization is not very advanced and, therefore, still conducting procurement the old-fashioned way, do not expect it to stay that way forever. It is only a matter of time before change comes. Tomorrow the company may have a change of ownership, a change in development strategy, or it may even disappear. At that point, an important question would be raised: How much are you worth as a procurement specialist in the market, and what is the value of your knowledge and skills? It is smart to think about this as soon as possible and decide on your own professional development program—perhaps even changing companies.

13. Redefine the Role of a CPO

It is important for the procurement director to have the same level of authority as the head of production or the head of sales. The head of procurement must be on an equal footing. Otherwise, there will inevitably be clashes of interest and conflicts of authority. One of my management colleagues put it best: "A procurement director is not just in charge of purchasing but has a role whose responsibility is to look at the business the way the CEO looks at it and to ask themselves where the company is in its development now, and how to make sure it meets the needs of clients and the market in the future."

KEY CHAPTER IDEAS

- An organization is a living organism. Practices and team composition change over time, and not everything always works the way it is written in books and regulations. This is normal. It is important to organize the work and the accumulation of knowledge in the organization in such a way that it is passed on and understood by future generations of teams.

- Investment in the development of the procurement function is just as necessary as investment in any other function—the speed and quality of the procurement function determines the performance of the business as a whole. Matching the need for investment with the company's strategy and the function's goals will help make the case for it.
- To root the change, it is important to create a critical mass of followers and set up a Center of Competence. The Center of Competence should support change processes, manage the flow of ideas and projects, support the objectives of change implementation through an appropriate system of goal setting, and inform colleagues not only about the changes themselves but also about the goals of changes and expectations from them.
- The key to success is continuous development and skill improvement. Do not rest on your laurels; explore and implement new solutions and learn from each other—it is important to take the time for this today to ensure your competitive advantage tomorrow.
- The role of the head of the procurement function should be equal in rank to the roles of the heads of the other functions and clients to ensure interaction based on a fair partnership.

LIST OF RECOMMENDED RESOURCES AND LITERATURE

BOOKS

1. Albrecht, S., J. Wentz, and T. Williams. *Fraud: Bringing Light to the Dark Side of Business*. Irwin Professional Publishing, 1994.
2. Alvarez, S. *Lean Customer Development: Build Products Your Customers Will Buy*. O'Reilly Media, 2017.
3. Easton, S., M. D. Hales, C. Schuh, M. F. Strohmer, and A. Triplat. *Supplier Relationship Management. How to Maximize Vendor Value and Opportunity*. Kearney, A. Apress, 2014.
4. Ellram, Lisa M. and Y. Choi Thomas. *Supply Management for Value Enhancement*. Institute for Supply Management, 2000.
5. Flynn, Anna E. and Sam Farney. *The Supply Management Leadership Process*. Institute for Supply Management, 2000.
6. Goldratt, E. *The Goal: A Process of Ongoing Improvement*. Routledge, 2004.
7. Gordon, S. R. *Supplier Evaluation and Performance Excellence. A Guide to Meaningful Metrics and Successful Results*. J. Ross Publishing, 2008.
8. Grove, Andrew S. *High Output Management*. Vintage, 1983.
9. Haskins, Mark E. *The Secret Language of Financial Reports*. McGraw Hill, 2008.
10. Lockstrom, Martin. *Low-Cost Country Sourcing. Trends and Implications*. Springer, 2007.
11. Nahmias, Steven. *Production and Operations Analysis*. McGraw Hill, 2008.
12. O'Rourke, James S. *Management Communication: A Case Analysis Approach*. Routledge, 2019.

13. Quitt, Anna. *Measuring Supply Management's Budget Effects. Introduction of Return on Spend as an Indicator of Supply Management's Financial Effectiveness*. Springer, 2010.

14. Raedels, Alan R. *The Supply Management Process*. Institute for Supply Management, 2000.

15. Rudzki, Robert A. and Robert J. Trent. *Next Level Supply Management Excellence. Your Straight to the Bottom Line® Roadmap*. J. Ross Publishing, 2011.

16. Schuh, C., R. Kromoser, M. F. Strohmer, Perez R. Romero, and A. Triplat. *The Purchasing Chessboard: 64 Methods to Reduce Cost and Increase Value with Suppliers*. Springer, 2009.

17. Schuh, C., M. F. Strohmer, S. Easton, A. Scharlach, and P. Scharbert. *The CPO. Transforming Procurement in the Real World*. Apress, 2012.

LINKS

- **APQC®** (https://www.apqc.org/) (USA)—a global research organization that specializes in benchmarking best practices for various business functions. In the area of procurement, it provides data on several dozen performance indicators.

- **CAPS Research** (https://www.capsresearch.org/)—a benchmarking center specializing in research on best practices in business process management, particularly procurement and supply chain management processes. It offers access to an extensive library of articles and reports and publishes an annual flagship report, *The Metrics of Supply Management*.

- **Chartered Institute of Procurement & Supply (CIPS)** (https://www.cips.org/)—a professional organization that provides education and consulting services in procurement and supply management. Offers a multilevel procurement management diploma program and access to an extensive library of knowledge for subscribers and members and organizes international procurement management conferences and roundtables. Publishes an online magazine called *Supply Management* for supply chain management professionals: https://www.cips.org/supply-management/.

- **Institute for Supply Management®(ISM)** (https://www.ismworld.org/)—an educational, research, and consulting organization specializing in procurement and supply management. Offers an international procurement certification program. Publishes *Inside Supply Management* magazine and the leading report on global economic trends affecting the supply chain, *ISM Report On Business*®, and organizes international conferences and roundtables on procurement management.

- **Procurement Leaders** (https://procurementleaders.com/)—a global community of professionals in the field of supply management. It conducts international research and conferences for professionals in the field of procurement management, provides consulting services, and publishes a number of thematic reports.

INDEX

Note: Page numbers followed by *f* and *t* refer to figures and tables, respectively.